Schizophrenia:
a patient's perspective

Schizophrenia:
a patient's perspective

Abu Sayed Zahiduzzaman

authorHOUSE®

AuthorHouse™ LLC
1663 Liberty Drive
Bloomington, IN 47403
www.authorhouse.com
Phone: 1-800-839-8640

Published by AuthorHouse   10/21/2013

ISBN: 978-1-4918-2036-0 (sc)
ISBN: 978-1-4918-2035-3 (hc)
ISBN: 978-1-4918-2037-7 (e)

Library of Congress Control Number: 2013917587

Contents

To: Samiya Zahiduzzaman

Acknowledgment

First of all I would like to thank my family doctor, social worker and various psychiatrists who have taken the time to find solution for me to better function. I would like to thank people from the Day Hospital: the occupational therapists, social workers, psychiatric nurses, residents, psychologists, psychiatrists, and patients who showed me light in a dark zone. I would also like to thank my parents who have shown me support, love and affection in my time of trials, my little sister who made me realize I can function like a normal person. And my wife for being there by my side. Furthermore, I will always remember those of you who prayed for me and wished to see me better. Thank you also to Afiqah Yusuf for the first round of editing. My mind made me feel weak but your kindness and support strengthened me. I would also like to thank Khalid Hussain (Shaheen) for designing my cover page and the back page.

Abstract

This book talks about mental illness and how one can be affected by schizophrenia. One can also be affected with other types serious mental illness while being treated with schizophrenia. This illness is like a golden chain that links other illnesses to it. In this book not only do I discuss about schizophrenia, but I also describe how one can be surrounded by other illnesses and issues relating to them.

I want to send a message to readers so that they are aware that people often have negative thoughts who struggle with mental illnesses. People judge those with a serious mental disorder. This book is divided into three parts. The first part discusses mental illnesses in general, with a focus on schizophrenia, and how I struggled with the illness. I also describe various themes related to a person who lives with insanity. You may find advice that can be helpful to you or to someone you know who has a mental illness. The second part discusses some theories I created and believed to be essential in various types of living. You may enjoy reading them and you can interpret them differently based on your own judgment. The third and the last part of this book talks about my experience on how I coped and dealt with depression, psychosis, and schizophrenia while being treated in a hospital. I was part of a program in a hospital in Montreal called the Day Hospital. During the day, I attended the hospital and learned and developed skills to overcome and fight my illness.

The illness became a part of my life and became a regular routine overcoming it. I had no choice but to accept my illness. After being diagnosed with this serious illness I realized that I was not the only one who has seen life differently. I had entered a dark zone and to leave, I had to search for the light to continue on with my daily routines.

This book is resourceful to people who live with this illness and for those who live with a person with mental illness. I hope this book will help me share the lessons I learned with the reader, their peers, families, friends, colleagues, acquaintances, and mostly their loved ones.

Schizophrenia

Is there a way to know some signs of mental illness? Usually, people with mental illness will not openly admit that they have an illness until they are accepted in the society. When an ill person feels safe and secure, only then he or she will discussed the condition honestly. It takes a lot of courage and motivation to reveal to others one's condition. When an ill person suffers from a mental illness, he or she may confide in a friend or even a stranger to for advice or just to be heard. It is not easy for someone to suffer from severe illness and disturbance. The following information are some warning signs of mental illness. Usually when one is ill there are "marked personality changes". They are "also unable to cope with problems and daily activities". Also they may have "strange idea or delusions". Some have "irrational fears". Others feel "sadness" for a prolonged period time. Some show "marked changes in eating or sleeping patterns". Many can have both "extreme highs and lows". And certain people "abuse alcohol or drugs". Furthermore, a number of people may have "excessive anger, hostility, or anxiety". Moreover, some can have very "violent behavior", (Haycock, D. A. p. 68). By noticing these behavior changes in an individual one will be able identify and function with the ill person. Being able to identify someone who suffers from mental illness, allow one to recommend him or her support and help from a practitioner. The patient can then receive help more quickly and the chance to heal is better.

Health professionals use a clinical manual to diagnose someone with a mental to illness. This manual is called the DSM.

DSM:

Multi-axial assessment (p. 27)

DSM assessment is conducted using 5 axes that categorize issues that client is facing.

AXIS 1—Clinical problems e.g. dementia, depression, anxiety, schizophrenia, eating disorders, substance abuse.

AXIS 11—Personality disturbances and mental retardation e.g. paranoid personality, schizotypal personality, borderline personality, antisocial personality, histrionic/dependent, obsessive-compulsive personality.

AXIS 111—General medical conditions e.g. neurological, endocrine, neonatal or antenatal complications, respiratory/digestive/circulatory.

AXIS IV—Psychosocial and environmental factors e.g. primary support group, social environmental, education/occupation, economic/housing, access to heal care, legal conditions.

AXIS V—Global assessment of functioning e.g. rate from 1 to 100, charts progress or deterioration.

Schizophrenia

Schizophrenia is like a complex puzzle with many moving parts that still cannot be solved. Some may say it is a mystery, a mystery that has been since many centuries. We still do not know the exact answers, but we have hypotheses. Schizophrenia is described as a serious mental disorder. Those with schizophrenia are not being able to distinguish between reality and the imagined. People with Schizophrenia are suffer from delusions, hallucinations, disorganized speech, the inability able to think properly, and social withdrawals. This serious illness can occur at any time of life. Most of the time however, it occurs during late adolescence or early adulthood. One with this brain illness may not be able to work or function the same way as before the illness. Scientists believe that Schizophrenia may have genetic factors. More precisely, if someone has this illness within your family, you may get it as well. People with schizophrenia may experience symptom differently. One with this disorder may feel labelled or stigmatized, and others may take advantage of the patients in various forms. Usually, people who have Schizophrenia experience symptoms that last for at least 6 months. Some with medication may be stabilized while others may take more time. In the following paragraph I will be describe my personal experience in this journey with schizophrenia.

A person suffering from schizophrenia commits "social withdrawal or isolation". One shows "little interest in speaking or being with others". One can have "preference for spending time alone". An ill person may have some "sleep disturbance". He or she might also show "little motivation, energy or ambition. One may have "little interest in previously enjoyable pastimes, hobbies, sports, or other activities". One can be "easily distracted". One may have "reduced concentration, difficulty paying attention or remembering things". There is a chance that the person's goes grooming, self-care, or personal hygiene habits deteriorate". Some sick people show "problems performing or functioning in school, at work, or at home". Many have "difficulty understanding what others say or what they are reading". Many show "lack of emotional display", "little facial expression", have flat monotone speech, and even the "inability to have organized speech". Many people will have "conversations that include statements irrelevant to the topic, use inappropriate choice of words, and have unconnected flows of speech". (Haycock, D. A. p. 69). When one notices the signs of Schizophrenia, one should immediately recommend the individual to seek for help and meet with a health professional, psychologist or psychiatrist.

Someone with Schizophrenia may show a lot of emotional changes such as "depression, exaggerated feelings, fear, guilt, rapidly changing emotions, inappropriate affect and lack of emotions", (Haycock, D. A. p. 97). In this context, having these symptoms will make the patient very disorganized and have unexpected behaviors. When one is fearful, he or she would constantly be worried about being hurt or being attacked. One does not feel secure with anyone, not even with friend. A person may look for security by isolating him or herself. Often one will feel blue and will have a different idea about life and the surrounding and constantly feel empty or even depressed. Feeling guilty is natural for those with schizophrenic as they frequently blames themselves. They will also feel guilt for not being able to focus. Often there are drastic changes in emotions that lead to severe pain and even tears. They will feel a negative energy that leads to crying while describing a certain situation or scenario. This will affect the self for a certain period of time.

According to the Schizophrenia Society of Canada, 'Schizophrenia is a serious mental illness that affects 300, 000 Canadians. Finding the causes for Schizophrenia proves to be difficult as the cause and course of illness is unique for each person'. It affects both men and women equally, with men, schizophrenia affects to around 20 year olds, whereas with women, it affects those in their late 20's to early 30's. It could take up to 10 years to properly diagnose someone with Schizophrenia. This serious illness is divided into different subgroups such as Paranoid Schizophrenia, Catatonic Schizophrenia, Disorganized Schizophrenia and Undifferentiated Schizophrenia.

The defining feature of the paranoid subtype (also known as paranoid schizophrenia) "is the presence of auditory hallucinations or prominent delusional thoughts about persecution or conspiracy"

(Bengston p.1). Basically, the patient fears that others want to hurt them. The patient suspects that strangers or closed ones will talk behind their backs and create speculation. The patient will not be able to see their friends the way they used to. There will be a change in behaviour with more anger and anxiety. I am diagnosis with paranoid schizophrenia. When walking on the street, I will always turn my neck to look back if there is someone behind me that tries to harm me. It is an irrational feeling of being spied on; it seems that the world is against me, and that I am part of a network. The network wants to use me for some uncanny reason. Not knowing where to turn to, I was fearful for many reasons. For a long period of time I felt that I had supernatural powers. I was able to see certain things; when closing my eyes the pupils of my both eyes were like a theater screen. More precisely, I would see different types of forms, pictures, sometimes faces; it is like watching movies by closing my eyes. At the beginning it was cool and enjoyable, but with time it became a nightmare. It seemed that I was in a different dimension. I felt like I was surrounded by an external force, like gravity is pulling me from different directions. I had the power to see objects with the speed of light. It was very fast and very clear. I felt that the rapid eyes movement REM, were showing things as fast as possible and I had to remember what I was seeing.

Those with paranoid schizophrenia often deal with anxiety. One can have excessive stress or feel worried about certain things or situations. This leads to sleeping problems and can cause other illness. Not being able to sleep at night can change the mood of a person. Sometimes one may sleep for a few hours and the next day one has to go to work after not sleeping enough. This affects the patient mentally and physically and causes them to not be productive at work. Not sleeping enough will lead to suffering and will create stress in one's life. Feeling stressed out can damage the mind. Showing a lack of interest in a task or loss of motivation is normal when someone has strong anxiety or is severely stressed out.

For a while I had cognitive distortion with emotional reasoning. For me it made me believe that I could see certain things. I had some visual powers. That made me feel a few things, for example, I would feel that people are trying to hurt me for no reason but I will not realize I would be hurt until I get a "flashback" of seeing this scene in a different angle. I also believed people wanted to control my mind and take charge of my body. This made me become suspicious in situation when people are be against me for no reason. It seems that I was in a war where I had to fight to protect myself. My mind would work non-stop for 24 hours a day and I was often tired. I could not do regular tasks. Furthermore, when I am in my thoughts, I had less concentration on regular tasks and my mental sharpness went down. This led to my feeling very weak and sick. Hence, I would not be motivated to do activities or to spend quality time with my peers and family.

There was a time where I did not want to shower or wash myself. For me it was like a computer application in me that was deleted. I kept my nails long and dirty. People would be confused when they saw me, when they know that I was usually very active and very friendly. Having good hygiene used to be necessary and important for me. However, when I was out of reality, it was extremely hard to balance my life with good judgment and decision-making. Looking at me, people were confused and that made me confused. People did not know about my beliefs and projections of them were of people who had different opinions of me. Most of the time, people would react and act according to their beliefs not mine. Slowly, when my health deteriorated, I was losing contact with the reality and started ignoring my friends, colleagues at work, and family. It was an extremely hard moment for me and for my peers, coworkers and my family.

Sometimes I would hear noise and people talking about me. I felt like it was a message that they wanted to send to me. Hearing voice was disturbing and horrifying, especially when I was alone. We say walls have ears but in this case they also have mouths. By now you should be able to figure out my perspectives on my illness. There are various events that happened within a day that most patients forget. The mind seems to block the majority of the disturbances and worries for a certain time. There would be a period that I could spend hours with some irrational thoughts invading my life. Shortly after, I would forget 90% of my thoughts, actions, and reactions.

Only 10% will be in my mind and is expressed to psychiatrists or psychologists. Ten percent may seem small but it is 10% that the practitioners have of me.

What happened with the rest of 90% of information? Certain percentage will be deleted from the memory, other information will be short term memory, and some in the long term memory. Information in this case will be like book in a bookstore, where a person will only get the information they go to the store and grab a book. Therefore, one may share the information with someone or may keep it for themselves. Towards my life experience I have learned that it is important to be honest but it is not good to be too honest. In this case, patients or myself will have various thoughts in our minds and most of the time one may not share the secret information that has invaded our mind. However, the information may come back when one feels terrible or faces a difficult situation.

Having paranoid thoughts can be disturbing and diminish our intelligence. Having paranoid thoughts is associated with strong emotions such as negative feelings. Our behaviors may change due to different circumstance. One may react by having bizarre movement or become violent. When one is violent, it may occur due to excessive negative feeling or when projecting things. Certain people may see things which others do not. Being violent is not acceptable but how do you control your own action? The patient will not notice any triggers or stressors as the patient is occupied by so much information in his or her mind. Do not try to control the patient by manipulating him or her by showing an interest in a book from the bookstore. If you want to help them find out how the patient is suffering and educate yourself with the disorder.

Being too emotional can break relationships. One may make fun of certain situations but the patient may take it personally and have negative feelings. Being paranoid schizophrenic is a challenge, living daily with severe negative feelings can bring one to suffering intensely. A simple situation can become a chaos. Sometimes, emotionally one can feel that he or she is being tortured. The intense negative feelings can be dramatic and intolerable. The mind is totally blocked with sorrow, sadness, and pain.

Someone with paranoid schizophrenia will slowly withdraw from reality. One will chose to have very limited friends and will isolate themselves from his or her friends. The patient believes that his or her friends want to harm him. By now the patient has probably had multiple psychotic episodes. It is natural for patients to believe that people are there to harm them and continue thinking this particular situation until they are seen by a health specialist.

Some believe that people with schizophrenia are violent. However, most schizophrenics are not violent and are not dangerous. Although there are a certain percentage of people who become violent due to some external factors, most of the cases are not violent. Most of the time, people can become violent because they are already affected by the outside world, and have irrational beliefs and suffer from them. Therefore, when paranoid, people feel pain and worries. Some may say that a paranoid schizophrenic are making up stories. However, this story may occur in one's mind or may happen during a particular period of time but cannot be prove. When listening to the story one may judge that it does not makes sense. Through hallucinations or delusions, the patient would experience difficulties in his or her life. If some sort of drama occurs, the patient would say it has happened and would strongly believe that the story happened for real.

When undergoing treatments, it is very difficult to maintain a stable relationship with the family, spouse, or with the outside world. One feels tired and weak from the medications. Medications have side effects that could affect the relationship with the spouse. For example, with having a lack of sexual desire, the partner may wish to have sexual intercourse but one may feel exhausted and may withdraw from having a sexual relationship. He or she may show lack of intimacy and passion. If the partner does not show any sign of desire then the patient may not show any sign of arousal. Slowly, this could create conflicts with a couple. If the spouse does not show any support or understanding with the patient then the relationship may not work. The wife or husband has a primary role of supporting and showing love, affection, and honesty with someone who has schizophrenia.

In disorganized-type Schizophrenia, the predominant feature is disorganization of thought processes. As a rule, hallucinations and delusions are less pronounced, although there may be some evidence of these symptoms (Bengston p.1). When talking about this symptom subtype, the patient has a different type of thought than a normal human being. Basically, the cognitive part of thought in the mental process is different. When discussing about one's experiences on this matter, one could spend hours with the same thought constantly thinking over and over of the same situation or scenario, and this followed by emotional withdrawal. For example, one will subconsciously attach an emotion with the thought and as a result one would have an irrational feeling. In a severe case, one might not be able to do regular activities, such as taking a bath, dressing, brushing his or her teeth or even preparing meals, and one will lose touch from doing certain things before like one was ill.

The cause is unknown and the disorganized-type schizophrenia usually begins before age 25. The Symptoms are "Active behavior, but in an aimless and not constructive way such as bizarre and inappropriate emotional responses (laughter), difficulty in feeling pleasure, false, fixed beliefs (delusions), grimacing, lack of motivation, seeing or hearing things that aren't there (hallucinations), strange or silly behavior, and speech that makes no sense" (2012). Having such symptoms can be very difficult for a person who is living with disorganized-type Schizophrenia. There are many different types of Schizophrenia. Behaving in a certain way can make a difference from one person to the other. In this context, being able to function and be organized and having normal behavior can be challenging.

The predominant clinical features of Catatonic Schizophrenia involve disturbances in movement. Affected people may exhibit a dramatic reduction in activity, to the point that voluntary movement stops, as in a catatonic stupor (Bengston p.1). This is a situation where one moves constantly or is fixed to stay in one place when one is ordered to do so. An example of the situation is when one paces continually for hours and hours without it. Instead of walking outside, one walls inside. Moreover, there are some more signs and symptoms that describe the Catatonic Schizophrenia such as "physically immobile, waxy mobility, excessive mobility, uncooperative, strange movements, and echolalia" (2013).

The ill person may not be able to move or even to speak due to biological factors. One may remain in a fixed position for a certain period by holding their body not being able to distinguish from the surrounding is also another challenge that the patient face in this particular illness. On the other hand, Waxy flexibility occurs when a patient remains in the same position as when someone leaves him or her. For example, when an individual moves the patients: leg in a position, the patient will remain in that position for a long period of time. The ill person may not even realize that this happened and would stay fixed in the position where he or she was. When someone has trouble with a certain things other may do the opposite. An example of Excessive mobility is when a patient may decide to move from one place to the other without any reason. Some may pace from one place to the next by walking in a straight line. This may happen when there is something in the patient's thoughts or if the patient has too much energy. Furthermore, the patient may be over excited for no specific reason.

Some patients may not realize their own behavior or when others are moving their body. This happens when the patient is uncooperative. The patient would not say a word in regards to being moved, while others may not respond to any instruction. Also the patient can develop some strange movements. He or she may move in an inappropriate way or be in an unusual posture. Then they may show some awkward grimace to other for no reason. Some examples of unusual behavior are repeating certain sentences or simple words continuously and being extremely obsessed with something in particular. Echolalia is repeating what others say, while Echopraxia is copying or duplicating other's movements.

"The undifferentiated subtype of schizophrenia is diagnosed when people have symptoms of schizophrenia that are not sufficiently formed or specific enough to permit classification of the illness into one of the other subtypes" (Bendston p.1). This subtype is one of its kind. One is considered to fall under this category until can prove otherwise. "In some cases, undifferentiated schizophrenia symptoms change often, resembling the symptoms of various types of schizophrenia at different times and defying classification. In other cases of undifferentiated schizophrenia, symptoms are stable but they don't match the description of the symptoms of other types of schizophrenia" (2011).

The Undifferentiated-type Schizophrenia has many of the same symptoms as those with other Schizophrenia subtypes such as Catatonic symptom, delusions, hallucinations, disorganized thought, and various form of emotions. "A gradual worsening of "negative" symptoms often occurs in cases of undifferentiated schizophrenia. Negative symptoms result from the loss of mental function. "Positive" symptoms such as hallucinations or delusions result from excessive mental functioning. Negative symptoms associated with undifferentiated schizophrenia include: Deadened or dulled emotions, improvised or impaired speech, inability to feel pleasure, loss of interest in activities, and social withdrawal" (2011). This subtype is considered a subtype of schizophrenia and requires a treatment plan.

The treatment options are similar to those required in other types of schizophrenia. After finding the right diagnosis, the psychiatrist can better decide what needs to be done next. What need to be prescribes as medication or therapy, if the patient should be followed by practitioners. This type of disorder can stem from complications of other types of illness and may be paralleled by some common disorders. This type illness might be genetic and may change mental function. Research is ongoing to understand this subtype of schizophrenia better.

Residual-type schizophrenia, is diagnosed when the patient no longer displays prominent symptoms. In such cases, the schizophrenic symptoms generally have lessened in severity. Hallucinations, delusions or idiosyncratic behaviors may still be present, but their manifestations are significantly diminished in comparison to the acute phase of the illness (Bendston p.1). Patients who are in progress of getting better from schizophrenia are typically termed as "residual-schizophrenia". They usually experience least one episode within a few years and are recommended to regularly see a shrink. One with this disorder shows no positive symptoms (delusions, hallucinations, disorganized speech). Most of the patients can maintain a stable life with a family. Residual-type schizophrenia is "a type of Schizophrenia in which the following criteria are met: Absence of prominent delusions, hallucinations, disorganized speech, and grossly disorganized or catatonic behavior. There is continuing evidence of the disturbance, as indicated by the presence of negative symptoms or two or more symptoms listed in Criterion A for Schizophrenia, present in an attenuated form (e.g., odd beliefs, unusual perceptual experiences)" (2013). From the Schizophrenia Society of Ontario website, "Schizophrenia is a chronic illness—most who are diagnosed will require various levels of treatment for most of their lives: 30% recover quite well, and are eventually able to resume their previous level of functioning; 30% recover to a lesser extent, but are usually able to live independently, 30% require extensive help, such as living in supportive housing or in a care facility. Sadly, the remaining 10% do not survive schizophrenia, usually due to suicide" (2011).

According to the DSM-IV-TR (Diagnostic and Statistical Manual of Mental Disorders) 60%-70% of individuals with Schizophrenia do not marry, and most have relatively limited social contacts.' (p.302). When one's partners knows about one's symptoms, he or she may investigate more about the disorder, and may not react positively. When your partner has no idea about the illness, it is difficult to reveal this to her or him. It is a shocking moment, it is hard for an individual, and it is controversial for a married couple to know that Schizophrenia is in your roots. What will happen to your offspring. Will she or he become like you? The relationship that you have built may collapse because a partner cannot accept the fact that you are Schizophrenic.

After being in a relationship for a few years, I have discovered that my interpersonal relation with others is weak. I do not know how to deal with people, and I have trouble being surrounded of people. I am not the same person I was a few years ago. I was very prudent, worried that people may comment on me or may hurt my feelings. I did not call my friends like I used to do. With my partner, there was a communication gap. I feared that I may lose my partner. I saw my wife differently because of the illness. It seems that there is no love between us. There was a big chance that it could not work out well.

At work it was even worse. It seemed the world was against me: all co-workers are talking behind my backs, my boss wants to hurt me. Have you ever felt like this at work? If you did then you may have a symptom. When you feel ill, you may not be able to work the way you used to, your performance at work may worsen. Your motivation will change. It might seem that everything is negative. People around you may help you, whereas you may feel that they want to hurt you. However, one may take advantage knowing that you are ill. It is important to be alert!

Having a good education is really important to have a pretty good job with a high salary. For a person who is schizophrenic, completing school, college or university is very challenging. In my case I was very lucky to complete my Bachelor of Arts, majoring in psychology before I become ill. The symptoms appeared slowly. At that time I thought I did not have schizophrenia. It was not until I was hospitalized and had psychosis that I was diagnosed with schizophrenia. I felt that my education was useless: even though I completed it, the result was not worth it. I was not able to practice and attain my dreams.

Not being able to care for myself was demotivating. Luckily, I have wonderful parents and a sister who helped me during my time of trial. It was extremely difficult for them and for myself, for many years, they supported me and helped me. Their perception about Schizophrenia is different from mine. In the following paragraph I will discussed one with education, family, friends, money, career, relation and sexual difficulty.

Education and Schizophrenia

Having the proper education is important. Having knowledge about our own illness can make a big difference and can change our lives. Knowing our weaknesses and strength can help us overcome the dark periods. We should ask a specialist on mental health to educate us and our family members. I felt as if my intelligence dropped by a vast percentage after my schizophrenia diagnosis. How can we educate ourselves of schizophrenia? Hospitals are a prime source as an educational centre. If you do not go to the hospital, then you can drop by a Clinique. You can choose to read articles on the internet, newspapers, books, watch documentaries, or ask someone with the illness. If this fails then you should ask a medical doctor. The more educated you are about the illness, the better your chances are at developing a good relationship with those who suffer from schizophrenia.

Family and Schizophrenia

Schizophrenia can bring a lot of stress to a family. For some, it might become a nightmare to not know how to cope with the schizophrenic, what to say to them, how to behave in front of them. In many cases, it takes a lot of time before one obtains a diagnosis. One with the illness may have changed his or her behavior while waiting for a diagnosis. Love and support play an important part in treatment and recovery. The partner needs to show care, affection, gentleness and be a good listener. When ill, you are out of reality the more time has passed the more necessary it is to show that you are there for that person. A partner has to show an understanding towards the patient by reassuring him or her that you will fight until the end of the treatment and recovery. If this fail then the relationship will fail.

Being a parent of someone with schizophrenia is not an easy job. Knowing that his or her child is severely ill can change one's life. This could have an impact emotionally, psychologically and socially for the parents, siblings, spouse and the patient. It is extremely important for the parents and sibling to show support, care and loves and reassure the patient they are there for the patient and their door will always be open for the patient. It is really essential for the parents and the siblings to educate themselves about the illness that their child is struggling with. In a time of trial it is significant not to create any kinds of stress. The parents have to stay calm and willing to acknowledge that the patient may react to any kinds of destruction. The more support the mentally ill gets the more quickly they will recover from the illness.

Friends and Schizophrenia

Those with Schizophrenia will choose to have a limited number of friends. When a patient slowly starts isolating themselves due to the illness, a friend needs to show support. Usually, the patient will confide in a friend about disturbing scenarios in their life. He or she may say that at this moment they are not attending school or not working or that his or her marriage life is falling apart. A friend should be open to talk. Someone with schizophrenia will choose not to discuss about his or her situation to those they do not trust. In this case, it is best to ignore what one is going through due to the illness.

For most of us we all want to help our peers by showing a sort of empathy. We show that we are concerned and we would like to help when a friend is going through a severe situation. Having schizophrenia, I hated to know my friends or even people from my community are discussing about me. One should not insult a handicap or mentally ill because of their health condition. Even though some people think that creating rumors about others is amusing, it insulting and to divulge private information others is wrong. It is important to know that a friend who helps you is a true friend.

Money and Schizophrenia

With schizophrenia, it is difficult to organize one's thoughts in everyday matters. Money is impossible to track and plan when one suffers from this disorder. It is not surprising then that a lot of people and with schizophrenia end up on the streets. How can one survive without money?

There are many ways to overcome difficult financial situations. At first it is really important to be frugal in a positive way. When one is struggling with finances, saying "I will not purchase unnecessary gifts for myself this month and I will save some money for the next month". This helps thinking could help you believe that you do not want to throw money away.

Planning for a possible financial crises is also important. What you do not have can hurt you but what you have cannot hurt you. Keep money aside and you will see it will be used when needed. In a relationship, when only one person works, it is prime that this person controls the money. The reason is simple: one who brings the money will know where it is being spent, while the opposite partner may or may not value the money. A person may not realize how much it costs to securely manage a family lifestyle when ill.

Knowing where the money is being spent and what are you doing wrong on dealing with the money can benefit yourself and your relationship. Challenge yourself to do the right thing. Discuss with your spouse all types of obstacles when you share valuable bills. Keep track of all the expenses and eliminate unwanted expenses. Use only what you have at the moment not what you expect to get; what you have use it for the present and if you have extra save it for the future. Do not assume that you can spend more than what you have by justifying that it will be paid in the future. Keep control of your finance. Keep control of your own action. Do not let anyone walk over your head by agreeing to spend money that you do not have.

It is preferable not to show any types of weakness in front of your partner. This could be seen negatively and be stressful to the opposite partner or in your family. An example, if you tell your landlord that you have been ill for a few months and that you have a financial crisis, this could affect your credibility to your landlord. Your landlord might evict you if you did not pay your rent, forcing you and your family in the street. Do not take negative experiences as weaknesses, consider what is meant to happen as happening for a good purpose. Try to change a negative situation to a positive one. In this case the husband and wife have no choice to build the relationship stronger. Stay away of stressful events. One way to do this is to spend time with your kids or pets, listen to music, watch TV, and movies, read books or write a journal, go outside and do some jogging and play sports. If you feel alone then bring your wife or husband or even your children with you.

If your mind is frozen, and you do not know what to do, talk to a smarter person than you. It could be a friend, your parents, your brother or sister, anyone whom you trust. If this does not work talk to a professional, such as a social worker, health practitioner or even a lawyer. They can help guide you through hardship. The main goal here is to go back on track by gaining control of your situation. By being more optimistic you will feel happier. You will feel better knowing that you have survived a difficult period. If you are overloaded with debts you are not the only one in the country. Ask a financial planner to help you revamp your finances to pay off all your debts as fast as possible. Keep a record of how much get paid and how much you want to spend on a regular basis. One advice for reducing worries, is to forget about buying expensive toy such as a car. You can reduce stress by choosing to purchase fewer materials or unnecessary expenses by being wise. One should use money to create a secure future by putting aside a certain amount so that you can plan to have control of your money. Make a commitment to save money.

Financial Planning

Budgeting: Most people work and have a plan in how to spend money they earn. Some people spend money continuously while others try to put money aside. It is really necessary to take the time to realize how much we spend and how smart we are in dealing with money. In my observation, I have realized that some of my friends do not manage money properly. It seems that they spend money that they do not have. Then they end up borrowing money from their friends or from the bank. We should not wait until a financial crises, instead we should plan in advance. If we tend not spend money correctly it could lead to a severe deficit especially when we have mortgages, loans, lines of credit, car loans, furniture loans, etc. We are influenced to spend money by the people around us. We tend to spend money when we are with others. We feel proud to spend money in front of others.

We are all influenced to purchase luxurious things such as cars, clothes, house decorations, and vacations Most of the time, people would use credit cards to treat others. What they do not realize is that they will end of up with a large debt. My advice is if you spend more than what you earn, then you should pay off your debt, destroy your credit cards, and use only cash, checks or even debit cards. This will allow you to protect yourself and give you peace of mind knowing that you do not have any debt. Being in debt can be very stressful for everyone. For someone with an illness such as schizophrenia or even mental illness, it can be even more difficult to manage and budget money.

The more money you save the more beneficial it will be for you. It is really important to put aside money, at least 5 to 15% of your earning for the future. You will never know when you would need the money that you have saved or even use it for retirement. CBC reported than senior citizens in Canada are not prepared for the future and their retirement. People will not have enough money even with a pension. According to CBC, a person at the age of 65 will not be able to live their life healthily and with wealth. Only one third of the population; will be wealthy while two-thirds will suffer.

It is advisable to protect ourselves by not investing too much money on something you are unsure of. Do not buy property, items or any kind of things that will drop in value. Buy something that will have an impact for the future. For example, buy something that can help you gain more money when you end up selling it. Do not be easily influenced by people who give advice in getting those materialistic things. Some may influence you to invest money in real estate, bond, stocks, and shares, it is up to you to decide where you would like to invest your money. It is really good to research before investing. There are various types of products offered by different financial institutions, therefore find something that will gain value and will make you proud of your decision. If you are unsure about a product or even any kind of information, ask the sales representative, or even inquire about the product and any kind of information.

When you make a bad financial decision, do not become emotional. Don't panic when your stocks or shares drop. Do not blame yourself or even your financial advisors. Making money is based on luck. When you can put a limit on your emotional states you will be capable of handling financial obstacles. You should focus on making a wise decision after having difficult moment in your financial life.

You will feel secure to have money in your bank account. Having money saved up can help you plan your future. Some can build a solid relationship by using their money. For example, saving money for marriage can help you buy an expensive and luxurious car, a dream house, travel, wear expensive clothes, give nice gifts, and eat in luxurious restaurants. You also can invest on yourself: you can spend money on education by getting a degree that counts. Plan ahead for a future transaction and choices. When you think about finance and money, planning your investments or savings can be useful for many of reasons. A person who is schizophrenic can make difficult and painful financial decisions. Some make terrible mistakes by taking a big amount of loans. Some may file for bankruptcy while others live on the cusp of losing money. Many people do not have enough money to survive and, certain percentage become homeless. Others live with their family or a foster home. Depending on the province and country, people with mental illness may get some types of support but majority live on the streets. In the first world country people with mental illness are privileged to be cared for but a lot of people still suffer.

One way for a person to understand their finances is to understand how much they spend and save money on a daily, monthly and yearly basis. It is necessary to budget and understand your personal finances. The budget is based on your income and your expenses. When you understand your budget you will be able to stay out of debt. Once you can stay away from debt you will feel much better and wealthier. You will feel good about yourself that you have saved a certain amount and when time comes you can spend the money wisely. You will feel good to have good credit, and you will understand value of money. Find a way to save money. Be creative and brilliant when dealing with money. After all it is your money and you should have discipline in your financial planning. Create a list for yourself on how to make money and how to save money. The bank and financial advisors are experts in saving money or planning one's income better. Trust yourself and make good judgments.

Career and Schizophrenia

Students graduating from college or university can gradually seek employment. Most of us are privileged to have a career choice in our early 20s or 30s. Making a career path is not an easy path if we do not know what will fit us. Choosing a corporation or organization and spending our lifetime with that company is daunting. The job that you want should suit the lifestyle you want. If you are unsure then keep your options open and keep searching for a better opportunity. It seems that there are many people who are willing to encourage others to keep studying or keep working. Among the younger generation, there is a race for the right job. The pressure is humungous, it seems that the sky will fall on us. Most of us are still young and may not care about keeping a certain job. We may be unsure of what we really want to do. In that case, it may be preferable to take some time off from school or work to figure out what you really care about and what is really important to you. Use the skills that you already have in your current work. However, education will lead to a better career.

Education, is a great thing to add on your resume. Keep searching for better opportunities by keeping your options open. You may never know what other opportunities may come to you when you have a college or university degree. You will never know what is useful until you have to utilise what you have learned in the past. Education will help you choose a profession of your expertise. Having knowledge is great but with time it is always beneficial to continue learning to develop more skills and enhance life. Being flexible is an asset nowadays. A person may prefer to hire someone with many qualities and skills. Having diverse interests could be beneficial in the long run as it can open other fields in careers. Put all your strength and effort into doing something because it could be rewarding. You will never know when you may get promoted based on your performance or loyalty.

It is demoralizing to work in something we do not enjoy. In this case, one will be discouraged and will develop negative thoughts and attitudes. It can be stressful to reject what others do. In a place where one is acknowledged and appreciated, one will feel fruitful and one's self-esteem will boost. Not wanting to do what we are asked to or hating the daily routine will misbalance us from reality. If you are not sure of what you want, you can volunteer at a place that appreciates your services. There is nothing wrong with dirtying your hands and showing your motivation. When the employers see that you can do a good job they might offer you a paid position. Volunteer work can help you build a strong network and could be priceless.

If you are not sure about something, you should ask as many questions that come to mind. In a particular job field that you have doubts about you should inquiry about the downside and the upside of the job. Learning the both sides can help you understand if a job fits for you or not. When choosing a job, do you feel that you will benefit from it or will you consider it monotonous? If it does not work for you then you are still not convinced about the information that I have mentioned. In that case, you should ask your peers, parents, teachers or even career counsellors about their opinions. When you have all the information, you may take it to the next level. You should have a good sense of how previous experience, research, additional training and belief can help you decide on a career.

Relation and Schizophrenia

In our lifespan, we will experience different types of relationships. We all have all types of relationships such as those between friends, lovers, families, co-workers, acquaintances and strangers. Depending on the relationship, one may develop any kinds of feelings, enjoyment and self-growth. Whereas, some may treat us differently based on various circumstances. The relationship can be healthy or even unhealthy, worm or cold, happy or unhappy, satisfying or unsatisfying. Do you consider your relationships to be strong? The following information discussed will give an idea about a situation where one stand. A good relationship between two friends needs to have compromises and respect. Among co-worker if there is no security and comfort discussing or helping each other then the relationship will be cold. When talking to your lover, one cannot be violent, one has to be truthful and one has to be able to resolve conflict by supporting each other. Between family members, one needs to take the initiative by asking his or her parents or sibling they are well, if they need any kind of support, and to show them that you care for them. With acquaintances, it is important to talk freely up to certain limits. Whereas, with strangers you may greet them with kindness.

It could be difficult to maintain a relationship with someone with schizophrenia For example, with a lover, one cannot manipulate him or her or the relation will break. One also cannot be easily jealous about any kinds of situation. One should not threaten to leave or criticize them of their behavior or even insult them. With friends, one cannot call their names or make fun of them for no reason. This could lead them to not be a true friend. Among co-workers, one should not make one feel bad about any kind of situation. Whereas, an acquaintance should not dictate anything to people they do not know. A stranger should not comment on how others are dressed. There could be various reasons for not wanting to keep a relationship with others. A person can bring a lot of stress to others by saying unwanted things or by disrespecting his or her beliefs. A person should not judge others based on their disability, ethnicity, race, sexual orientation, gender or other personal beliefs.

A healthy couple will stand strong, and will not have problems resolving conflicts. They do not need to have a mediator in between their relation. They feel warm and enjoy spending their time together. They are happy to laugh together. One will support one another when one is down. When one goes to work, the partner shows interest in knowing how it was or show some form of caring while he or she was not there. To keep it positive, one may cook something for the partner who is sick or would him or her wish to gets better. A couple would show concern or understanding of each other. Furthermore, one feels warm to be surrounded by or her lover's family members. When one is unsatisfied with something one keep it privately within the couple. Personal and confidential matters should be discussed between husband and wife or boyfriend and girlfriend. A healthy relation does not need drugs or excessive alcohol. One cannot be happy if one is not satisfied sexually or unable to communicate properly and honestly. Having intimacy will create a sort of bond between the couple. To keep the relationship together, it is required to have more good time than bad times and to feel proud about your relationship that you have built for such a long period of time.

Unhappy relationships could start by not communicating properly with each other. When you are at home, and the partner does not pay attention to you, ignore you when you speak, spends time with his or her friends by pretending to be on the phone or does not show interest for you. Basically, an unhealthy relationship is when a couple does not want to make time for each other. In to disagreements one shows excessive temper and raises his or her tone with the partner. Instead of showing support and motivating the other, one will discourage them. One may be extremely rough by pushing or grabbing the partner strongly by threatening him or her. One may throw certain objects to take control over the person. One may show unhappiness of not being able to control the other's finances. One may also discourage the other from doing something by showing dissatisfaction towards someone or something. All the above could break up a couple. Both the male and female will go through many triggers and stress. Both will feel different when not together.

Health can play a primary role in establishing a secure relationship between a couple. When ill, it is important to be honest to your partner. Sometimes one may choose not to mention it as he or she does not want to create extra stress. Basically, what you do not know cannot hurt you. One may keep it confidential, especially when one is mentally ill or has schizophrenia. The majority of the population may not know about this illness, therefore it could ruin the relationship. In this case, one can reveal that it is good to be honest, but sometimes it is preferable not to be fully honest. When revealing the truth, it all depends on if one can accept this illness. When you choose to accept the illness you will, appreciate the partner for being unique and sincere. Therefore, one has accepted the mate decision by showing mutual respect. Hence, the mentally ill partner will feel safe by knowing that the relationship can succeed or collapse. Both couple can choose to take two different directions.

Sex and Schizophrenia

When it comes to mental health, sex is one of the topics often discussed. Sex, unlike other topics in this book, should be treated as for information purposes only. One should be advised that the following section might be sensitive. Not all relationships are perfect. A couple may not fully be aroused when making love. Many may encounter obstacles such as sexual dysfunction. One may have sexual problems and may not know what to do. It is believed that in a healthy relationship, for a couple typically perform sexual intercourse at least twice weekly. The more a couple have sex, the more healthy their relationship becomes.

People may not know how to cope with a highly stressful period. As a result, may have difficulty being aroused. Feeling burning during intercourse could be a sign of pleasure or pain. Someone who takes medication on a regular basis may show signs of sexual problems. Depending on the medications, one may have multiple side effects that would impair performance. Moreover, when a couple have a dispute he or she may not be in mood for intimacy, passion. In reality, when things do not go as planned, you may not have sexual desire. When one is in mood and the other shows discomfort the feelings and attraction may disappear.

Disability

When sick, it is extremely hard to go and to do work every day. Missing many days at work can be seen as a sign of laziness. It can also put one in danger of losing his or her job. Sometimes the employers may not believe you until they see you or hear your story. While working for a company there are many advantages and disadvantages of being on disability leave. If you have been working for many years you have the insurance you have paid on previous paychecks. In that case you, like me in my previous job, are lucky to have support from your company and your insurance company. Sometimes even the government can support people who get sick. Having the privilege of being supported by your company or the government can help one to live life without tension and worries. Obviously, your paychecks may not be as much as while you were working but you get enough to survive.

Having a company or organisation supporting your health and sickness can be a sign of generosity and kindness. When being on sick leave, the company allows you to take the time to heal yourself. If you want to change your career, this can be done while on sick leave as well. What is great about the system is that you can find others who have the same illness. This can motivate you as you would know that you are not alone in the treatment process. You can benefit from the time off by taking different classes such as cooking lessons or computer classes. While undergoing treatment, you may learn how to manage stress and educate yourself of other types of stressors or triggers. You can also take the initiative to get involved in volunteering or even participating in various organization before going back to work.

On the other side, the disadvantages of being on sick leave can be disastrous. For example, when returning to work, you have to face the stigma from coworkers. Many may ask questions about why you were on leave or more details about the illness. This can affect the self-esteem or even trigger flashbacks of being ill. Sometimes, there is social isolation at work. Finding the right people around you can be difficult. Talking, behaving and being yourself can be challenging especially when recovering from an illness. People may have different judgment about you or your illness. Furthermore, following a daily routine can be hard for someone who was ill. However, most people attend work after their recovery. If you get enough support then you may have the facility to a transition to another place. It is necessary to have a good relationship between coworkers, supervisors and health professionals as they will help put you on sick leave and they will allow you to better work. This will help you better find yourself.

Culture and schizophrenia

Based on the Schizophrenia Society of Ontario, "Schizophrenia affects 1 in 100 people and occurs in every race, culture, and socio-economic group" (2011). No one can actually tell if the disorder originates from a continent, country, city or area. In some countries the majority of the population is not even aware of this illness. In third world countries, the government does not pay much attention to mental illness. Mentally ill people in certain countries are not be treated like other people with other illness. For example, in Bangladesh, there are many poor people with mental illness and they may not know about their symptoms and illness. Many people become beggars and live on the street. There is a vast population who are homeless. No one can tell what illness they face every day. When people with mental disorder act differently to others, some may say that they are haunted by ghosts, or are victims of black magic.

Other personal beliefs and Schizophrenia

We are all human beings and we all think differently. A personal belief is based on the perception that we have on something or someone. Our beliefs may protect us from the unknown. Dealing with schizophrenia, one has many different feelings and ideas about the unknown. Often one wants to be cautious about someone or something. The personal beliefs can described as having the following thoughts; 'if I do not perform well on something people will say that I am not good at it', or 'if I do not call my friends, people will say that I have no friends,' or 'if I do not have a girlfriend or boyfriend, one may think that I am homosexual,' or 'I must do this perfectly if I want to reach perfectionism'. Sometimes we value what others think about us more than what we think about ourselves. This is one reason why a schizophrenic may not be able to deal with society and withdraw from reality. The conception others have of us is somehow more important than the real fact. It is natural and normal not to be accomplished at everything; it does not mean that you should take all critics seriously. If you take the bus and the metro (subway), you would be astonished to hear what other people are discussing. Many people do not realize what they say in public. Listening to them, one will understand that we are all humans and it is normal and natural for people to gossip others. He or she has the right to choose a certain lifestyle according to their beliefs.

Not being able to express yourself properly can damage your health. Keeping sorrow, pain, doubt, inside of yourself, can put you under stress and this may bring future conflict. Not knowing how to handle a certain situation may misbalance one mind and thoughts. It is great that you have your own beliefs about a certain situation or thing but thinking rationally is the main aim here. It is your life therefore you should take control of your situation and conflict. Never let anyone walk over your head just because you do not share the same belief or have the common goals. It's great that you are independent; therefore if you think that you do not need help do not ask for it. Do what you have to do and understand if this is right for you. When lonely, it is always good to be with someone you trust. If you cannot build trust with someone then you have to work on this matter. It can take one second to many years to build a relationship. Hence, the bond that you have created may be destroyed within a fraction of second due to misunderstanding, painful events or mistrust. You may stay away from people to reduce problems, worries, misunderstanding and unwanted dilemma as a result. This may help you for a short period of time. However, when you have stopped contacting people you may feel lonely. It is important not to isolate yourself due to interpersonal crisis. Think positively. If you have problems, others have their problems as well. Therefore, if they can handle it, you must be able to handle it as well. Furthermore, if others can be happy, you may find happiness within yourself as well. If there is something or someone that you value the most, focus on that thing or person. Do not think about being in the center of the universe, but find the centre of yourself. Since you do not control others, at least you can control yourself. By being yourself you will see that other will want to be a part of your life and they will let you be a part of theirs.

Negative symptoms

The negative symptoms of schizophrenia is 'absence as much as a presence: inexpressive faces, blank looks, monotonous and monosyllabic speech, few gestures, seeming lack of interest in the world and other people, inability to feel pleasure or act spontaneously. About 25% of patients with schizophrenia have a condition called the deficit syndrome, defined by severe and persistent negative symptoms'. (2006). Patients with negative symptoms have trouble keeping jobs, cannot be independent rarely maintain relationships, and find it difficult to concentrate has difficulty expressing or thinking logically, or cannot perform a social tasks in a proper way. One with this disorder will face many obstacle from not showing any interest in expressing and revealing feelings. One may not feel like doing activities or would prefer to spend time alone or at home, where, one feels secure and safe.

Those with schizophrenia also develop cognitive symptom. One may perform negative tasks poorly due to the illness. Researchers believe that due to the illness, one has limitations on completing certain tests and are inapt at keeping an attention on something. In socializing an observer cannot distinguish between patients with schizophrenia and those with social communication disorders. One may lack motivation and social skills. Due to the illness, a patient experience social anxiety and emotional disturbance.

Based on my observation, the best treatment for patients who have schizophrenia is getting support from spouse, children and family members. Obviously, the more help we get the better informed we become and the better the chance of recovery. In the hospital, practitioners, nurses, educators, occupational therapists, tailor the treatment based on each patient. Psychotherapy, group therapy, cognitive behaviour therapy or any other types of therapy can help patients recover. Another type of assistance that one can get is companionship between patients to patients and staff. If you have difficulty finding a job, there is support to search for employment, and to look for housing.

With therapy one with schizophrenia will develop social skills. Therapy helps an individual learn how to express their feelings, how to behave in front of others, and provide a space for the patient to ask for information and make requests. The use of proper gesture in front of others help in adjusting facial expressions, and body languages can also lessen insolation from others. The more therapy patient gets, the better the outcome. Patients who undergo all kinds of therapies tend to feel much better at the end of their rehabilitation. They can find happiness, make friends easily, have more knowledge about their symptoms and are ready for employment.

Have you ever heard someone with Schizophrenia talk? Sometimes, what one says just does not make sense. During my early symptoms I was not able to complete certain sentences. I would let others guess what I wanted to reveal. It was like playing charades; I would start by saying something then use my body to show the word. I felt that I needed to have the English or French dictionary by me all the time, because I was wordless, not knowing what to say or which proper word to use. The proper word to describe this type of symptom is disorganized speech. It happens mostly in severe cases, especially, with psychoses. It seems that it was very hard for me to mention a single sentence. Luckily, I speak three languages, when watching TV, I had a hard time understanding what actors or actress were saying. I had to understand through their body language. It was like putting a big headset without hearing any sound. You feel only the pressure. People who work in construction wear soundproof headsets. The feelings that one might get with those headsets is almost the same feeling that I was having.

Psychosis

Psychosis is a common symptom of Schizophrenia. People who usually suffer from abnormal condition of the mind are usually known as psychotic, in other words experiencing psychosis. When someone goes through psychosis, usually one does not have any contact with the reality. One may experience delusion or hallucination by having a certain belief and not being able to think properly. The sensory perception of the brain is affected. This also impairs social interaction and the daily activities. In the following paragraph I will describe the main symptom of psychosis, i.e. hallucination, and delusion.

When hallucinating you experience life through images; basically one may see certain things or hear specific sounds. One may see things that do not exist. One might be excited to see things at first sight or be horrified. It might be really dangerous for the self or even others around the patient. Certain medications may cause hallucinations. When one hear a sound where there is no sound, it could be hazardous. The mind could be controlled by an inner voice telling one to do something or to go somewhere. This happens when one is severely ill.

When delusional, a person may feel enlightened or confused, or they might have ideas that are truly false. One has a strong belief that a network is against that person, he or she is being spied upon, attacked, insulted, threatened by someone, discriminated against and is a victim of a certain thing or situation. One may say the their thoughts were taken away by an outside force, that external thoughts have been put into one's mind. Hence, delusions are a misinterpretation of perception.

Negative symptoms, have nothing to do with thinking negatively but it is a lack of motivation. One becomes very emotional, has trouble expressing him-or herself, is inapt at doing any activities, and cannot communicate properly. One does not have or need pleasure, one mostly loses interest in life. He or she has difficulties with relationships, for example, is not happy with the spouse or partner. This symptom can also be confused with depression.

Cognitive symptoms affect the thinking processes. Such as memory and how the thoughts are organized in your brain. This part of this brain manage daily tasks for work or education. In the next few chapter, one will discover more about cognitive symptoms of schizophrenia.

When I had Psychosis I was not functional. I could not think in a proper manner. My thoughts were deranged. My mind functioned slowly. Most of my memories were blocked due to my illness. I had no idea what exactly happened to me. My only memory that I had is that feeling like I was in a mouse trap. Sometimes it was like I was part of a video game, where each level was a scene in my mind. It seems that I was trapped in that game and I needed to do something to go on to the next scene. I felt like someone controlled my mind. It was like a message sent to me by showing some images, graphics, or even movement. When I had Psychosis, I did not realize that I was unconscious. I was hospitalized for one month and when I was in the hospital, it seems that I was awake where in the reality I was not. In my mind I was constantly moving and projecting image. It felt like I was moving and doing regular activities. When I came to, it took many months for me to feel alive and real.

Alien & Mafia

A very small percentage of those with Schizophrenia may reveal that he or she was attacked by an Alien. One may have strong beliefs that an Alien is controlling his or her mind, that he or she was captured and experimented on. Others may believe that they are a part of a special project of the Mafia that the mafia is controlling his or her mind, observing every detail. The mafia wants to use them for future projects. This paranoia exists in those with Paranoid Schizophrenia.

Verbal Abuse

Verbal Abuse can damage a relationship and hurt others emotionally, and psychologically and it may be more harsh than physical abuse. When using nasty and cruel words to punish someone, one will feel wounded and one's self-esteem will suffer. A minority of the people with schizophrenia may go through verbal abuse either from their peers or their loved ones. When doing these kinds of act, one will develop a sort of negative feeling towards that person whom one used to admire with utmost respect and kindness. The love and affection that one has for a spouse or even a friend can transform. Verbal abuse cannot be seen or has no records, whereas, physical abused can be traced or marked our body. Verbal abuse can occur at work, at school or at your home or even outside. Verbal abuse can be as harmful as physical abuse. Some example of verbal abuses are 'criticizing, insulting, yelling, putting others down, swearing, screaming, being rude, threatening, and blaming for something' (2012).

When the heat is on and people want to blame you for something, never feel unnecessarily guilty unless you have done something meaningful. Establish a boundary with others person by telling them that their words are harmful to you. When others want to verbally attack, they usually target your emotional and mental states. You are fragile, so seek for help, either through therapy or individual counselling. Look for support, either from your family members, friends, professionals or someone who is willing to give you good advice and listen to you. Obviously, it is painful to hear strong and meaningless words from someone who loves and cares for you. Therefore, be strong by not paying attention to those unwanted words or sentences. When a difficult situation occurs and others try to disrespect your values, walk away from the tense situation. You will win the battle when you decide to take control of the circumstances others have placed into your heart and mind.

Coping mechanism

'A coping mechanism is a strategy or behavior a person uses to deal with a negative, stressful, or uncomfortable environment. The person may or may not know that they do it, or why they do it, but it helps them feel better about the situation' (2012). For example, when feeling stressed out, someone may smoke cigarettes. There could be various reasons why one becomes stressed out. In most cases, one may not even know why or when they become stressed out. Many smokers are less tense after smoking. They are able to continue with their daily task or daily routine. Chain smokers are addicted to cigarettes, whereas others use strong and hazardous drugs, which can cause them to become severely ill or even cause mental instability.

Stress-relievers such as smoking, and drugs can be addictive. Side effects or even other types of illness can arise from these coping mechanisms. I would recommend frequent exercise as a stress-reliever. Getting fresh air by walking or running can help one cope with stress and be healthier. Let the mind and body adjust to each other follow a rhythm. The mind and body work together. When the mind is satisfied the body would respond accordingly. When the body is please the mind would feel peace.

Strategies

We are all human and we react to things differently. Some are able to cope in a decent way while others get lost easily. Many seek to find what could be a successful coping strategy. The following information is based on strategies related to coping with mental illness. Some techniques are as follows: 'deep breathing, listening to relaxing music, resting the body and mind by doing Yoga or Chi Kung, meditating, occupying yourselves by thinking about or doing something, comforting yourself, being creative, talking about your problems, try to work on your problems and expressed them'. (2009). You can also write a journal or even a book. You can watch TV, listen to music or browse the Internet. You may wish to read articles, newspapers, and magazines. Find yourself an activity that you would enjoy. There are many ways of reducing stress or avoiding conflict, it all depends on you as you are the prime person in charge of your own body and mind. If you know that something triggers you then stay away from that thing or that person. If you pace frequently and repeatedly, you would need to find out how to stop pacing. A solution could be to walk outside or to sit down, or to do something else. When you can cope with such stressors, you will find your own strength.

Depression

What is a Depression? 'Depression isn't just a temporary mood swing or a sign of personal weakness. It's a serious medical condition with many emotional, cognitive, physical and behavioural symptoms' (2011). It is estimated that at least 1 out of 10 Canadian will have depression in their life time. Those who feel depressed usually do not admit it. In most cases, one will feel blue throughout day and night. A depressed person loses interest in something or stop finding pleasure in their favorite events or activities. The patient will feel that life is not worthwhile or is worthlessness. Many have suicidal thoughts or the mind is covered with the idea of death. The majority of the time they will struggle with their emotions, will feel fatigue, may have too little or too much sleep, may not be able to think and concentre normally, will develop unexplained aches and pains, and gaining or losing weight. If you have these symptoms for at least two consecutive weeks, there is a chance that you are facing with depression. It is recommended to discuss with your Doctor if you experience these symptoms. In the following paragraph I will discuss more of symptoms of depression.

When depressed it is normal to have negative thoughts. These come from not being able to think properly. It seems that one is invaded with the same thoughts over and over again i.e. cognitive distortion. Sometimes one can overestimate the negative aspects of a certain situation or even scenario. Often people try to be a mind-reader: they try to guess what others think about or predict a behavior. A meteorologist may predict rain tomorrow; therefore we need to bring an umbrella. A depressed patient may think like a meteorologist by performing an action based on their prediction of others' thoughts and actions. In my case, I felt suspicious with my peers, friends, lover, family members, relatives and acquaintances and stranger. I believed that other people will try to harm me. Slowly, I isolated from society and tried to protect myself from unrealistic events. I feel like I was experiencing early symptoms of schizophrenia mixed with depression.

According to Smith, L., L., & Elliott, H., C depression causes one to have negative thoughts. The negative thoughts can start with one idea, for example thinking that one is worthless. A person may feel that something is missing in a certain situation or may want to commit suicide. One may think that he or she is a failure by blaming themselves. A person may not make proper decisions as their memory does not work accordingly. Furthermore, one may not look forward to much of anything. Then a person may feel that the world would be a better place without him or her. Basically, one is extremely pessimistic about things. Moreover, one cannot think of anything that sounds interesting or enjoyable as one feels that life is full of regrets. Also one cannot concentrate and mostly forget about what one has read. However, some patients may be high-functioning and not have any cognitive deficits. The negative thoughts make one feel more negative. When depressed, it is like being in a dark zone or atmosphere.

It is beneficial to know the symptoms of depression to figure out how to behave while having early symptom of depression. Often one may not go out and tries to have fun. One may not feel excited or amused while being with people. While depressed, one usually does not have a lot of energy as one does not feel like to exercise. On the other hand, being overly concerned with health and exercise is also another symptom of depression. When in a couple one might prefer not to spend time with his or her partner. At work, it is even worse: one would miss work often and does not feel motivated or productive. Furthermore, one cannot get the motivation to do something or to be a part of something. One would often postpone projects to other days. It seems that when doing a certain thing one will move at a slow pace and would not find a good reason of doing it.

Depression has a lot of impact on how we communicate or perform an activity with family members, friends, peers, coworkers and acquaintances. Smith, L., L., & Elliott, H., C also explain how depression affects the self and the surrounding while being part of a relationship. Usually one may start by avoiding people more than the usual, including friends and family. One may also have more difficulty than usual talking about his or her concerns. Some may be unusually irritable with others. In most of the time one will isolate by being alone. He or she also believe that no one cares about or understand him or her. When it comes to having a physically intimate relationship, one may not have the desire or be aroused due to lack of satisfaction, motivation and desire. Between friends one will let down those who are close to him or her by avoiding phone calls, or simply not talking as a regular friend would do.

The authors of Depression for Dummies; Smith, L., L., & Elliott, H., C discussed about how people suffer while having a major depression. Basically, a person will feel inability to concentrate or even making decisions. One will not be able to distinguish between right and wrong. Often he or she will have repetitive thoughts of suicide. One may think about committing suicide, or even ponder about which methods will be appropriate when taking their lives. Having disturbing thoughts can cause a major change in sleep patterns. Some may sleep during the day, others during early morning or a few hours a night. Often one will stay awake for a certain period of time. These lead to extreme fatigue and will compound the loss of interest about life. When tired, one can only function slowly and would feel agitated easily. Hence, one will have low sense of personal worth. A person may have various change in appetite and increased or decreased weight. Having different types of emotion can foster intense feelings of guilt and self-condemnation.

It is not easy to have depression, what is even harder is experiencing profound loss of who you used to be. A few examples are believing in the positives often one thinks that one is incapable of doing certain things. Other may have difficulty with relationships. Feeling less secure is also another tension that one may feel. Having a low self-esteem can make one feel less valuable. A change in one's status due to medical and financial reasons can make one feel empty or even worthless. This leads to various negative situations, for example, one may seek friendship and experience more rejection. Others may go to a job interview and realize that he or she failed the interview. When one may wish to take a risk in doing something or for someone, he or she may feel humiliated due to the negative feelings. Sometime, one may face different types of problems and realize that as much effort one puts in, it feels it will all be useless.

Some effective therapies can help one feel more motivated and reduce his or her symptoms. Therapies such as Cognitive therapy, Behavior therapy and Interpersonal therapy can help patients find a solution for depression. With Cognitive therapy one will learn about how people think, perceive and interpret events. Many may learn some techniques that can be used in the real world. Behavior therapy can help one change their behaviors. There could be many different types of situation or even scenarios to improve one's behavior to bring pleasure. From that point of view when finding pleasure one will be able to figure out how to focus on something and how to solve certain problems. Interpersonal therapy focuses on getting enough evidence to modify problems in one relationship. With enough evidence one will learn to support one's idea and feelings to reduce depression. Various type of therapies can also solve issues involved in a major change in life, such as grief, loss, divorce and for some it can be their retirement. Obviously, there are many different types of therapies and it is important to attend the right therapy for you. It is up to the person to identify if a type of therapy was useful or useless to them.

Obsessive Thinking

Obsessive thinking is the act of thinking about a certain situation or scenario repeatedly over a period of time, sometimes for many hours continuously. Most of the time, the thinking is negative and sometimes emotional. Some may do a lot of self-analysis, while others may create something like a drama in their mind. Based on the situation one will focus on thinking and might continuously day dream. People usually become absorbed in thought right after watching TV or a movie, reading books, articles, listening to the radio, or looking outside or hearing from others. These actions are useful to overcome obsessive thinking but you must be careful as the thoughts can deranged and disturbing with time.

When people have obsessive thoughts, the thoughts may come in various forms. Some have worries, others feel anxious from thinking. Some people also behave differently or be moody. When being engrossed with deranged thoughts, one may become angry. One may not like to be disturbed. Sometime one may have out-of-reality thoughts in their mind. This leads to emotional disturbances self-blame. It can be very difficult to be stable while having irrational and obsessive thoughts. Most people can find a solution to manage their bizarre thoughts. There is psychotherapy such as Cognitive Behavioral Therapy that can help an individual to better manage and overcome their obsessive thinking.

Overcome obsessive thinking? The following are some information to better manage one's mind. Try these tips and it might work for you as it did to me. I was often able to combat obsessive thoughts.

1.) **Take deep breathes.** You will be surprise to know that people do not breathe properly. Practice taking deep breaths and you can feel much better. There are many different exercises and techniques to teach one to breathe correctly.

2.) **Try to relax.** Relaxing can be anything that makes you feel comfortable and releases worries, tension, stress, fears, and mostly thoughts. Each person is different, therefore, relaxing varies from one person to the other.

3.) **Try to distract yourself.** Distracting is tricking yourself to not think about a something constantly. Do what makes you happy and instead of focusing on one thing you should focus on positive inputs and outputs. Practice by yourself as you are the only one who knows when you are invaded with obsessive thoughts. Find out what makes you change your thoughts. Being able to focus on something can help you forget about the obsessive thoughts. When you are able to focus on another task, you will be able to overcome unnecessary thoughts that travel in your mind. Prepare to combat with all kinds of weapons such as the tips above and below.

4.) **Exercise often.** When you do physical exercise you will feel much better. Exercising will not only help yourself emotionally, physically but also mentally. You will also be able to distract yourself when exercising. Try walking: it not only helps you be in better shape but helps you feel released from difficult moment.

5.) **Breathe some fresh air.** Find where you feel most absorbed by your thoughts. Know the places that can change your mind and subconsciously shape your thoughts. More precisely, if you think obsessively when you are in a certain room, then you should avoid being in that room. Find an alternative solution. For example, breathe some fresh air where you will feel better and less fearful.

6.) Take a hot or cold bath. Taking a bath or a shower can help a person feel better. You are not only cleaning yourself but it makes you look better in front of another person. When your head is wet you no longer think about imaginary thoughts but you are only concerned about putting a towel on top of it.

7.) Start a conversation with someone else. What might help you the most is to have a conversation with an individual. It is one way of distracting yourself. You will take control of your weird thoughts by changing them to positive ones. It also helps one to start have new ideas, topics, experiences, news, gossips and share verbal jokes and other types of conversation. Interacting with people will aid in dealing with unnecessary thoughts in your mind.

8.) Do something productive and meaningful. Have you realized that most of the time, we tend to think when we have nothing to do. We do not have time to think about ourselves when working or doing something productive. Our thoughts happen to be in our mind when we take the time to spend it with obsessive thoughts. It is amazing how it is possible to change our mind and taking control. Try to take control of your thoughts by working. See if you are able to overcome and change your own thoughts, emotions and feelings. You will take charge of your own health. Think positive and you will feel positive.

9.) Meditate. Meditating can shape your mind and improve your thinking at the end of the day. When you have a difficult moment with your mind, try to meditate. Control your mind and you will control your thoughts.

10.) Make a list of your thoughts and compare and contrast. Take a sheet or paper and write down the thoughts that make you feel uncomfortable. Write down all your negative and positive thoughts on the papers. You will be amazed at your own thoughts. This exercise helps people realize their good and bad thoughts. It helps you see yourself and find out what makes you feel unhappy about yourself along with what makes you feel good about yourself. Write down all the obsessive thoughts in your mind and try to distinguish reality from fantasy. You need to be able to understand your thoughts as they are very intimate and confidential information. Not everybody wants to tell or write our fantasy thoughts on a piece of paper or even share with others. Therefore write down what you feel safe and want to write from your heart. If you want to share your thoughts with someone else you may do it, if not you keep it for yourself and understand the connection between thoughts. This should keep your mood in balance and you would be able to focus for a certain period of time. Find out the right from wrong, true from false, good from bad thoughts, and you will be more optimistic about your own self. If you can compare and contrast your own thoughts you will be more rational and you will be able to overcome any fears, worries, tensions, and any negative aspects and thoughts in your mind.

11.) **Try to think on positive aspects rather than negative one.** More you are positive more you feel positively. If you can change your thoughts positively instead to thinking negatively you will take control and believe that there is not negative thinking in your mind. When being positive your moods, actions, behaviors, health and thoughts are shaped in a way that you do not see how you are better externally and internally.

12.) **Do something you enjoy.** The more you trap yourself with your thoughts the more worried, emotionally unbalanced, tense and deranged you will feel. Therefore, find something that you enjoy doing. If you enjoy playing sports then find the time to participate in an activity. If you enjoy reading then read more to escape from weird thoughts. You need to be preoccupied by something you enjoy. It will make you feel better and healthier.

13.)Use positive input such as what is real and or is not real.
Apart from yourself no one can read your mind. We have not reach a technology that can read our minds. It is necessary to distinguish true from false thoughts. Acknowledge what is possible and what is not realistic then decide on thoughts you can believe in. Making clear decisions and having good judgment can be healthy. If you can see the difference between real and what is not real then you will empower your thoughts.

Do not let your thoughts run your mind. You will feel much better at the end of day when you can control your mind and thoughts. You need to expect to be function well when you take care of your obsessive thinking. To heal you need to accept yourself and change your way of thinking. You may feel pain and chaos when your irrational thoughts take control of your mind, therefore do not let this happen. Try to think for once that you are normal and you can feel normal when taking the above tips mentioned. You are looking to stop having obsessive thinking for once and have rational thoughts pass your mind. Remember, everything is possible and it is a matter of trusting yourself. If you need help they are many ways to better prepare yourself and better control your beliefs, fears, tensions, worries, and thoughts. Your journey can be painful and very long but your patience is needed. You need to believe that you will overcome any kind of hardship and you are capable of using many resources to get healthier. With time, you will get over such thinking and slowly realize that you are no longer controlled by these thoughts. Your obsessive thinking will reduce and you can take control of your thoughts by controlling your beliefs, fears, tensions, worries and obsessive thoughts. You are a better and healthier person by connecting your mind and thoughts together.

Emotional

In the Wikipedia emotion encompasses the following 'Affection, Anger, Angst, Anguish, Annoyance, Anxiety, Apathy, Arousal, Awe, Boredom, Contempt, Contentment, Courage, Curiosity, Depression, Desire, Despair, Disappointment, Disgust, Distrust, Dread, Ecstasy, Embarrassment, Envy, Euphoria, Excitement, Fear, Frustration, Gratitude, Grief, Guilt, Happiness, Hatred, Hope, Horror, Hostility, Hurt, Hysteria, Indifference, Interest, Jealousy, Joy, Loathing, Loneliness, Love, Lust, Outrage, Panic, Passion, Pity, Pleasure, Pride, Rage, Regret, Remorse, Sadness, Satisfaction, Shame, Shock, Shyness, Sorrow, Suffering, Surprise, Terror, Trust, Wonder, Worry, Zeal, Zest'. These words are not just words, each has a particular meaning, therefore it is used differently from one person to another.

Sometime you may feel joyful and other time blue. Sometimes you may not know from where you are getting these feelings. Sometime you are stressed out and some other times you feel rested. When you are sweating due to excessive heat or shaking when it is too cold for example, your body is reacting to some form of action. We all have feelings and most of us can feel differently in the same situation. Our body language could be the perfect example of when one is being too or not enough emotional. Being emotional could be a positive quality but this could be bad for health as well. Knowing our limit of being too emotional could be better for each of us in managing and balancing our internal and external feelings.

One can feel anxiety about something that has occurred; this anxiety is an internal response. One will feel and will become emotional by showing an external response, such as crying or obsessing about the situation that just happened. When seeing someone's body language, you will be able to pin point exactly what they are going through and how they feel. Other times, you may not show any kind of responses. Therefore it can be hard for an observer or even the self to realize how they are behaving or feeling. Mental health plays a primary role in helping us control our emotions. Our emotions change constantly. Knowing how we feel can help us decipher if we suffer from an illness. We all go through various feelings daily and we should not worry about negative feelings to a certain extent. However, someone of who is extremely hurt and stays hurt for a long time could be a symptom of sickness. Someone who is healthy can go through stress or negative feelings and be able to bounce back with a positive attitude.

A person who is healthy emotionally may have high self-esteem or high self-confidence. Therefore, when confronted by a negative situation, they can fight back to protect themselves by controlling their emotions. One tends to be capable of dealing with any kinds of criticism, blame or sorrow. One is able to adapt to different environments because he or she can regulate their emotions. One can have a positive attitude with others. One will learn and develop skills to better impact others. Being mentally ill or schizophrenic can be challenging, thus overcoming negative thoughts and emotions by implementing positive outcome can make a difference.

Cognitive

Cognition refers to thinking and conscious reasoning. Cognition helps us accomplish various forms of capacities. To better understand the cognitive parts of human being one must be able to view how thinking works. In the following paragraph I will discuss about aspects of cognition: 'memory, problem-solving, attention, reading, linguistic, verbal comprehension, math comprehension, visual comprehension' (2013).

Memory

Have you ever wondered what might happen if we did not have memory? Memory is the information we store and remember. How is information formed and stored as memory? 'The information processing models consist of a series of stages: input, storage, and output. Input processes consist of analyzing the stimuli. Storage processes include what happens to the stimuli in the brain: our brain codes and manipulates the stimuli. Then output processes prepare an appropriate response to the stimuli' (McLeod, S.A. 2008). Without the proper input, storage and output process in place, memory would not function appropriately. Human brain unlike other species are very exceptional and complex. Our brain is more powerful than a mini computer. Memory is discussed in details in the following chapters.

Problem-solving

One usually faces problems daily. Every problem has a solution. It is important to understand a problem to resolve it. It can be difficult to decide on a solution when there are alternatives. Therefore, one should implement new ways of seeing things. In About.com, problem-solving is defined as 'a mental process that involves discovering, analyzing and solving problems. The ultimate goal of problem-solving is to overcome obstacles and find a solution that best resolves the issue.' (2013). Being creative is extremely important, to find an answer for a complicated problem. Problem-solving goes hand-in-hand with decision making. With no problem-solving skills one can face severe obstacle in making decisions. To find the right way of overcoming obstacles, you can brainstorm. You can learn more by gathering information and understanding the facts that led to the problems. Another way of finding a solution is to think of all the advantages and disadvantages of problem either by writing it them down or by discussing them with someone whom you trust. Talking about problems also help you solve problems. It is best to ask yourself which strategy makes you comfortable. You can then prepare your plan for better decision-making and have the perfect solution to problem solving.

Attention

Regardless of whether you are in school, working in a business, surrounded by people or alone, sometimes it is hard to focus and to keep track of information. This could signify a lack of concentration. The inability to pay attention could make one not able to do regular tasks correctly. Doing a single task could take more time than someone who is more focused. Attention deals with many other brain functions such as the ability to 'think, learn, problem solve and store information' (2006). When attentive one can function at a very high level and even multitask. However, it is extremely difficult to multitask when the pressure is extremely intense.

Verbal comprehension

He or she who excels in verbal skills can be extremely gifted in school or work. The better your verbal ability, the better chance you have of succeeding. Being able to understand a short story or a novel after reading it, could help you feel accomplished and allow you to discuss it. The better your linguistic skills, the better others can understand you. The more you comprehend, the faster it is for you seem to learn things quickly and the easier the learning process. People with high skills can enjoy leaning new languages, learning new words, and understanding poetry.

Math comprehension

One way to improve our thinking process is to perform mathematics. From the beginning of childhood we start by learning simple numbers and equation. In adulthood we learn theories and are able to implement what we learn. Mathematics helps to better grasp information and it develops us to function. When challenged with various mathematical problems in school we learned to find the answer to the problems. Later in life, when complex situations arise, we can deal with various obstacles. This can help us to better to read, comprehend, and solve problems. There are many mathematical games that cultivate our cognition, creativity and problem-solving skills.

Visual comprehension

Visual comprehension is learning from words, letters and numbers. Since the beginning time, human beings have created many languages to communicate with each other. Without words, letters and numbers, it would be extremely hard to understand each other. Various forms of images include be pictures, photographs, sculptures or even architecture. There are many other types of used depending on the culture and country. Within the modern society images are used to influence or even brainwash us. For example, images are extremely useful for marketing purposes. To attract something one will use many different types of presentation to transmit some sort of attractive information. It is a sophisticated way of manipulating human beings. Children, teenagers, and adults are bombarded by all kinds of images aimed for us either to purchase something but also to make them understand their past and present.

For others to understand what I see and my message I would describe the structure of an image, letter, word, or even number by printing it on something. Without the artist there would be no way of showing or understanding someone's image or point of view. With the use of 'motifs, logos, and brands', information can further shape one's mind.

Physical

It is important to be physically in shape. Doing exercises, training, and playing various physical activities can make us physically fit. This could help us be healthier physically and emotionally. When we are fit physically our mental state responds well. Someone with schizophrenia could have unusual physical changes, either a weight gain or loss. Due to being absent in the mind, do not realize that we need to exercise and we can gain weight. By not being fit, our mind may be shaped negatively and may damage our health. At that time, various things may happen; we may get emotionally weak. An example of this is we may feel blue, his or her moods may change. This could lead to develop other types of diseases or mental disorders. Therefore, it is really important to care for our well-being and to be physically in shape. It is believed that most of us connect more with our bodies when we have physical health.

Behavioral symptoms

In the article from Better Medicine a 'Behavior is an action or reaction to the environment or to internal thoughts and emotions. Behavioral symptoms are persistent or repetitive behaviors that are unusual, disruptive, inappropriate, or cause problems. Aggression, criminal behavior, defiance, drug use, hostility, inappropriate sexual behavior, inattention, secrecy, and self-harm are examples of behavioral symptoms' (2012). What are the reasons for behavioral symptoms? Major brain injury could lead one to have such symptoms. Also chemically imbalances in the brain as well as genetic reasons could also cause behavioral symptoms. It is widely believed that those who have a family history of mental issues or those who use likely to show behavioral symptoms.

Anxiety

Feeling anxious from time to time is normal but constantly living in fear, worries and tension is not normal. There are many different reasons why people feel anxious. Anxiety can start internally, externally, or more precisely; biologically or environmentally. There are many reasons why one can have anxiety. Feeling anxious can begin by being in a certain place, by looking or touching an object, and when being in a particular situation. Anxiety is normal when one starts a new job, starts a new relationship, or when one prepares for job interviews. Some signs of anxiety can include having trouble concentrating, thinking constantly about negative things, knowing what to do or how to cope in life, and not being able to deal with normal tasks. On the other hand, sometimes it is normal to feel anxious when one speaks or performs a seminar in public.

Some may show physical signs when anxious, such as headaches, sweating, trembling, difficulty in sleeping and feeling tired. How people cope with anxiety also differs. In my case, when I feel anxious I try to avoid going to a certain place or meet people with whom I feel uncomfortable. In my mind, before even dealing or being in a certain situation my mind already visualizes some sort of fears. Most of the time, I avoid awkward situations so that I won't feel tense. Since a few years I have discovered that I have some kind of social phobia, especially when meeting new people. I do not participate in events, programs or activities. Sometime I wonder if it is due to my illness or just a normal aspect of my personality.

How others behave around me also affect my anxiety. If someone is very loud and offensive I will develop an anxiety. My mind will automatically send a signal to my body and I will start shaking or even have irrational feelings. I will right away decide to avoid social contact or even interaction. It is really important for me to feel safe and secure with people. When I feel that others can hurt my feelings I kindly withdraw from people. People can bring about a panic attack. When I have a panic attack, I become very loud or would even start screaming in front of people whom I respect, care and love the most. They may not realize what I am going through. When dealing with this kind of action I am not functional. I cannot prevent the action or even tell them what I am going through. Sometimes, I can feel that I cannot control myself or that my brain will explode. When anxious I would have irrational and unreasonable thoughts in my mind. I may react differently and my behavior might look odd to others. Some other times, I feel dumb in front of people, and therefore feel that I must be alone. It is also one reason why I isolate myself after having severe emotionally negative feelings. In many situations I have tried to read people's mind by predicting how others may react or act to me. Most of the time, my prediction is a negative one. I feel they may not wish to value me or accept me as I am.

It is really important that I feel secure, rational, reasonable and accepted when being with people. There are not many people who will care to make you feel the way you really want. The only people who will give a shot are parents, spouse, siblings and maybe your best buddy or someone who knows your symptoms. For me it is usually my parents, sister and wife who have seen me in an anxious moment. Sometimes, they were able to tell me I am reacting in an unusual way. This made me feel like I was a failure, even though I was conscious about my action while they tell me to calm down or to take deep breaths. From feeling anxious one can also feel stress. The mind and body may react due to an overload of emotions. Sometimes, not coping with anxiety can lead to other types of situation and create further triggers to more anxiety.

Some anxiety triggers can occur in every aspect of life. Some examples are arguing with the partner when doing tasks. For some it can be financial problems. Others may feel anxious at work, not knowing how the supervisor will think of us or if the management team will ask us to improve our performance can also create tension. For many students, not meeting the standard requirements such as having good grades can be challenging. For couples who have relationship problems it is common to fear the end of the relationship. Some even have high expectations of the relationship which leads to more conflicts. Mostly, people will feel extremely anxious when they have a health issues. An illness can create other illnesses. It is like a chain: one illness is linked to another. If one can manage to prevent a trigger, one will be able to reduce stress and anxiety.

When feeling anxious or when having panic attack it is really important to stay calm. If one can avoid emotional responses, one will feel much better. Some tricks are to breathe for many minutes, for some walking can be another solution. Others may say that eating is an option to feel less anxious. A person can also go outside to take a walk. In my situation, I often pace in times of high stress, anxiety or when I feel nervous about a situation. It is one way to realise tension and to forget about my worries. Distracting myself by changing my thoughts helps me overcome certain tense periods in my life. I find a solution by being more creative, by staying calm and thinking positively. It is really necessary to find a coping strategy when you are anxious and do not know how to react. If you can balance your emotions, you will find peace within yourself.

Many people feel fear in different ways. Some may feel anxious when there is an obstacle to accomplish, others are fearful of not being successful. A person can also feel failure when they cannot fulfill a task. They may expect to do something in perfection. People may react differently to isolation. Many people may not appreciate being controlled by another person. These are some examples of anxiety in life. A trick is to keep a journal with you and when you feel stressed, uncomfortable, or disturbed, you can write down exactly what you feel and how you can find a solution to cope with the discomfort. Writing in a journal can actually be healthier and you may feel better in coping in a certain situation. Spend some time with your journal, try it as an experiment and see if it helps you feel better. Feel free to explore your thoughts, feelings and mind. Write down your deepest thoughts and feelings then read them out loud when you are calm or even when you are stressed out.

Sometimes, people who have religious or spiritual beliefs can find peace within themselves. One way of distracting their own thoughts, emotions, and feelings is by forgiving a mistake. When one feels anxious about a certain situation or an action he or she tries to modify their mental state by praying. Many people can actually control their mood and feel less stressed. Believing in a divine power can be a very powerful feeling for some, others may practice but up to a certain limit. Many people learn to worship a force or someone and find multiple ways to control anxiety. For example, if one feels fear about something, in the religion Islam there are some prayers that can help one to feel released. Some say that when mentioning the prayer, the Satan will leave us and we will have power of ourselves and become more courageous in facing any kinds of hardship. As a result, we will feel less worried and less anxious.

How can we control anxiety? There are many triggers and stressors that can lead to high stress that will end up as anxiety. Most of the time people who give seminars or speak in front of an audience feel some sort of anxiety. However, this can be controlled over time by practicing to be in front of people. Others can have difficulty expressing their opinions. Some may feel uncomfortable expressing in front of people for fear of disagreeing with others. By modifying their beliefs, they will feel much better and will be able to confront criticism. One can share advice by giving and receiving others compliments. Some people feel uncomfortable when they meet people for the first time. They may not know what to answer or even how to ask questions. Therefore one may not have eye contact or even avoid being in the center of attention. We are all human and it is natural that we feel in various ways. Any form of anxiety can be controlled, it is a matter of finding the right solution. When one can balance one's emotion and feelings, one will be able to cope with multiple types of provoking conditions.

Metabolic Syndrome

According to the Canadian Diabetes Association, Metabolic syndrome is a term used to describe a group of conditions that put people at higher risk of developing type 2 diabetes, heart disease and other heart-related problems, (2012). Basically, it centers around weight gain, diabetes, cholesterol, hypertension and heart disease.

To have metabolic syndrome, one must have the following 3 conditions 'high fasting blood glucose levels (5.6 mmol/L or higher), high blood pressure (130/85 mm Hg or higher), high levels of triglycerides, (a type of fat in your blood;1.7 mmol/L or higher), low levels of HDL, (the good blood cholesterol; lower than 1.0 mmol/L in men or 1.3 mmol/L in women), and finally abdominal obesity or too much fat around your waist (waist circumference of greater than 102 cm or 40 inches in men and greater than 88cm or 35 inches in women). The fewer symptoms one might have, the smaller the chance of developing type 2 diabetes and heart disease.

What could be the reason why one is able to maintain a good life style and balance metabolic syndrome? The following information are some examples of how to keep the body healthy by following a good routine. For a person to be quite healthy, they need to exercise frequently, follow the Canadian food guide to have a healthy eating plan, and to keep track of your blood glucose, blood pressures and cholesterol levels regularly. Studies shows that keeping our body healthy by exercising or even just walking for 30 minutes to 1 hour it helps to reduce the likelihood of illness.

Anger Management

We become angry at the people we love most. Some get angry once a week, others twice a week, while certain people get angry almost every day. It does not matter where one get angry or with whom one gets angry. It is important to be able to control the anger. If someone is unable to control their anger he or she may become aggressive. Being angry is linked to the nervous system and could have an impact on ourselves or even project towards other people. One can be angry at any time regardless of age, gender or ethnical group. Anger has no limit, one can become out of control due to external or internal factors. One may become emotional and may not realize how they are behaving. One may become angry by because of past events, present moments or even future plans.

When responding to the past, one may remember an event and the feeling can be intense. Repeating the same action or having a flashback about something can be toxic. It can make you mad. It is very difficult to identify some types of feelings when angry. It is very hard to be alert emotionally, thus those who are capable of dealing with certain situations have a chance to be healthier. Healthy people can identify their anger by controlling their emotion and by forgiving someone or a situation that has occurred to them. People usually get often angry when they enjoy less a situation, scenario or an emotional event that one felt in the past. Sometime one may have trouble identifying anger. This can impair logical decision-making. Therefore, one may start an argument or react differently. Usually people remember negative feelings and forget about positive ones.

If the anger within you, it would ruin your day and further aggravate you, causing more anger. Being present in the moment and dealing with anger is the main solution to this anger cycle. Find a solution to calm down your emotions. When you get very angry, it is important to find the triggers to that anger and find support to feel better. You need to talk to people who understand what you are going through. Explaining your situation to someone you trust or someone who wants to listen to you will make you feel better. The more information you give of your feelings, the better the responses. You have to control your temper by understanding your moods. It is important to not let anger fester within you, as it will propagate. Expressing and understanding your anger can benefit your health.

It is important to find people who will give feedback about your behavior and reaction whenever you become extremely angry. You do not want to repeat tomorrow what you went through today. People are usually open to advice and counselling. It is human nature to help and advice those who have problems. Even if some of your friend may not want to help, there are always those who will be kind and listen you. If you are someone who gets angry often then you may have hurt people whom you care about the most. Therefore keep track of when and where you get angry. One way of keeping track of anger is to ask people for feedback.

Now that you can identify anger you may able to face every day without conflicts. If this does not help you then finding a solution on anger is necessary. You need to ask questions about your situation and what is in your mind. Do you want to show anger to your enemies by being violent? Aggressiveness does not solve but create more problems. This will impair your health by making you more nervous and you may start a fight because you may not fear your opponent. Having strong feelings such as being emotional could lead to future revenge. Having a strong reaction can be toxic and people may become afraid of you. Therefore, it is mandatory to keep calm and behave in a proper way by being as diplomatic as possible. You must stay away from the emotion that cause more harms then happiness.

Have you ever rated yourself about how angry you are when you feel emotional? It is a feeling most people do not wish to have in their life. Everybody would love to avoid anger but it is something that we have to live and deal with properly. In most cases, people get angry occasionally, but a certain percentage feel angry all the time. When angry, people may mix their emotion with irritation and rage. Some may say that anger reduces with ages. However, you may still react to criticisms. You may feel that others are trying to dominate you or that they want to pit you against others. Having such thoughts can be natural and some may even react by taking drugs.

Drugs and alcohol can be addictive and can modify your point of view and health condition. Drinking too much can make you really ill, give hang-overs and even make you become out of control. Drinking can make people become violent by being more easily enraged. Depending on the situation he or she may not cope in the moment. Therefore, one should drink responsibly. Caffeine can also be addictive, hence there should be a limit of coffee amounts per day. Other people may smoke cigarette to reduce stress. Smoking can cause psychological and physical damage such as cancer and other symptoms. There are many severe drugs that are not healthy for mankind. Not being able to keep track of the self and not understand the consequences can be hazardous. It is recommended to stay as far as possible from illegal drugs and maintain a certain limit when using legal substances to better control the anger.

It is hard to figure out why friends or loved ones leave. When things just not go the way you want, it can seem that everything and everyone are mad at you. You may feel that you do not have enough resources to cope with anger. You may not be able to reach for help from others when angry. When angry you may blame yourself and feel pain. Having an argument or misunderstanding can be exhausting. Do you feel that you are tired after having a dispute? It is normal as anger consumes a lot of energy. It's like getting fuel for a car. When you press on the accelerator too much, the car goes faster and uses a lot of gas. Like driving too fast, one can lose control easily when too emotional.

Not being able to control the anger can indirectly cause various types of disease. Someone who smokes a lot of cigarettes can have heart problems. Others may have Metabolic Syndrome such as high cholesterol, high blood pressure, and can become overweight. Anger can impair our mind and hurt our body without us realizing it. Some may even hurt themselves because they do not have any hope or feel no love from others. Furthermore, anger can lead to serious psychological problems. Not knowing how to control or to behave can put ourselves in danger. Usually people only realize of their behavior or even their action after being violent or aggressive towards others or even towards themselves. Managing anger can benefit all aspects of life, either physically by motivating us to continually exercise or mentally by helping us monitor our behaviour. The better we can control ourselves the better our health.

When you cannot manage your anger at work, it can lead to bad relationships with clients, coworkers or even managers and ultimately cause tension. A person should firstly avoid conflict at work. When someone has conflicts with another at work, it can make others feel uncomfortable. Slowly it will cause negative feelings of anxiety or phobia. Having these types of feelings can hurt others mentally. The persons should have limited contact with each other when feeling people become too emotional at work. Maybe changing managers, teams, or even department can benefit the parties. It is important to explain your feelings and doubts about your team and manager to the proper department. It could be human resources or someone superior than your manager. If you want to continue working in your organization or company you should consult with someone about your feelings and emotion and keep yourself calm. Never become angry at work, it can ruin your career or even your life.

Being angry with your wife or husband can create a negative atmosphere in the relationship. With both of you going to war with each other. What is the proper solution to better keep the marriage or relationship alive? You have be willing to give in to your partner. You should not raise your tone. You have to start by understanding that anger makes the relationship more toxic instead of romantic. He or she may continue yelling, screaming or even shouting, but you can gain control by being warm, kind and nice with the opposite partner. It is necessary to put away all kinds of negative feeling and emotion such as suspicious, jealousy, stubbornness and disrespect. It is time to put an end to abusing each other by putting anger away from our emotion.

To manage anger, it is important to stay away from emotional disturbances. If there are triggers or stressors in the relationship, you should take a step back from your loved one. By keeping a distance there is a chance of not taking immediate actions. By taking control of anger, there is a better chance of not becoming too emotional. Sometimes it is a matter of knowing what to do when angry. For example, you can take deep breaths. You can also count until your anger dissipates. Others may perform exercise to feel better. Sometimes, it works when you walk away from a difficult issue or situation. Whereas, other may feel better by discussing about the anger or taking a walk outside.

To break free from anger, you must be able to express anger freely. The book Anger Management for Dummies suggests that "You need to use your anger to educate, inform and share that part of yourself that is hurt, sad, frustrated, insecure, and feels attacked with the person trapped into these feelings" (p. 67). You need to release your anger from inside of your heart, emotion and body. Now imagine anger as an object. Each time you feel angry put the object somewhere or stay away from the object until you are able to calm down. If this does not work try to understand what causes you to become destructive. Then, you can place the object accordantly. When you can balance the object in the right place at the right time, you will feel much better. After that, anger will become something like a joke. Once you can balance you will be able to understand and manage this emotion like other emotion. The object becomes like other objects and anger become like other feelings.

Anger Management for Dummies explains anger by that "when you react to anger, you are reflexive, impulsive, predictable and out of control. Whereas, when you respond to anger you are thoughtful, deliberate, unpredictable and in control" (p. 77). When someone reacts reflexively the other person should respond by being caring or thoughtful. Saying something nice can change the topic. Hence, this may lead to a better conversation. By predicting the response one can make a better judgment consciously. However, you cannot accurately a response, especially when you have a mental illness.

From this point of view, it is necessary to respond by being rational and try to take the situation under control. Knowing what to say to someone or what to do can make a big difference and can turn the argument around.

How should we behave or react when someone is out of control and is extremely angry. When being near a person who is angry he or she may not be cognizant of his or her action, reaction, and response. The best way to deal with someone who is angry is to be upset of that person. It is necessary to keep cool and calm. When the person is loud and noisy you are in control therefore you take control of the situation, either by walking away or by avoiding the person. You may also mention that you would prefer to speak naturally. When in an argument or misunderstanding, the situation will escalate and can bring about a high tension. In that case you need to find a solution by relaxing or going somewhere quit. If the person accuses you of something you should not pay attention to it and keep a distance. If you are blamed for a certain thing you must go where you feel secure. This will give the person a chance to reduce his or her anger. This will let them cool down and be in better charge of their action. The best response is to be calm until you feel the storm is over and normal conversation can resume.

Sometimes anger can lead to aggression. How often do we hear of people being bitten because someone becomes extremely aggressive? Aggression can damage and hurt people. Screaming, yelling or even hitting someone can be dangerous and against the law. When someone shows signs of aggression you should walk away. Others may not want to be and would like to find an alternative way of solving the problem instead. Having a compromise between you and the aggressive person will lead to in the right direction. Instead of arguing or using verbal abuse, one should seek alternative solutions by asking what the aggressor wants and why that person is reacting in that way. It is a matter of finding the right place for both persons to exchange sentences in a peaceful manners.

What happens to your body and mind when you get angry? Basically "your blood pressure goes up, in some case dangerously high. You feel like you're going to burst or explode. Your heart pounds. You feel a knot in your stomach. You feel overwhelmed. You lose your concentration focusing only on your anger. You feel depressed and unhappy. You feel ashamed, embarrassed, and guilty. You feel nervous and agitated. Other people have hurt feelings because of your anger. Other people become defiant. Other people become indifferent to you. Other people avoid you. Other people lose their respect for you", (Gentry, W, D. p.86). You lose your approach toward others and you feel much worse after being angry on something or on someone. Before getting angry at yourself give yourself a chance. Use various techniques to reduce anger such as taking deep breaths, changing topics, or even walking away from negative situations. You have to choose not to get angry at others. Be calm and try to understand their situation. Explain to them why you are getting angry. Get as much feedback as possible. When you get aggressive, there is a chance that others will be aggressive to you. Then you will end up with a verbal fight and misunderstanding. In order to win and gain control you have to play smart by talking smoothly. Let other be loud and angry but control your emotions and response. If you are lost and do not know how to balance your anger there are a few tips that can help motivate you to gain control of yourself and the surrounding: "you calm down more quickly. Other people maintain their respect for you. Other people are more likely to approach you. You're more likely to come up with constructive solutions to problems. You minimize future conflict. You're more likely to understand the other person's point of view. You and the other person leave the situation feeling good. You're more empathetic. You have lower blood pressure. You feel less agitated. You leave the situation not holding a grudge. You're a much more agreeable person" (Gentry, W, D. p.87). When you can cope with your anger you will feel much better and it will be easy for you to communicate with others. Thinking positively will make you positive and help you to deal with people positively. When doing this you can reward yourself by doing something good for you. Celebrate yourself as you have made a healthy choice; go outside or do activities that you enjoy with people that you love.

To better manage your anger, you need to avoid being "annoyed, disappointed, disgusted, displeased, dissatisfied, enraged, fuming, furious, indignant, irate, irritated, mad, outraged, pissed, and vexed" (Gentry, W. D. p.124). The more you think about tomorrow, the more prepared you will be for the day. Prepare yourself for arguments and stay away from people who make you angry. Take initiative for your health and try to respect other as much as possible. When you think of others, people will value you and have respect for you. Create a connection with others by knowing their strength and weakness. Use your strength with people's weakness; like that you can balance a situation without conflict. The better you know others, the more you will feel confident about your situation with others. You will then look better in front others; and you can appreciate your surroundings more. As a result you will feel better about yourself and have more self-respect. By being able to balance your emotion and mood you will be feel much better about yourself and also about others.

If you do not know how to manage your anger, you can write down on a piece of paper some Negative Emotions and Positive Emotions that you feel in that. Divide the paper in two parts and make a list of all emotions that you feel when you are in a bad and good mood. It is one way to understand how you may feel in an intense situation. By identifying your emotion you will know how Negative and Positive Emotions will affect you. It is important to be able to select the emotion from your list and analyze. Some examples of having Negative Emotions are being "afraid, agitated, alarmed, angry, anxious, ashamed, bitter, bored, depressed, frustrated, guilty, irritated, petrified, regretful, sad, sorrowful, unhappy, and worried" (Gentry, W. D. p.282). Whereas, having Positive Emotions can be considered as being "amazed, amused, appreciative, cheerful, content, curious, delighted, enthusiastic, excited, generous, grateful, happy, hopeful, joyful, kind, loving, optimistic, satisfied, and thrilled" (Gentry, W. D. p. 282). Now that you can keep a record of your emotion you may notice that perhaps you have more Positive Emotions on your list than the Negative Emotions. This can help you feel much better about yourself. What will happen if your Negatives Emotions overrule the positive ones? In that can you need to work on it. Talking to the right person about your feelings can be a good next step. If there is no one whom you trust you may search for a professional, such as a social worker, a psychologist, or even psychiatrist. Being able to identify your emotion, be it negative or positive will help you to keep track of your health and your situation.

Stigma

A certain percentage of people have a negative impression of mental illness i.e. stigma. It does not matter how gifted people are, if they have a mental illness, they are seen negatively regardless of race, age, gender, color, ethical group, culture, caste or even social class. People do not understand mental illness and may have false beliefs about mental illness. Therefore, the mentally challenged are discriminated. Having stigma puts a distinction between sane and insane people. Normal people see those who are mentally ill differently. Mental illnesses manifest themselves in various forms. A few people are afraid of the mentally ill because some react violently. Some individuals are targets of various stigma, and this stigma affects the majority of the population.

Some "sources of stigma are beliefs that patients are violent, fear of what is not understood; ignorance of the disease, negative media images of the mentally ill, fear of being associated with mental illness and unease with anything different" (Haycock, D. A. p. 239). Being subjected to stigma can be challenging. If one cannot find a solution then there are other sources for advice and help. One must be strong when hearing various types of comments and insults. It can be very difficult to accept it but with time a person can learn to reinforce his or her behaviors and change answers. One has to show a lot of courage and must be strong emotionally and mentally. If you know someone with schizophrenia you have to show a lot of positive attitudes by understanding the prejudice and one's moral. Mention to the ill person that it is possible to overcome and perceive the disorder in positive ways, which is by recovering slowly.

The Mental Health Commission Canada web site for suggests that "stigma is a major barrier preventing people from seeking help. Many people living with a mental illness say the stigma they face is often worse than the illness. Mental illnesses affect people of all ages and from all walks of life. It can take many forms including depression, anxiety and schizophrenia". Many people face stigma every day at work, at school, among friends, families, relatives and acquaintances. One may blame his or her family as the illness can be genetic. Not understanding the symptoms can make one perceive the illness negatively. People will ignore the ill person or start making fun of them. Therefore, the individual who is going through depression, anxiety or schizophrenia will withdraw from the social network.

When facing stigma, it robs one of their self-esteem and it is a challenge to face on a daily basis. It seems that people do not care about you or how you may feel. Being discredited internally can bring one to isolate oneself. What people do not understand is that people who are mentally ill do not chose to live in this manner. It is not our fault that we live with this illness. The challenged one has to live day by day with this problem. We need to educate other about the illness. The more educated people are in mental illnesses, the better chance there is for them to accept people with mental disorders. This is one way of reducing stigma and discrimination. With self-acceptance one feel the opposite of prejudice. To overcome the illness it is important to fight. What is difficult is to change people's perception as they do not know about the illness. Furthermore, self-acceptance cannot be achieved unless we strive for it.

Take the illness in a different way, more precisely see it in a different angle. If you work somewhere you have health care insurance if not you can get support from the government. There are some "potential sources of health benefits: one can get private health insurance or from health maintenance organization. Some will get veterans administration benefits. Others apply for social security disability income. Some apply for supplemental security income. Furthermore, there are also Medicare (medical insurance for the elderly) and Medicaid (medical insurance for low-income patients)", (Haycock, D. A. P. 240). If some people are stigmatized the system would not be in favor for mentally ill people or even someone with Schizophrenia. Obviously, one does not receive a lot of money from the system, but without it, one can barely survive due to the illness. Receiving money can be a big change in one's life especially if one cannot work while being sick or under treatment. In this context, the system is designed for everyone equally, thus, each individual is supported for their illness and diagnosis. One cannot know in advance who will end up receiving some benefits from the Health Care. Each individual is helped to benefit the whole population. This system works in Canada and it is a sign that many sympathize and help those who suffer from any kind of illness.

Reduce Stress

Reducing stress can be very difficult for some. Some techniques to reduce stress are to "get enough sleep, get good nutrition, find ways to laugh, find ways to be entertained, exercise, and practice deep breathing or meditation", (Haycock, D. A. P. 237). Not having enough sleep is common with people who have mental illness. Some people sleep too long. When ill one can experience lack of or too much sleep due to extended worries, tension, stress, having irrational thoughts and other external and internal factors. For me I could not sleep properly. My external factors occurred when at work I would have various shifts: For example one day I would work from 8:00 am to 5:00 pm and another day I will start at 2:00 pm and finished at 11:00 pm. Then I would need to spend some time with my family and prepare for the next day shift. My schedule was a mess and it was extremely difficult for me to balance my life with my working hours. It seems to me that I was totally disorganized due to awkward hours at work and with my sleeping pattern. Sometime I would sleep for 2 to 3 hours and I would go to work the next day. It was very hard for me to stay awake at work. Slowly I felt I was less productive. I felt really stressed about not being able to give 100% at work. When I would come home I would not want to do anything as I was incredibly tired. I lost motivation in doing activities with my family.

Getting good nutrition is also another factor that applies to our body and mind. If we do not feed our body well it will react negatively. One will feel less motivated to eating regular food. One may not feel like to eat normal food due to lack of taste. It is important to eat good healthy food especially when under high stress. Having awkward hours at work impair our body. Not eating at the same time every day has an impact on our eating pattern. Having a volatile schedule made me eat at various hours and sometimes I did not feel like eating at all. Some other time, I would feel extremely hungry from my medication. Within a few years I gained 60 pounds extra. I was tremendously shocked. I could not believe that I had gained that much. While under treatment, my goal was to have the right weight for my height but I exceeded by almost 10 pounds. I needed to work on my health to be better in shape.

Working with different hours every day made me blue and miss all my TV shows. It seems that I could not find ways to laugh. I felt my life was monotonous and I did not feel not happy. It is important to work to survive and maintain a family life. For me being a good husband and father was very essential. Having an erratic schedule at work and missing all my TV shows made me feel disoriented. Furthermore, not being able to give enough time to my wife and daughter was another issue in my life. I felt overwhelmed by the inability to fulfill my wife's and my own needs. Spending time with my little daughter was necessary but it seems that sometime even though I was giving enough time I still felt that I could have spent more time. She was our first child and my wife and I were not experienced in raising a child and there was a lot of stress between my wife and myself. Luckily, we managed to raise her and see her grow up. People were also saying that I needed to smile more and I was not laughing enough. When a person does not laugh it seems that his or her life has changed due to some negative factors that required serious attention. To better feel one has to find a way to enjoy a certain situation or find a solution to smile and laugh as much as possible.

I needed to find a way to entertain myself and my surrounding. People said I looked sick and tired. There was a time that I was a movie fanatic. I used to go with friends almost every week to watch two different movies. Then I would rent movies when I would have time. I loved movies. The idea, creativity and fascination that producers and directors come up would transport my imagination to another dimension. Watching movies was a way for me to spend time with others too. I used to keep myself entertained. If it was not watch movies I would spend time playing sports. Playing hockey during the winter, baseball in the summer or swimming was a way for me to keep busy. I had a few friends who were involved in producing cultural shows in which I was involved. It seems that my life has changed radically due to early symptoms. Lately, I lost motivation in entertaining myself and my surroundings. Due to my illness I lost touch with my childhood friends for whom I had the utmost respect and with whom I shared my sorrow and happiness.

It is also important to exercise, practice deep breathing and meditate. During my early adulthood I was extremely active and energetic. I needed to move around. Otherwise, I would feel stressed out. I used to play various sports with friends and acquaintances which helped me to keep in good shape. However, as more time passed, I slowly stopped participating in sports. I would isolate myself more. It was a sign of my illness but I did not realize it at the time. It took many years to seek for help. I neglected to admit that I was getting ill and I used to isolate myself by ignoring all my friends and not answering their phone calls. I did not know about my symptom and do not have any memory when being hospitalized. With time I learned that I had schizophrenia and had no choice to accept it. It took me a while to reveal to my friends and my surrounding that I had a mental disorder. Still now some do not know about my illness. Hopefully by reading my book they will understand and forgive me for not telling them earlier. At the Day Hospital I also learned some tricks to practice deep breathing. We would gather in a group and have a session on breathing and meditating. After performing the exercises on breathing and meditation, I would feel released and feel mentally much better. I learned how to focus and let go of my anxiety. I helped me calm down and control my panic attacks. After all there are many different ways to keep our body and mind in shape; it is a matter of balancing and practicing a routine. It takes dedication and self-care and the willingness heal to get better.

Conjugal relationship

It is a happy sight to see two people together. With a marriage, couple choose to show the world their commitment to each other. It is a promise that they will be faithful, show care, love, affection, and compassion to each other. They will share the same house and the same bed, have a faithful sexual relationship and be true to each other, keep the right attitude and honesty by sharing their thoughts, values, and morals. Couple have to be open in their personal conversations. Preparing meals for each other as well as doing grocery, and buying each other gifts on special occasions is necessary. It is also important for couple to take care of each other during an illness. A relationship will come out strong and solid when it is put to the test. This can help bring a couple be more true to each other.

Conducting regular tasks such as preparing meals, washing and drying clothes, and shopping for each other are important while maintaining the married life. One can be invited to participate in various activities held the communities or by friends. This can enhance and diversify the relationship to include the family, peers, friends, neighbors and spouse. Maintaining a good understanding among family members is essential in a couple. Understanding the partner's financial situation can make the relationship work better. One has to value his or her partner when spending money and asking for valuable gifts or even for necessary things. Both people in the relationship need to have a financial arrangement and compromise to better balance and budget their wallets. Ownership of objects or valuable things such as gifts and property need to be agreed upon that they belong to each other. Therefore each person has the right to use the things until there is a court order for a separation or even divorce. Children are equal responsibility and rights to both in the relationship. Usually, if the woman does not work, she would stay home and take care of their child or children, and the same goes for the man.

What causes a relationship to fell apart? Usually between couples it is easy to misunderstand each other, which leads to bigger, more detrimental fights. If there is a serious problem, both parties need to fix the relationship; otherwise it will sink. Couple then become fed-up with their relationship and no longer trust each other. They may not want to break up if there is a child or many children involved. They need to understand both sides and share same thoughts, feelings and worries in order to better function as a couple. It is natural to make silly mistakes and one should ask for forgiveness. Hence, one should forgive each other. Being rude or telling cruel sentences can hurt one's feeling or break someone's heart. Knowing the limit is the prime line here. Up to what extend should one undertake a conversation, situation, or even scenario with his or her mate?

What happened in the past with a relationship should be kept in the past. A couple should move forward in the present by acknowledging to be truthful to each other. Being on the same side with an open mind will open many doors to the couple. This will give the couple a second chance to value and share respect with each other. Basically, a couple should decide what both parties want. Do both want to maintain the relationship and are willing to change their bad habits? Do they want to continue with the same misunderstanding? It takes both people in a relationship to fix or destroy the relationship. One needs to ask question, about the relationship and what typically causes conflicts to prevent the same circumstances. In dealing with doubts, worries, confusion, and criticism, one has to think about future behaviors, and conditions and plan accordingly. If both couple want to be together, both need to work and find a structure that will help maintain a healthy relationship. By being thinking for the future, the couple will enhance each other.

Counselling

The meaning of counselling changes depending on each individual and the expertise, they seek. When one seek for counselling one is looking for a person with whom one can consult, exchange ideas and opinions, obtain professional advice in a private environment discuss about various areas of one's life such as physical health, mental health, personal problems, family, personal relationship, career, education, work along with, emotional environmental, internal and external factors and dealing with difficulty and distress. The main goal is to find a way of healing by learning to solve problems and find solutions in a peaceful way. My experience in counselling, involved practitioners conducting interviews and my taking part in, psychotherapy, group therapy, and Cognitive Behavioral Therapy alone and in a group. For me it was very helpful to get support from various professionals. They all helped me overcome many obstacles by stabilizing me and finding the answers for my different issues.

1.) Getting started

Usually, one of the professionals will conduct an interview to find out with whom you will be placed in the health centre. You can also choose go to a private Clinic where you can have your choice of psychiatrists, psychotherapists for counselling.

-Connecting with the Client

The professional may start by simply greeting you and asking how your day was or what can the counselor do to better assist you. The counseling usually start either by letting you tell them what is on your mind, and what has occurred within the past few days. It can depend on how you and your counsellor connect with each other. Being able to communicate with your counsellor can be a sign that they understand your situation. It can also be important to feel at ease with the counsellor. Sometimes people are afraid or are too shy to open up and to start a conversation with an unknown person. The more at ease you are with the counsellor, the more efficient the therapy can be and the, more quickly one will get answers to your situation.

-Finding the problem

Finding the problem can be difficult especially when you just started meeting. Most of the time, there is a solution to every problem. However, if you cannot discuss your problems it might take more time to understand what you are going through. The more you explain your condition, the more the therapist can suggest you an explanation. The main focus here is to help you feel better by letting your emotion and feelings be released with the discussion. Sometimes we may think that we know the answer to the problems but by talking to the therapist you may realize that you got the problem wrong to begin with.

-Listening to various situations

The practitioner will listen to your story and may ask you multiple questions about your mood and emotion. It is important to tell the truth so that he or she can see the different solutions to your situation. Listening is a two-way street. Most of the time, the clients has a lot to say, while the professional does the listening. It is also necessary for the patient to listen to the practitioner's advice. Listening is a skill because it can help better understand and solve something mysterious. As patients, we will tend to have severe negative feelings and become overwhelmed and preoccupied with a problem before meeting a counsellor.

-Asking questions

The counsellor may ask you some questions to better understand your situation. Obviously, it is very hard for them to put on your shoes, but they are trained to face many issues. The more questions you can answer, the better the therapy. You also can ask questions to the counsellor. You have to accept that you are in a critical situation and that you need therapy. Therefore, you need to find what will help you to overcome your sorrow. Sometime one can be so hurt, mentally down, or out of touch with reality, therefore, it is really hard to answer or even ask questions. In that case, the counselling can be very long as there might be periods of silence.

-Observing

Observing works in two ways for both patients and counsellors. The counsellor observes by keeping calm and handling the situation continuously. It seems that they are very energetic regardless how you are in front of them. They seem to know how to react in front of patients. Sometime, a patient may have a panic attack, or start crying, others can be agitated and rude. By observing you, they can make a decision either to continue with the therapy or end there until you cool-down. Observation plays a prime role in counselling. It is hard to judge a cover. Hence, one may observe a client and his or her reactions after certain questions or silences. Sometimes a counsellor may reinforce a situation or even a behaviour simply by talking. In a conversation, one may stray out of topic but the best method is to follow what the client is anticipating with his concerns or even body languages.

-Writing information down

If you are told to write an information down, it is usually important. In cognitive Behavior Therapy, the therapist will tell you to write down your reflections and concerns on various aspects. One may even give you some homework to better analyze your motivation. Writing on a piece of papers or even computer can become therapeutic. For some people writing is one way of focusing and avoiding negative memories. This can lead one to feel positive and cope with unnecessary distraction.

2.) Supporting the client

It is important for the patient to receive as much support as possible from the health specialist. One can be deranged and have irrational thoughts and therefore cannot make decisions or are inapt at finding solution. When the patient is discouraged or even feels isolated he or she needs extra support. A person needs to realize that there is someone who cares for the client and is willing to listen to what they have to say. In many health systems such as some mental wards or even hospital, patients receive enough support from specialists, psychologists, nurses, occupational therapists, and other health professionals. Obviously, a person who needs extensive assistance will get enough time from the health expert. Whereas, someone who is in process of healing or getting better might not get enough time by the professional. For a client, not getting enough attention can be sorrowful. The health professional can be thought of as the team captain with the patients as players. The captain leads the team by motivating people, making them happy and hearing what everyone has to say.

-Finding stressors

When having the interview with the professional it is important to find out what motivates you. Telling the truth can benefit you. One will be able to distinguish solutions by asking you of certain situations, reactions or even problems that have happened. The more you talk about the psychological process, the easier it is to find answers to help you feel better. Knowing what triggers us can help us find solution. We need to sincerely ask what is important for us and what we want to find out in knowing the triggers. Knowing the triggers can benefit a person cope with said triggers.

It is important to identify the stimulus that causes stress. By looking from different point of views and from various angles, you may find different types of answers to your questions. Until you find out the causes of stress, the counsellor may not be able to solve your stressors. Therefore you have to start from ground zero, and detail every action and reaction. You will realize that the more open you are with the counsellor the more released you will feel. Knowing what causes stress will help you in many ways. For many having high stress can be a sign of being agitated, nervous, and anxious. Some may cope with high stress while others will fall apart. For a person with mental illness having high stress means differently and can be more dramatic. A person with illness facing high stress will be affected differently. For some many symptoms may appear. For example, one might start hallucinating or even having delusions.

-Understanding the problems

By finding your stressors your counselor will be able to guide you through your dark journey. One will have the answer to all your issues and circumstances. When you can retain the information shared by the practitioner you will see the light and experience different types of positive emotions. By discussing with the counsellor, you will get a better idea on how to deal with various topics. If you do not agree with a certain solution you may ask for an alternative scenario. Most importantly you play a main role in understanding the problems by implementing solutions in real life. The more you understand your crisis the more confident you feel, and the better a chance there is for healing. When one knows what exactly causes your problems, the health specialist can prescribe medication accordingly. It is really necessary to take all of your medications. It is one way for you to heal quickly.

3.) Offer solution

The counsellor may offer you many solutions to your dilemma. You may take consider the solutions as choices and you have to make a serious decision based on the offer. A solution may not work at 100%. It may help you better grasp your emotional and mental issues and help you identify other problems. One may help you better grasps emotionally, mentally and identifying your problems by finding a resolution. The counsellors have many years of experience and based on that they have seen, many patients go through similar situations.

Most of the time, a practitioner may not tell you what you have to do but will mention there are various situations, scenarios and solutions you may choose based on your judgment.

-Emotional support

Usually the counsellor will find a range of tactics to offer emotional support. They will help you show internal and external emotions. We usually remember the negative memories more than the positive ones. We often forget when we have fun and enjoy in a specific moment, whereas we always recall pain. If the pain is more than happiness one will start suffering until one receive support. The patient then has to put a lot of effort into willingly adapt change and accept internal emotion. Sometimes medication is the only solution. Counselling may be another option but if one cannot cope emotionally one will have even more difficulty dealing with people.

-Mental support

When you feel that your mind is not functioning accordingly due to severe pain and feelings, you need to have some sort of therapy. You have to change your environment and follow a new routine. For example, you may have to stay at the hospital you are deranged. It is important to find out if you have a mental illness or if it is just worries, sadness, tension, fear or anxiety for a temporary period. You may meet a doctor, psychiatrist, or psychologist to better understand your symptom. It is necessary to be open and honest about your thoughts, and emotions. Many people may not know that they do have mental illness until they are brought to the hospital or start counselling. When one feels better mentally one is able to make decisions in life.

-Identifying problems

Identifying problems is not an easy task. Sometime it can take a lot of time depending on each client and how open they are with the counsellor. A client may take more time to open-up whereas, other may talk right way after meeting with the counsellor. When the client identifies his or her problems the counsellor can take various approach to give service and to reassure the client. It is necessary to find out if the problems are due to emotional, mental, physical, environmental, internal or external factors. By knowing the real cause the specialist will be able to guide you with extreme precision. A psychologist or a psychiatrist is trained with different ways to better identify and help you identify problems. It is important to trust their judgment, capacities and abilities. If you cannot identify your own problems then it will take more sessions before you can heal.

4.) Coping Skills

Coping skills can start with avoiding negative talk to yourself. Do not compare yourself with others because each individual is unique. If you label yourself expect others to do the same. Do not try to be psychic but know that you can control a certain situation. If you feel hopeless you have to find what makes you feel better by finding a solution. Do not put too much pressure on yourself by having overly high expectations. If you feel too emotional, take advice from other people or even a professional. Describe your problems it is one way of letting them go from your heart. By talking to someone you will feel released. Try to open up to society instead of isolating yourself. By being present at an event or surrounded with people you will see that other may not wish to hurt you but to be with you. Take control of yourself by boosting your self-esteem and confidence. Take initiative in something and involve others to participate with you. You will feel self-respect and people will enjoy being with you.

-Listening

Both counsellor and client must listen to each other. A good counsellor should have listening skills. It takes a long time qualify as a counsellor and many hours of experiencing different situations to better help a client. A client would prefer to have a therapist who can motivate and reinforce them mentally. Usually, the client prefers to have someone who can mentally stimulate them with positive advice and creative solutions to his or her answers. The client wants to feel secure and safe with the counsellor. The client may present with symptom of depression, worries, tension, financial issues, personal problems and addiction. Therefore the counsellor must know how to guide the client and make them feel comfortable.

-Finding solution

Depending on the client and therapist, counselling can consist of only a few sessions to sessions over years. For every session, there is a new obstacle. Finding a solution works in two ways: first, we must share our experiences and feelings of ourselves. Second, we must overcome any obstacle before we can see any result. Be flexible and reasonable in setting goals and you will feel much better knowing that the goals are achievable. Aim for positive and realistic goals.

-Working on skills

With the counsellor, you will learn tricks to make you better as a person. For example, if you had an addiction, you would be told to be honest about it to the counsellor. Even though you might be tempted to lie and hide it, you still need to tell the truth to your counsellor. The more open you are the more you will develop skills. The counsellor may ask you to write down a certain aspect of yourself that you would like to cover up. If you feel that you are weak on a certain aspect, then you will need to work on that in that way, you can build yourself by accepting your thoughts, emotions, feelings and memories of a difficult moment. If you do not take your life seriously then no one can take your life seriously for you. To see change in your life, you have to first agree to change on your own and show the environment that you have committed to following any kind of changes. By allowing yourself to change, you will automatically develop new ways of skills. This will give you new ideas about life and help you start a new beginning.

-Explore various approaches

There are many approaches in counselling and psychotherapy. However, the diverse approaches are similar in practice. Mostly, it is important to listen to a client by identifying his or her problems and to understand, the clients experience to find solution. The therapy needs to be confidential and make the client feel safe and secure. The counsellor need to focus on the client's problems by making the client feel comfortable. One kind of therapy is Cognitive Behavioural Therapy (CBT). This approach helps us learn to act and think in a certain way using our perception of life. The Systemic Family Therapy focuses on the individual, couple and family. The main goal of this therapy is to better interact with the family in exploring dilemmas. The Humanistic and Integrative Psychotherapy focuses on developing our awareness of our inner and outer self. In Psychoanalytic Psychotherapy, the therapist and client work together to identify the client's distress and difficulty. It focuses on understating memories and feelings that disturb the mind and cause pain. The Psychodynamic Therapy is a non-medical approach that focuses on items that are usually meaningless to the majority. For example, dreams and verbal mistakes can be explained with Psychoanalytic Psychotherapy.

5.) Provide professional support

Those with a mental illness require support, both financial and emotional. Doctors provide such a support in health. Nurses do their part by caring for people and listening to problems. A nurse may even go to your house to better assist you. In the mental health system, psychiatrists, psychologists and psychotherapists are in high demands for support. People need constant support to heal. Certain help centres are open for the mentally ill for 24 hours a day. In non-profitable organizations experts can provide support by sharing resources in health.

-Recommending various resources

Depending on your need, the practitioner may direct you to another health expertise. For example, if your family doctor cannot prescribe a certain medication, you need to see another specialist to receive support, there is nothing wrong with that. You must know that the specialist wants to help you. If you feel uncertain about a situation then ask for as many resources as you can. Ask many questions and you will get many answers. Knowing more can only help calm, satisfy and motivate you. Sometimes, you just need to talk to someone, and get reassurance. With support, you will feel much better.

6.) Negotiation with the client by asking (What, When, How, Why, Where, Who and Whom)

Doctors rush through assessment especially residents. As a result, they don't get your whole picture and will give you unhelpful advice. As a doctor, you should help the client understand their issues. Do not be afraid to say no if their issues are out of your boundary. The patient should be satisfied after meeting you. For the patient, it is important to be flexible for the next meeting. After all you want to be healed and the practitioner is there to assist you in that healing process. It is mandatory for both patient and specialist to listen to each other. If the patient does not listen, ask him or her to pay attention. As you are the health professional you have answers to most of the question, therefore take the time to educate your patients. Your time is very valuable, therefore, the more precise you are the better the patient's response. One will get much more information by asking the questions What, When, How, Why, Where, Who and Whom. For example, what is your client's expectation? How can you better help him or her? Why the patient is in front of you? Where is he coming from or going to? Who should you call in case of an emergency? Whom should you talk to on his or her behalf? The patient may be bombarded with questions but he or she will feel satisfied in answering them. A patient will know that you need information to better fulfill his or her need.

7.) Resolving the problems

Resolving problems starts from having good communication skills. While listening to each other; both patient and health professional both have the responsibility to communicate properly. If one cannot communicate there will be missing information. The patient or the health expert need acknowledge the other that they understand the issue. You can use body language to express yourself or even to show that you are listening. When counselling, it is necessary to first define the problem to then resolve it. Once you acknowledge the problem you can try to analyze it. Knowing the nature of the problem can guide in finding information in the situation. One must understand that the most important aspect of analyzing a situation is too involve the right person and the right people. Once you have the fact, focus and collect more data by attending to the situation more. Connect ideas and create more possibilities to have more options and answers. When you have multiple answers you can choose the best solution. With experience one may evaluate and learn from experiences and mistakes. When you are done with the session you may ask if the client was satisfied with your counselling. This can guide you to improve your next session and understand your strengths and weaknesses. Find out if the client feels motivated and if you were able to build his or her self-esteem. When you believe that the client is ready to function by him-or herself, ask if there was a change since he or she started counselling with you. Did the client improve since they began with you?

8.) Survey

If you want to gain feedback on your expertise then you have to do a survey with each client. First of all, you need to create a questionnaire. Then you need to determine who you will interview. In your case it will be your patients. The main goal to keep in mind is what information you want to put on your questionnaire and what would you like to learn from it. If you want to know if the survey works, then you have to start from somewhere. You can start by asking if the client is satisfied with your performance. Once you have all the information you can analyze the results. Doing survey is one way of getting feedback from people. If a patient is satisfied with your service then he or she will return to see you again.

Phobias

We all live with different types of phobias. One must undertake various types of technique in order to overcome. Some examples of phobias that the human species face are when taking medication. Some women have a phobia of having menstruation, many people have phobias of insanity, others of injection, some of dying. There are some who have phobias of animals and heights.

There was a time when I feared that medications will harm me. After my psychosis episode, I did not want to take any kind of medication. For some time I refused to take medication, and this refusal kept me from getting better. I would spend time obsessing about the prospect of taking medication. As soon as I heard people talking drugs it would disturb me. I would imagine that the medication would allow people to control me. After many months, I finally accepted the fact I had to take medication.

Some people fear animals. Usually, the phobia develops from a negative experience. When I was younger, my friend and I decided to play with two small dogs. The dogs were very loud and furious meeting me for the first time. I did not realize they were dangerous.

They both attacked me for no reason and bit my feet. It was amusing for my friend but since then, I felt uncomfortable being near small dogs. Slowly I developed a phobia of small dogs. When walking on the street I would stay away from small dogs. However, I slowly overcame my fear and now I do not mind them.

A common phobia is of heights. At great heights, the heart beats faster and people may feel dizzy. Some may even experience stomach and vomiting. People would avoid going on the airplane or even crossing the bridge. Others may fear using ladders or looking down from the edge of buildings. Some may feel anxious or may have panic attacks. There are various techniques to help one overcome phobias such as one of heights. One way of overcoming phobias is by undergoing Cognitive Behaviour Therapy (CBT). It is important to identify if a thought is rational or irrational. First of all, one must understand what makes him or her fearful. One way of identifying what causes the distress is by writing the cause down. The cause could be something such as specific thoughts, fears, worries, pictures, images, graphics, people, animals, objects. This should help an individual clarify his or her thoughts. When you can identify what makes you feel anxious, you can be alert so that the same reaction does not happen again. It is necessary to write down exactly what is in your mind. Try to find out if the situation is true or if it is false. Try to be realistic about your situation and scenario. Find some ways of coping. Find someone who can guide you and help make you feel better. Sometimes listening to people's advice can be helpful. Take negative thoughts and replace them with positive ones. The better you can manage you fear, distress, and phobias the better you will feel and the more chances you will be able to take.

Insomnia

All humans need to sleep for certain hours. It is believed that a normal person will sleep for 7 to 9 hours daily. Interrupted sleep will affect the body and mind. One will feel tired and may not function properly without enough sleep. For someone with mental illness such as schizophrenia, sleeping can be dysfunctional. Due to medication one may sleep too little or too long. Antipsychotic medications are very powerful and can affect our mind and body. For example, Zoloft made me tired even when it helped me out of my depression. If sleep is missed or of poor quality for long periods of time, both the body and mental health will suffer. This will lead to further complications within the body.

What are the symptoms of insomnia? People with insomnia have trouble falling asleep. Usually it take at least twenty minutes for those with insomnia. Often they awaken during the night and cannot get back to sleep. Some would wake up earlier in than they would like and worry about being able to get a good night's sleep. They don't feel refreshed when they wake up in the morning, and may feel sleepy during the day. Therefore, they would use stimulants like caffeine to keep themselves alert during the day. (Vukovic, L. p.12). Usually, people have insomnia due to high stress in their lives. For some people, having a new a schedule at work can throw off their sleep schedule. A new born baby can be a cause of lack of sleep. It can be very difficult for parents to take care of their infant. Insomnia can be either acute or chronic. Acute insomnia occurs only occasionally. Chronic insomnia is quite different: it persists for more than a month and can even continue for years. Insomnia both acute and chronic, tends to affect older people and women more (Vukovic, L. p.13).

Exercise can help resolve insomnia. You can walk, cycle, practice yoga, which will all provide an excellent way to relax. Feeling too stressed could lead to insomnia. It is important to balance our body and mind in a proper way by taking care of ourselves. It is necessary to be in a calm environment. Not having enough sleep due to noise could also be a reason why you are not sleeping. Feeling hungry or thirsty, can make it difficult to sleep. Then it is necessary to snack before bed. Feeling constantly hungry all day can also prevent sleep. Eating well will help us sleep well. Calming the mind is also important to better sleep. Sometimes it may be difficult to sleep due to excessive emotions, such as fear, anxiety, tension, worries or even joy. One way of better sleep is to take a warm or cold bath. Doing physical exercise during the day is essential for a good night's sleep. Humans need to move to feel released. Doing daily exercise will help a person sleep better and boost physical stamina. It also enhances your mental outlook, self-esteem and mood. When one spends enough time outdoors, one will also feel much better due to sunlight. Regardless of the activity you decide to do, aim to exercise or play sport for at least 45 minutes at least 3 to 4 times weekly.

Having bedtime routine such as taking a bath, preparing a hot drink, reading poetry, books, watching an entertaining TV shows, listening to radio show, listening to music, playing with their children, makes bedtime comfortable. It is important to feel peaceful and quiet before going to sleep. If you live in a busy road, near an airport, a train station, choose a place where you may sleep comfortably. Noises are one cause of not sleeping well. While sleeping you need to stay away from loud noises. After a good night's sleep, you will feeling good and will feel very enthusiastic of the day. It is necessary to identify what keeps you from sleeping and how can you sleep better. If you sleep well then you will have a better day compared to others who did not sleep well. Your performance art work and home will gradually improve with good sleep.

One way to better sleep is by employing a breathing technique called "relaxing breaths". This easy exercise slows down your breathing and helps you feel calm and relaxed. It is an excellent stress-reliever that can be practiced at any time. Sit in a comfortable position with your back straight and bring your attention to your breathing. Relax and inhale through your nose to a count of five, counting at a pace that in comfortable for you. Hold your breath for a count of five. Open your mouth slightly and exhale to account of ten, keeping your exhalation smooth and controlled. Repeat the exercise for a total of five complete cycles. (Vukovic, L. p.108). This will help you better breathe and will make you feel better. You will feel that you have taken control of your body and mind. People do not know how to breathe properly. Once you know how to breathe and you practice the breathing exercise regularly you will realize that your sleep improves and you will feel better.

How do we fall asleep and what should we do to better manage our sleeping patterns. It is necessary to go to bed only when you are sleepy. If not you may stay awake for many hours and this could make you feel disturbed. While you try to sleep and you are awake you may think about everything and nothing. It is important to maintain a regular schedule of sleep and waking. Use your bedroom only for sleep and sex. You will see the impact on you and your partner. When going to your bed you will be more motivated to sleep or even to have sex. Try not to take any daytime naps. This could be one reason why you may not fall asleep at night. As mentioned earlier, exercise regularly but avoid vigorous exercise within three hours of bedtime. It is wise to exercise during daytime and night you use that time only to sleep. Let your body and mind relax. Thirty minutes before bedtime, engage in a relaxing ritual such as reading, listening to music, or taking a warm bath. This can help you better manage your bedtime. Sleep in a cool, well-ventilated bedroom. Before sleeping avoid large meals within three hours of bedtime. Give enough time to digest what you have been eating. Also avoid drinking large amounts of fluids one hour before bedtime. More precisely, avoid drinking caffeine in all forms. It is also necessary to not use nicotine or consume excessive amounts of alcohol. (Vukovic, L. p.99). When you can employ these normal steps you will see the change in your body and mind. You will take control of sleep. Give enough time to yourself and invest time to acknowledge what will make your sleep better. Slowly, you will see the change in you and in your environment.

What causes insomnia? "Different situational, physical or psychological factors can cause the sleep disorder. To deal with insomnia and alleviate sleeplessness, you may need to make behavioral, environmental or psychological changes in your life" (Drake, J. 1999-2013). In most of the time, stress is why people have insomnia. Due to some situational factors, such as a conflict with peers, family members, pressure at work you may feel tense and worried and would not be able to sleep. Physical disturbance such as pain or other kinds of discomfort can impair sleep. Having constant psychological episodes such as delusions, and hallucinations can also be one reason why one might not sleep well. Medication can also disrupt sleep. A person may sleep too much or too little. When suffering from insomnia, he or she may have behavioral changes; they may become angry quickly, may lose patience, and get frustrated easily.

Take note of your stressors so that you may have a better perception of what causes you stress or what triggers you. Knowing your own response to stressors can motivate you and help you find a solution for sleeping at a convenient time. The more you learn about yourself, the more you can control your stressors and gather information on why you have problems sleeping. It is important to learn to cope with insomnia. If you still have problems then you should consult a professional who can help you. A therapist may be able to help you deal with insomnia. He or she may give you tricks how to better manage your sleep. If your problem is chronic then you should consult a medical doctor as soon as possible.

The Problem

There are three types of insomnia: you cannot fall asleep, you wake up several times during the night, or you get up very early. (Newman, M., A. 2010). Insomnia usually occurs for a few days to a few weeks. Until you can figure out what causes the insomnia you may not realize what the problem is and why you lack sleep. You may feel tired, short-tempered, in a bad mood, which would go on until you restore your sleep. If you cannot sleep, do not force yourself. Instead, go to bed when you feel tired and ready for sleep. Once you have been sleeping well you may function better but most importantly you are in shape and you will feel like yourself. If you cannot sleep well for a few weeks then your situation is serious and alarming. Therefore, you should consult a doctor, psychiatrist or even a psychologist.

Myth versus fact

1. Myth: Dreaming is essential to be psychologically healthy.

Fact: There is no convincing evidence for this. The reason why we dream is something of a mystery.

2. Myth: Daytime naps are useful if you have difficulty sleeping at night.
   Fact: Quite the opposite—napping during the day can make it more difficult to sleep at night.

3. Myth: All adolescents are impossible to get up in the morning—it's just the way they are.
   Fact: It is true that adolescents often have a special need for sleep, but not all are difficult to rouse in the morning. Where this is a problem, there is likely to be a reason that can be put right.

4. Myth: Old people don't need much sleep because they don't do much during the day.
   Fact: Apart from the fact that the second half of this statement is often untrue, the amount of sleep needed to function at your best remains very much the same throughout adult life. There is likely to be a treatable cause if they do not sleep well.

5. Myth: The effects of not sleeping well are obvious to anyone, including yourself. You just feel tired.
   Fact: Actually, inadequate or poor-quality sleep can affect you in many different ways, both psychologically and physically. Other symptoms besides fatigue get overlooked instead of being dealt with.

6. Myth: If you don't sleep well, it's just one of those things and you have to put up with it.
   Fact: Nothing could be further from the truth. Careful enquiry will almost always reveal the reason why you are not sleeping well. This could be any of number of things. Once identified, the cause should be treated effectively. It is true that most people probably have occasional brief spells of not sleeping well, perhaps for no obvious reason. However, if the problem persists, there is likely to be an identifiable cause that should

be dealt with because of the potentially serious consequences of persistently not sleeping well.

7. Myth: Some people haven't slept for years.
Fact: This cannot be true, else they would not have survived! People who say this think they haven't slept because they only remember the times when they have woken in the night and have forgotten the rest of the time that they have, in fact, been asleep.

8. Myth: An alcoholic drink at bedtime is a good way of helping you to sleep well.
Fact: It may help you to get to sleep but is likely to disturb your sleep later in the night.

9. Myth: If I can't get to sleep, I should stay in bed and try harder.
Fact: This is likely to make matters worse because you will probably be tense and frustrated. Being in bed will become associated with being awake instead of going to sleep.

10. Myth: If you sleep longer at weekends, you can make up for loss of sleep during the week.
Fact: It doesn't work that way. Regular bedtimes and waking up times are important, otherwise your circadian body clock get confused.

11. Myth: The only treatment for insomnia is sleeping pills.
Fact: This is far from the case. In fact, the use of sleeping pills is rarely appropriate. Instead, depending on the reason why you are not sleeping well, one of a wide range of treatment other than medication can be used.

12. Myth: Daytime naps are good for you.
Fact: They can be for some people but, alternatively, they may be a sign of abnormal sleepiness that ought to be investigated.

13. Myth: Some people are just sleepy heads. There's not much to be done about it.
Fact: If you are persistently very sleepy, something should (and usually can) be done to correct it, because the consequences can be serious.

14. Myth: Snoring is a joke or at worst a nuisance.
Fact: It's not funny if someone else's snoring keeps you awake. More to the point, it can be a sign of serious condition (obstructive sleep apnoea) that needs to be treated.

15. Myth: Nightmares and night (sleep) terrors are basically the same thing.
Fact: Not so. They are different in a number of ways, including their causes and the type of advice and treatment required.

16. Myth: You should wake up a sleepwalker.
Fact: No. It is difficult to wake a sleepwalker and, if you manage it, he is likely to be confused and frightened.

17. Myth: Eating cheese give you nightmares.
Fact: Research has shown that there is no support for this idea.

18. Myth: Having children inevitably means that you have a bad time through loss of sleep.
Fact: Actually, children's sleep problems can usually be avoided or helped, and their parents' sleep protected, if appropriate advice or treatment is provided.

19. Myth: Women just worry a lot. That's why they don't sleep as well as men.
Fact: This may be true in some cases. However, there are other quite different possibilities that need to be considered and dealt with if necessary. (Stores, G. 2009).

From the book Sleep Deep: Simple techniques for beating insomnia by Karen Williamson, human beings spend a third of their lives sleeping. We need to understand our body clock and determine all our highs and lows in the day. Injury, poor performance, and depression are the results of not getting enough sleep. It often happens that we struggle to keep our eyes open during the day but cannot sleep later on. If that is the case, the chances are you have insomnia. As a result you may choose stimulants such as caffeine. You may have trouble to function without your morning coffee. Even if you rest you may get up easily due to noise. You have to juggle work and home life, which would be stressful. For some people baby on the way can be a cause of not sleeping properly. When the baby is born, taking care of the little one can be hectic and very stressful. Usually the first baby is very demanding as we are not experienced and we learn how to take care of the baby as it goes. Walking up in the middle of the night for nighttime feeding or to change its diaper can be demanding. When your loved one can't stop moving all night long, this could be another reason why you may not get proper sleep. Working the overnight can also impair.

It is a common for travelers to put their sleep pattern back on track. Sleeping problems can occur on a long journey or simply on your way to work after a bad night's sleep, sometimes driving a car when exhausted can even be fatal. Some people with sleep troubles do not realize they are due to snoring. You may have gone to bed early, yet wake up feeling sleepy and continue to feel tired all day long. Problems with sleep may stem from stress, you need to find techniques and strategies to calm-down and reduce nighttime worries. For a depress person, the chances are that he or she is not sleeping well due to their depression as insomnia is common in this illness. At night one may not realize how important is to breathe properly, this can be one reason why it is hard to fall asleep. When there is no alternative solution to sleep problems, you may be required to take medication, such as sleeping pills. Sleeping pills can help put you to sleep but its long-term efficacy is questionable. Avoid relying on medication to put you to sleep. Rather, use your mind and brain to control your sleeping pattern and time. Use mind power to dominate your sleep. Sometimes you may not feel sleepy due to hunger, therefore eat some snacks if you have to. Also the filter you are, the better you will sleep. Exercising and keeping yourself healthy can help you fall asleep quickly. Having a good mattress also matters; if you bed is too soft or you have an old mattress, it is time to replace it with a better one. You will see the change in your room and the comfort that will bring. If you think that you need to change some habits do so. It necessary to try all kinds of tools that will give you a good night's sleep.

While working, I had tremendously problems sleeping. In many occasions I would stay awake during the night and feel sleepy during day. I felt without energy during the day after sleeping only 2 to 3 hours a day. This went on for at least one year. One day I decided to monitor why I could not sleep, I later realized that my sleep problem were due to my work routine. I needed to be flexible at work, I had to work anytime they scheduled me. For example, I would finish work until midnight, then I would start the next shift at 8 am the following day. Working up to 50 hours weekly was very demanding. I needed to be on top of everything to keep up with work. I managed for a year until I collapsed one day. I was also addicted to caffeine; I would have at least three to four cups of coffee a day plus a soft drink at work to stay awake and work. Later, I realized that I was consuming too much caffeine. My stress level increased and I started feeling panicked often. My mood changed and I lost the desire to do any activity. Slowly, I lost control of myself and I started having symptoms of mental illness, such as hallucinations and delusions.

One day I mentioned to my family doctor my symptoms and lack of sleep. She was astounded and worried. Without hesitation she recommended to spend some time at the Day Hospital in Montreal in a psychiatric ward. As time passed, I was getting worse and it seems that I entering a dark zone. I finally took a sick leave, and my work at the bank then ended there. It took me a while to accept my illness and to agree that I needed to be monitored by professionals. When being monitored I had to take multiple medications that made it difficult for me to sleep regularly. What I have realized is that some medication kept me awake while others would be used to put me to sleep. The side effects of all the antipsychotic medications keep me from doing and functioning well. The medication trial lasted for a few weeks until the psychiatrist decided to put a limit and reduce medication. I have mentioned to the psychiatrist that I felt like a zombie when taking the multiple medications. Can you imagine taking various medication until one suit your body and mind. More precisely, you feel stabilized only when right medication works for you. It was a difficult period for me and with patience I have found light in the dark zone. I was not the only one having the symptoms, I made a few friends at the Day Hospital who were in the same shoes as me. They would understand me and I would understand them as well. With time I was able to juggle my sleeping pattern and I would be able to go to bed every day at a certain timeframe and wake up early in the morning every day. However, what I have realized is that when you have an illness, there is a chance that you may get another illness. It's like a chain connected to each other. Therefore, if you are in good shape and healthy, try to stay healthy. Do what needs to be strong mentally, emotionally and physically.

It is really important to ask many questions to better manage insomnia. You can start a pro and con list to see which aspect in your life need to improve and which of these is difficult to change. When you can track the difficulty of falling asleep, you will have a better chance of recovery. After all it is your body and your health therefore, you should take care of it by managing your sleep. There could be many unobvious reasons why you struggle to sleep. Therefore monitoring your life is necessary. Try to answer the following questions "How do I feel when I do get to sleep and wake up? Tired? Irritated? Happy? Excited? Do I have any stress or excitement that may cause my insomnia? Can I get rid of it? Who will it affect if I can? Should I get rid of it just because I can't sleep right? What kind of insomnia do I have? Is it problems getting to sleep? Problems staying asleep? How do I feel about having or the general thought of insomnia? What have I been doing to get rid of insomnia already? Is it working? What effects does it have on my insomnia?" (Pensiero, P. Wade, L. Herrick, J. & Zack). These questions should help you find out about yourselves and your sleep. Remember, the more you know about yourself, the more you can manage your insomnia. Slowly, you will feel better when you know how to cope with insomnia.

Early Symptoms: A Short Story and Theories
of Love, Life and Marriage

Early Symptom 'Short Story'

I do not understand this: I'm attractive, smart, sensitive, accomplished. Why doesn't she flip for me? Why Can't I find love? How many times have you lost sleep asking yourself this question? Usually, love begins within the first few minutes of meeting. A good impression is the secret to love that people may not know. Basically, a first impression could make someone like or loathe you.

Everyone has different ways of impressing others because they do not want to feel like an outcast. Most people talk about their accomplishments to others so they will be admired. A connection can start with eye contact, followed by a luscious smile and a delightful conversation. Everything materializes so fast: this simple natural behaviour of mankind occur every day.

Everybody has two antagonistic behaviors: within them a deep and dark side, and a bright side, a side that gives a perfect image. Furthermore, usually, people camouflage their true image, to hide a secret or something personal.

This story is one about Bob and his observations of his environment. Bob had a close friend named Jack. Bob and Jack were always together in school. They used to play sports on the same team where they became good friends. They developed trust between each other. They lived in the same area, and went to school every morning together, and walked back home together. Both of them had different characters and personalities. Jack was not too chubby nor too pudgy, but built. He was very conscious about his behaviors. He is hazardous when furious. At other times when he was jolly, he was restless.

Jack spoke French very well and would help those in trouble. But other times, he would make fun of individuals. Sometimes, he would chuckle for no reason, as if he had done something wrong. Jack had two faces depending his mood: one side of his good personality and the other side a vile character. But he was a smart guy. Bob on the other hand was always nice to everyone, he respected his elders, friends, and teachers. For Bob, there was no special cast or class. He had a religious view of women. He tried to be the perfect gentlemen. If someone would need help he would be the first to please that person. Bob was very sensitive and fragile like a porcelain vase, he would not even hurt a little fly. Bob had difficulty speaking and writing French.

For Bob, everything started in school. He was startled by his own behaviors, and he had a feeling the odds were against him. At the beginning of the term, his goals were to do well by keeping his grades over eighty percent, and to not make too many friends, so he could be a little more serious. He knew almost everyone in his school as it was a small and private school, but he could not pay attention to people around him to concentrate on his studies.

His friend Jack was serious too, but he wanted to have fun and study at the same time. Bob thought that keeping a little distance from his friends may help him get high marks, one of the primary reasons for choosing a private school. Furthermore, he wanted to stand out to pretty girls. Pretty for Bob was not a simple word, it meant something else. Someone is pretty because of their personality, not because of their physical appearance.

As silly as it sounded, for Bob staying away from all kinds of attractive flowers was the only to do well in school. Without realizing it, he was making a fool out of himself to others. It was his last year in the private school. He did not know how to give a perfect image to others. When the two friends were on break, they would be in the library. At the time girls walked by Bob and Jack.

Bob was joyful to smell their perfume. From that point on, he noticed that some of them were coquettish. They were purposely letting, him smell their fragrances. It took him several days to realize how people were judging his character, and he had to observe them precisely and analyze them to clarify his mind. He was astonished by watching their behaviors, it seemed the he was some sort of alien that people were interested in. They were interested in finding out what was inside of this treasury.

After smelling all kinds of aroma, Bob was trapped by one that made him dream. The lovely bird had such a beautiful fragrance, and she was such a beauty, pretty like a rose that each time she would pass near him, he would become passionate. He could not handle this anymore, and he had to do something by trying to get close to this marvelous person. Not only that, she was gorgeous, she spoke with a seductive voice. Listening her whisper to another person gave him the perfect image. She was like a model that all men dreamed to possess for themselves. From that point on, Bob decided to open the door of his heart to this girl.

Bob wanted to do everything perfectly in a very gentle way, because he did not want to mess up by giving her a bad impression about himself. He thought that giving her a vile impression of himself will make him less important to her. He begins to think about everything and nothing, things that made no sense. Furthermore, it was hard for him to begin a conversation, but once he was introduced, he had no trouble chatting with that person. He believed that if he would start speaking to that beautiful flower without being introduced, it would be an act of flirting. So he thought about how he could be introduced to her. At that time, Jack did not know that his friend Bob had an eye on someone.

One day, Bob and Jack were in the library doing their school work and at the moment, Bob saw the princess of his dreams passing near him and without waiting tells Jack to take a good look at her, and that Bob is interested to know her. Consequently, Jack tells him, to go for it, but Bob explains to him that he would prefer to get introduced. After a few minutes of reflection, Jack says, "if you want I will talk for you and tell her that you are interested to know her", but Bob declines, by saying that it will be too obvious that he is interested in her.

In school there was a perception that, science students were better then social science students. Science was considered more difficult than social science, even though social science students had in their pocket an immense amount of reading and writing that people were not concerned about. However, those who study either are both equally intelligent regardless of the program. In an institution, each student picks a program that they are interested in, not because they are not capable to get in other programs.

One day, our two friends were in the library doing their usual work. Jack was introduced to a guy named Jon, Bob classmate. Jon was shocked to meet Jack, simply because Jack spoke excellent French, compared to Bob. These three gentlemen were waiting until classes ended because they had a student Union meeting. Jon seemed to be very clever and knowledgeable about everything, and he started asking peculiar questions to Bob and Jack. Bob was startled to hear such odd questions from Jon and he felt guilty that his French was not as sophisticated as Jon's.

The time came for the first day of meeting at the student Union, people were introduced and were explained the rules of the meeting. The room had all kinds of tapestry on the wall. One student represented two hundred from that school, and had a lot of responsibilities. For that reason, each student had to choose a role and if there were too many students interested in the same activity, they were to speak before others would vote. Six positions were available in the Academic Council and Bob was interested in one of them.

A lot of students wanted to be in this Council, but only six places were available. They were given a few minutes to prepare, but Bob was not sure about the roles of the Council. He asked Jack what exactly people had to do in the Academic Council, but he did not know so Jack could not help him. Bob usually gets very nervous and panics very quickly when he has to express himself in front of a crowd. Giving a speech in front of thirty-five students was not a great idea for him; but he had no choice if he wanted to be in the Academic Council.

Bob knew that he was not able to speak French well. He began to give his speech and was saying things that were out of subject, and making many language mistakes. Moreover, his speech only lasted a few seconds and at least two minutes were recommended. Everybody was astonished to hear his speech, it was really not good at all. Jack's speech was marvelous, it was really something, very intellectual. He sounded to be like a real prime minister. However, Bob had a sphinx like smile on his face, and Jack was happy for him. When these two were coming back home from school by bus, Bob asked Jack about his speech; if it was good or not, so Jack replied that it was good but a little too short. Bob knew that Jack was not telling the truth, but as a friend, Jack would not want to make his friend feel bad by saying that his speech was worse then bad. However, Bob insisted to know the truth, so Jack told him that he made several mistakes by speaking and it was too short, also it was out of subject. Bob felt a little bad to hear that, but he was happy to find out the true image that he gives in front of the other students.

At night, Bob could not sleep pondering why he could not speak without making mistakes? Why did he have so many difficulties expressing himself? Is he an abnormal person, an outcast? He was asking himself some pretty odd questions. He had so many questions to ask but nobody was there to answer. A shiny little tear dropped from his eyes and he fell asleep. The next day, he woke up prepared for school, and thought that he would ask Jack about himself about his faults, and what he should do to improve. It seems that he was distracted by the thought of giving a bad impression to others. Jack did not know what exactly to say, he began by telling his friend that maybe he should read more French books or watch more French movies.

It was early in the morning, Jack was still essentially asleep, it was not the time to ask questions. From that point, Bob seemed to be a little depressed. He started hallucinating, it started as a little thing which later became very big for him. He was telling himself, why he had no means of being known, understood, or loved. For once, he felt very lonely, his friend who was near him was sleeping with a big smile. He was probably dreaming. After the bus stopped, because it was the terminus, and Bob had to wake up his friend.

Bob then sees his dream girl walking with an Asian friend. Bob and his princess made eye contact for a few second. He was so happy to see her in the morning that he said to Jack "from tomorrow on we will come early to school so I will see her". Jack only wanted one thing, and that was to see his friend happy, so he agreed. The next day they came early in the school, so Bob would be able to see her, they but realized that the princess was not in the same building as the other day, so they could not see each other.

From that moment on, Bob was focusing less on his studies because he was becoming blind by her beauty and he started to have true feelings for her. Unfortunately, love is an extreme power that is held inside of a human being and it can radically change the human mentally. It was that case with Bob, wherever he was, his mind was on that girl. He wanted to know her name with utmost desire, it seemed that whoever will tell him her name will be a lucky person because he would reward that individual. Unfortunately, no one could help him. He had no choice to wait until something really happened or to pray to God to help him. Bob appeared very despondent, only because he did not have the courage to talk to the girl. Who would want to go out with an immature boy? The girl seemed to be very clever and serious by observing her, one might conclude that she will keep her distance from of a guy. She won't show anyone that she is interested in them.

As days passed Bob's mind was slowly leaving his studies. It seemed that he was losing his concentration because of that girl. He was always talking about her to his friend. One time Jack got bored of listening to Bob and he did not know what to say anymore. Once he got angry because he was revising his notes and Bob was talking without knowing that he was disturbing his friend.

Jack and Bob had many courses, and in one of Bob's classes there was a girl named Vicky. Once in the library, Bob saw Vicky with the girl he dreamed of and he really wanted to know Vicky. Knowing her would be the best way to get introduced to his princess. Finally, one day after class, Vicky introduced Bob to Mela, his princess. He was now able to speak to her. Hearing her voice made him joyful and he was really excited to meet her. He told Jack that he was introduced to Mela. Jack was surprised to hear this and started teasing Bob. The next day, Bob walked into the library and saw Vicky with Mela, so he saluted Vicky. Her friend Mela made the first step by greeting Bob. Slowly they started a conversation together.

Mela asked about Bob's life, his age, hobbies what he likes to do and so on. She told him that in one month it will be her birthday. Time was running out and Bob wanted to surprise Mela with a birthday gift. He did not know what to do or what to get for her. Jack was also waiting for him to head back home. Basically, Bob was stuck with two major decisions: Jack or Mela. Suddenly, Bob heard his inner voice speaking to him, 'you don't see Mela every day, so don't miss your first occasion, leaving her would be an act of not caring for her. You see Jack every day, so let him wait for a few minutes'. Jack was not happy as he had to wait for Bob more than an hour. Later, Bob called Jack to apologize and tell him what exactly had happened, but Jack was really ticked off at him, so decided to not to listen by making all kinds of noise over the phone.

Bob was losing his patience waiting for Mela to call him, so he decided to call her. They talked again without noticing the time. After a long while, they bid farewell to each other. For the first time Bob seemed very happy. That night he slept well with a smile on his face. The next day, Mela came first in his mind when he woke up; he was already thinking of when he should call her. They talked for an hour again. Mela was the type of girl Bob dreamed of. When Mela talks she does not stop, she could talk for an hour without getting tired. Bob was a good listener, he would be able to listen to Mela for very long time. It was a dream which came true for Bob, they were made for each other. She was showing Bob how important he was for her, and he was getting more and more carried away by listening to her seductive voice. One might conclude that she was manipulating his mind, she seemed to be very harmless, but it was too early to find out her true character. She was hiding her true image.

The true image of Mela was coquettish, she would so have liked to be pleased by a gentleman, to be envied, to be wanted, to be sought after by Bob. That was one part of her personality, and Bob was not yet conscious about that. And he won't be conscious about it for a while, until he began analyzing her character and personality. It would be too late when he finds out. However, at that time, they were exchanging information about each other. The next morning at school, Bob was telling Jack every single thing that he and Mela been talking of, and Jack was listening very seriously, for once he seemed to pay attention.

Later, they went to fast food restaurant where they were ate and talked and laughed. Near them, an old lady was observing strangely. The old lady did not appear too happy nor angry. They stopped laughing, and they started asking to themselves questions about that lady. Bob was shivering and he was panicked by her look towards them. Jack was shocked to see how she was fixing her eyes on them. Suddenly, it was so quiet, you could not even hear a fly. The old lady seemed to be a wizard, she had big yellow eyes, a long nose and her curly hair carried shades of red, black, white and pink. She did not smell good, and she was wearing a long dark and dirty overcoat.

The two friends thought that she was a tramp. Jack said to Bob; that Halloween was a few months ago, and Bob was laughing. The old lady walked towards where these two friends were sitting. Jack's heart started beating faster, Bob was sweating and grumbling. All of a sudden, the old lady spoke with a nice voice. "Young gentlemen, may I sit near your table, if you do not mind?" The two young fellows were astonished hearing her talk sweetly and told her make herself comfortable. As she put her car keys on the table, the boys saw that her fingers were decorated by luxurious rings made of diamonds and gold. Jack was amazed and Bob could not believe what he saw. Jack complimented the lady on her rings. She replied; "My husband bought all these but he died a few months ago". Bob felt a little bad, and he said to her that if she needed someone to talk to that he was there to listen to her.

Suicide

Suicide is purposely hurting and ending one's life. Society sees it differently based on its religion, culture, belief and philosophical perspective. Hence, one's act of committing suicide is seen negatively or positively based on one's perspective. For instance, in first world countries suicide is seen mostly negatively, whereas, in the third world countries committing suicide could be seen positively. An example of a negative view is one ending his or her life because one could not cope with the pain. Whereas, a positive way of seeing suicide is when one sacrifices their life to protect a nation, country or even a family reputation. On the other hand, in countries such as Canada, we have a better understanding of the social problems and their effects; as a result, the individual is not necessarily looked down upon committing suicide. Regardless, killing oneself is not the right decision; and he or she instead should seek for appropriate help. The number of suicide attempts are unclear and could vary from one place to another some are declared, while others are incorrectly judged as accidents. Many people believe that "women attempt suicide more than men but men successfully commit suicide more often than women", (2013).

We often hear about people ending their life. Often one wonders why someone would take his or her life. What was the motive for someone to commit suicide? It can be very devastating for the family members and those close to the victim when a person chooses to take their life. Usually a person who wants to commit suicide leave "suicidal notes, say direct threats, give personal belongings away, talk about or is preoccupied about death, feels hopeless, and isolates themselves socially. They also show abrupt changes in appearance, show more risk-taking behaviors, and activities, experience weight changes, have severe depression, feel helpless and might act like he or she does not care" (Wiley, J. & Sons. 2013).

A suicidal person often leaves suicidal notes to others or even to their family, for example, a poem or a message about themselves or even about their pain and suffering. In 2012, there was a young teenager who committed suicide after being bullied in her school in Vancouver, B.C. victim mentioned how she was disliked by her peers and other people in her school. She had a difficult time in school. She mentioned how people were rude to her and were disrespectful toward her. This affected her mood and motivation. She blamed her surrounding for not letting her to live. When a situation like that occur, it affects not only the individual but the society. Not being accepted in an environment can lower the self-esteem and cause various types of negative thoughts, which may lead to suicide.

One will use direct threats in a conflict with others. When we have something on our mind that bothers us, we would express it unintentionally when in rage or sadness. This helps people identify those who may be suicidal and allows us to take action to help them. Some may even record themselves in a video and put it, online e.g. You Tube so people can see and hear about their sorrow. One might ask what has happened in their mind and why they behave so differently. Could it be possible that they do not feel loved by certain people or feel frustrated with themselves?

When a person decides to give their personal belongings away it is difficult to understand why they did it. Perhaps it is a way of sharing their valuables with others. It can be a sign of love, care and affection towards a person. It can also be an indirect message to others. The message can be simple, one will commit suicide, therefore, he or she takes the positive decision of sharing and giving away their valuable belongings. If you know someone who is giving people his or her belongings you should notify their family members, or someone who cares for that person. Try to convince the person to not take his or her life. Find out more information about that person. Ask many questions that come your mind to understand the motive behind the decision. You can become a life protector for a person who is in danger and who is deranged emotionally and mentally. In this type of situation, you have a prime role to play and your duty is to protect that person and give back his or her belongings.

A friend may be talking about or is preoccupied with death to you. Unintentionally, he or she is giving information about themselves and their intention. It is really important to support them by giving them good feedback and using positive reinforcement, and helping them understand that talking about death is not a good subject to talk about. When someone talks about death he or she often sounds negative. You want to avoid negative thinking and to share negative information. One should change the topic to life and birth. He or she will feel simulated by having a positive pep talk. Give a chance to the person who wants to harm himself or herself by simply listening to the conversation. By listening, you will win trust and faith that you really care for that person and understand what he or she is going through.

When one feels hopelessness, one often ask themselves or others the following questions: "Why bother? Nothing will work out. I'll never be happy. My relationship can never get better. I'll never be able to get what I want. There's no use in trying. There aren't any good men (women) left. I'm too old (ugly, poor, boring, damaged, etc.). I can't compete. I'm cursed. The world is against me" (Oprah, 2013). Have you ever felt like this? One may say that most had felt hopeless once in their lives. It is normal and natural to feel like that. However, what is not normal is to think about these things constantly and to build negative feelings and thoughts about yourself, until you feel like hurting yourself. You believe that you need to punish yourself. You may feel discouraged, degraded, demoralized, and disorientated. The more you spend time on negative discussions or worries, the worse your mood become. Give yourself a chance to discover positive situations. When you feel lonely do not isolate yourself, go out and be with your friends, try to do physical exercises which might help you physically, emotionally and mentally. When you try to do something it may feel like the devil is whispering that you will fail. Do not obey or listen to that voice. Try to find what is real and what is not. You may blame yourself for not being successful. Based on your actions you should be able to distinguish between right and wrong, bad and good and use your consciousness when making a decision. Being spiritual can be essential and believing in God can change your thoughts and give you inspiration to better manage your life. You will also feel much better when you laugh or when you make someone laugh. When you feel strong, motivated, faithful, and passionate, you will feel and discover hope for yourself.

Social isolation and loneliness can affect a person emotionally, mentally and psychologically. People may be too scared to deal with others. Therefore, a person may choose to isolate him-or herself from society. People with a mental illness are afraid and are apprehensive to mixing with people. Schizophrenic, will stay away from people and often think that others are talking behind their back. Sometimes they feel that people want to hurt them. "Some studies have suggested that loneliness can be linked to a number of psychological and physical difficulties, including depression, substance abuse, increased smoking, increased anxiety, reduced medical care and compliance, increased stress levels, reduced satisfaction with life and decreased self-esteem and increased blood pressure" (Ankrom, 2009). Based on the previous quotation; people may have different reasons for feeling lonely. One should try to be engaged with society and meet new people to feel better about themselves. Loneliness is just not being alone but it has a lot to do with how we feel, and behave with people. It is necessary to be in the reality to better function and deal with various stressors and triggers. When one faces various obstacles one is then able to overcome difficult situations.

One may notice a change in appearance in someone who is about to commit suicide. He or she may look differently and may gain or lose weight. One may also exhibit more risk-taking behaviors and may not participate in daily activities. This can leading to severe depression. When feeling depressed one will eventually have suicidal thoughts and a desire to harm oneself. This feeling of helplessness might prevent the victims from taking care. When people have irrational thoughts he or she may not feel responsible for their actions. For a person who is suicidal, it is normal to think negatively and to blame themselves for everything that they do. Some may also blame others for not letting them live or even be themselves.

The causes and effects of suicide all vary from one place to another. A person, who is willing to harm himself, could do so because of a loss of a loved one through separation or death. The surrounding could also be another reason why one wants to kill him or herself. Not being able to deal with suffering is another way of seeing the pain. The majority of the time, one end one's life due to mental illness, such as chronic depression. Depression is not the only mental illness, which is a risk factor. For example schizophrenia, anxiety, manic depression, eating disorders and substance abuses all contribute to suicide. Hence, one's mental health plays an important role in one's life. Being able to cope with such disorders takes a lot of energy and courage.

By observing a person behaviors one can conclude that he or she may become suicidal. The following information are some common signs of a suicidal tendency. Usually, when one becomes depressed and withdrawn from society, is at risk for attempting suicide. Also one often becomes careless; one may say that he or she does not care about certain situations. Some may even give away valued or meaningful possessions. Suicide is a high risk especially when one abuses drugs or alcohol. Consuming a lot of drugs and alcohol can become dangerous for someone's health and change one's perception about life and people.

If you know someone who is suicidal you have an important role to play with him or her. It is necessary to be able to talk quietly with them to find solutions to a problem. Then one needs to find actual facts and ways to help the person. If you cannot help that person, you can refer to someone who is qualified and experienced in the field. You can call non-profitable organizations, the emergency, hotlines, professionals. There are many resources available in Canada and also in many other counties. You have to better understand by gently asking questions to better help the person who wants to commit suicide. Try to take a different approach to understand that there are many options to solving a problem. Try to help the suicidal person by showing alternative options. An example would be to tell them that people would prefer to see that person alive. Suicide is not an option.

There are coping strategies to better handle the risk of suicide. If you are thinking about committing suicide, keep in mind that you may not be alone in that thinking. You may feel a lot of pain, disturbance, anxiety and worries. You do not know what action to take and you may react badly to someone who is willing to help you. Therefore keep yourself calm and think twice before acting. Give yourself a second chance. Do not blame yourself for no reason. No one is trying to take over your mind. Let you tension go away by waiting for a few hours or even a few days until you find someone to discuss about your situation. You may have irrational feelings telling you to do an action. Put a distance between your thoughts and feelings. Do not let your feelings take over your thoughts and your thought take over your feelings. Try to balance both at the same time. Often people try to escape from reality by hurting themselves or ending their lives. In this context, if you cannot balance your feelings and thoughts try to feel them. I you can feel your emotion then you will feel that you are alive. If your thoughts say to end your life try to feel death with your thoughts. If your thoughts cannot feel death then try to live and give yourself another chance. You may be angry on something or someone, there is no need to hurt yourself just because people do not value, care, appreciate or even give attention to you. You may have lost someone you admire, and love. You wonder what to do and how to cope. By giving yourself some time you will be able to overcome the situation. You may feel hopeless or even left out, fear of rejection or guilt. In this case, talk to someone about your concerns and seek for help.

How do I Overcome Suicidal Thoughts

For a person who is constantly thinking about committing suicide it is necessary to find a way to overcome suicidal thoughts. One should not stay and continue thinking about harming himself or herself. The best tactic is to perform some activities, such as swimming, or jogging outside, to distract yourself with something that you usually enjoy doing. When thinking constantly about suicide it is hard to concentrate on other things, therefore you have to find a way of being in the moment. Think of what you can do to help yourself by avoiding negative thoughts that go through your head. You should not think about what might happen if you disappeared from this world, but instead on what might happen if you choose to stay with people you care about the most and with individuals who admire you. Sometimes writing on a piece of paper can help you realize what you have achieved and that people care about you. When seeing on the paper you will be able to judge by yourself all negatives and positives action conducted by you and others. This will help you distinguish many ideas and thoughts about people and yourself. How many people appreciate your company and how do they care for you? When feeling suicidal you can also write down some phone numbers on your papers and you can contact them when you feel lonely. It can benefit you to write down some crisis numbers in case you need to speak to them to get better advice about everything and nothing.

Promise to yourself not to do anything wrong. Make good decisions for yourself. If you can think about negative thoughts realize that you may as well think about positive thoughts. It's much more fun to think positively than negatively. Sometimes you may even lough about your own behavior and thoughts. Hence, when you feel sad and down do not decide to take an action right away. It is understandable that you are going through a difficult moment, therefore wait at least a few hours to 24 hours before taking any decision about hurting yourself. Give a chance to yourself and be kind to your body and mind. Remember you made a promise to yourself earlier that you will give a chance for you. Know the difference between thinking and acting. This will lead you to a better mental environment when you can control your behavior and thoughts. If you feel down or suicidal, do not hang out with people who take drugs or even drink alcohol. Do not mix alcohol and drugs when you are thinking about suicide.

When you feel better you should remove dangerous things from your house, such as knives, weapons, drugs, razors and other kind of things that might be hazardous. If you take medication, put it somewhere safe and you will not try to overdose yourself on pills the doctor prescribed. If you have any doubt about yourself talk to a doctor about your symptoms or even about your thoughts. If you feel unsafe then find someone with whom you feel secure and safe to discuss about your matter. It is understandable that when you feel blue it is painful but you must overcome your feelings and take the pain day by day and eventually you will feel better. Give yourself the time to live, and to survive even though you may be convinced to harm yourself. If you feel lonely or hopeless, just by waiting a few hours to days you will see that you have managed to find solutions to your problems. You will feel light instead of darkness.

One way to overcomes suicidal thoughts is to discuss them with someone you trust the most. They should be able to guide you with better advice and show you the way safely. When you cannot trust anybody and not even your close ones you may try to discuss it with a stranger. They might even be more helpful than someone you trust. Do not feel shame, embarrassment or even guilt for your actions as you have not conducted anything wrong, therefore there is no reason why you should hide your secret. You may feel much better letting things go from your heart. Release your mind from unwanted thoughts. By sharing thoughts and memories you will feel much more secure and released. Allow people to help you as it will give you trust and hope.

You may ask why you feel this way. To answer that question, one often feels severely in pain when thoughts are overwhelmed with various types of emotions and feelings. Some may see the pain more severely than others, and one may cope less well than others. Suicide is not an option but it is a painful solution. Just the fact of thinking about it make it more complex and painful to deal with it. The impact of pain in yourself can distort your thinking by making you very vulnerable and emotional. One should discuss with a professional such as a counsellor, psychologist, psychiatrist or other health professionals. There are always many solutions to a problem. When you find that solution you will change your mind and feel better about yourself. With their guidance you should be able to cope and feel better about your experiences. It is natural to feel sad "at least once in a blue moon", therefore you should not pay attention to the idea of hurting yourself just because you are not feeling well. There should not be any reason why you should take your life. Take life as a gift and open that gift and see yourself flourish and grow older.

Who can you approach to get advice when you are suicidal? You may have mentioned to someone about your plan to commit suicide. It is important to tell from your bottom of your heart. Tell exactly what you will tell to yourself. Be open-minded and honest as much as possible. If you feel that you cannot tell them word-by-word, then write it down. When writing it you will feel differently and you can see exactly what is wrong and what is right with you. If you think that a person who you trust does not understand you, then find someone else. You may encounter bad experiences but this should not prevent you from telling or writing it down. There are always people who are ready to give advice and help people who are in need. Talk to someone on a daily basis. Tell them whatever comes to mind. Do not think what the other person will say but think about the positive things that you can say to better create a communication between you and your friend. It might help to plan what you want to do and how you intend to follow your routine. Furthermore, if you exercise it will make you feel much healthier. Plan to go outside with friends or family members. Go see a movie in a theater or plan something meaningful. This will make you feel happier. You can also ask a person to walk outside with you for at least 30 minutes. If you feel nothing then force yourself to participate in activities or just take some fresh air.

Now that you have some ideas about yourself and what to do when you feel blue or alone, there are also certain things that you should avoid doing. Avoid taking drugs or to drink alcohol. You will feel healthier not consuming dangerous substances. Avoid being alone. The more time you spend alone the more you will feel alone. Find an alternative solution to change your thoughts. Do not do things that can hurt yourself, such as listening to sad music, watching sad movies, or doing something that make you feel sad, they could increase your negative thinking. You should think positively and do something that stimulate your mind. Find what changes your motivation. What will make your mood change. Volunteering can help you and bring a new interest. You may meet new people and you may enjoy being with them. Find healthy solutions to better guide your mood and satisfaction.

The Suicide Theory of Me, Myself and I

An example,

"Me" says: Me wants to commit suicide.

"I" says: I should live to help others.

"Myself" says: Myself will take the final decision about whether "Me" should commit suicide or "I" should live to help others.

I define "Me" (-NEE)

"Me" has sexual desires. If "Me" wants to do something more exciting (according to "Me") then killing people or animal will take place. In addition, behaviors such as fighting, jealousy, dishonesty, shyness, unfriendliness, sadness, paranoia, phobias and psychological disorders may be controlled by "Me". Anything that is considered as 'bad' in our society will be controlled by "Me". "Me" can take care of all the negative memories (loss of parents, or loss of a loved one, divorce, more precisely it is all sorrows in "Me". It is the unconscious mind that louses unconscious pleasure, unconscious satisfaction and unconscious desires. Basically, the unconscious Negative Extreme Energy (-NEE) will dominate to take an action and to fulfill "Me" Furthermore, when there is a misbalance or a chemical misbalance in the brain, "Me" is defiantly taking over "Myself" and "I" personality. When one is using the "Me" personality, one may behave rudely, may not be respectful toward others, will not be tolerant, may not be understanding or merciful. This is why people behave in an abnormal way because it is controlled by "Me".

I define "I" (+PEE) as being controlled by the conscious Positive Extreme Energy (+PEE). It is always seeking to do something good. The "I" is gentle, calm, seek for peace, and believe in doing good actions, such as helping others, helping sick people, and controlling "Me". The "I" will always be in conflict with "Me" and will always disagree with "Me's" decision. The "I" personality is very tolerant, very understanding, and very merciful toward others or things. The

"I" knows that "Me" will cause trouble; therefore "I" will always be in conflict with "me" and will always disagree with "Me's" decision. When making love to another "I" will be patient and will ask the consent of the individual. The "I" will not try to hurt anyone; the personality will care for one or another and will love one another. "I" is the conscious mind, the conscious pleasure, the conscious satisfaction, and conscious desire. Basically, the conscious Positive Extreme Energy (+PEE) will dominate to take an action by fulfilling the "I" personality. Furthermore, the "I" personality will consciously look for "Me". "I" may not function well when there is a misbalance or a chemical misbalance in the brain. The "I" can also be seen as a 'normal' individual.

I define "Myself" (-NEE+PEE) as:

"Me" is the Negative Extreme Energy (-NEE), whereas, "I" is the Positive Extreme Energy (+PEE), which is the opposite of "Me". "Myself" is the in between (-NEE+PEE). The "Myself" personality is like a Judge that makes the final decision; it is like a balance that determines which side is the heaviest before taking an action. The "Myself" personality can be seen as super conscious. The "Myself" personality always stays neutral between (-NEE and +PEE). However, the super conscious will always weights between right and wrong, between happiness and sorrow and will be able to distinguish between sane and insane before making a proper decision. The super conscious may choose to do something bad or it can be the reverse as well.

I was asked of these two questions in the past:

1. If a new drug were to be made legally available that increased happiness by ten percent, but reduced the length of life, how many years would you be willing to forfeit to use the drug? How did you decide upon this number? What if the drug were illegal?

   My answer was, first of all, I have no intention to use drugs to increase happiness. If I go through depression I would rather use anti-depression. If it is written in my destiny that I will live for a longer period of time then I will, if not I will die. In my opinion happiness comes from both Nature and Nurture. One can also consider happiness as a self-fulfilling prophecy. If every morning I tell myself I am happy, there is a big chance I will be happy until the end of day.

2. If you could sell years of your life to people willing to buy them, would you sell any? Why or why not? If you would sell some, how many would you sell and for how much money?

I think those who are interested in selling years of life to others for money are those who will be interested in committing suicide. Basically, it is brainwashing an individual. I am not interested in selling years of my life or to receive from anyone. I take life as it is and as a gift.

Hypotheses on 'Me' 'Myself' and 'I'

Based on those two question it is very easy to find out if one is suicidal or not. If the 'Me' personality (-NEE) would be suicidal then I would answer 'Yes' to both of the answers above. But I am not suicidal; therefore my 'I' personality (+PEE) said 'No' to the above question. The super conscious was able to distinguish between right and wrong automatically (-NEE+PEE) by answering the above questions. The person who asked me these two questions in the past I believe had either the intention to commit a crime by using me or wanted to see if I would commit suicide.

The decision to commit suicide is controlled by 'Me' the Negative Extreme Energy (-NEE). The—NEE is overloaded by sorrow or emotion and cannot be controlled anymore that 'myself', the super conscious, has no choice but to agree with 'Me'. The math and the proper formula between 'Me' and 'I' is as follows:—NEE+PEE=TEE. When 'Me' dominates 'I', the TEE (Total Extreme Energy) is negative overall and 'Me' would choose to commit suicide. If 'Myself' dominates the TEE is positive and the self would not commit suicide.

This equation can be used for any kinds of problem or actions or to understand psychological disorders or disturbing behaviors.

I also believe that we all have at least three multiple personalities. "Me", "Myself" and "I". Each of them functions differently and each has its own goals. The 'Me' personality functions unconsciously, the 'I' consciously and 'Myself' functions by the use of the super conscious. To live a healthy life, the three multiple personalities should be fulfilled. If one is not fulfilled and gets into conflict with 'me' or 'Myself' or 'I' then one will go through suffering (e.g. depression, arguments, unhappiness, stress, anxiety, suicidal tendencies, insanity, or psychological disorders).

3 stages

Stage One (Healthy): This stage represents a healthy person, a normal being without psychological disorders.

Stage Two (Normal): This stage represents someone with conflicts with 'Me' and 'I' personalities, there is a little suffering.

Stages Three (Abnormal): This stage represents someone with psychological disorders. The self is abnormal, and is out of touch with reality. Chronic suffering occurs here.

Level One: (-NEE+PEE): occurs when someone makes a decision and when—NEE+PEE has a conflict of interest.

Level Two: This level occurs when (-NEE) takes control over (PEE).

Level Three: This level occurs when (PEE) takes control over (-NEE).

Final Level: This level occurs when '"Myself"' personality takes the final decision between (-NEE+PEE).

Upper Level: This level occurs when "Me, Myself and I" are satisfied equally.

Lower Level: This level occurs when "Me, Myself, and I" are not satisfied. There is a possibility of suffering for the individual then if there is a chemical misbalance in the brain.

Stage one occur then it is associated with a Level. (Stage + Level)

If Stage One is not fully satisfied then it goes to stage two. Stage two is associated with a level.

If Stage one and two are not satisfied with a level then it goes to Stage Three. Stage three is then associated level.

Understanding a Disorder

Some examples of activities that increased the Positive Extreme Energy are as follows:

1. Doing well on a test.
2. Working part-time, making money even though it is not enough.
3. Meeting new people.
4. Studying for 8 hours daily.

Stressors: (-NEE)

These are some examples of stressors that increase the Negative Extreme Energy:

1. Losing 2000$ in Casino
2. Breaking up with the girl friend (Emotional hurt)
3. Need to pay credit card (stress)
4. Arguing with a friend (blaming yourself)
5. A rumor being created (anger, frustration, shame)
6. Burning out because of studying too much (Burnout, tired, fatigue)

As you can see in this example, there is more of the—NEE than the +PEE. Let's use "Myself" personality to solve the problem by putting numerical Value.

-NEE+PEE= Answer

-6+4=-2

-NEE is taking control over +PEE and there is a conflict between—NEE and +PEE, therefore, suffering occurs. This person is going through Depression.

Obsession about Words

I define obsession about words as using words to better understand a particular symbol or meaning. In my belief, when someone wants to end their life, they would obsess about words in their thoughts before taking an action. In the first Phase any word comes to mind. In the second Phase, slowly one gets more in depth with the words. In the third Phase, one begins to put the puzzle of words together. The Fourth Phases is when finally thinking constantly about the meaning for the words. Phase Five occurs when one is able to accept the word most relevant to oneself.

In phase 1, we think constantly about any word that comes to mind. In most cases we wonder why we think like this and why these words enter our mind. Words flood our mind and it seems that we cannot get out of it the flood. In this early Phase, we only start doubting if we are rational. We may compare words that are valuable. For example, we may think about the words "care, nice, beautiful, shames, respect, critical, hurt, and sensible". These words are in your mind along with the situation they are associated with. Therefore, we become very sensitive unconsciously obsess about words in this phase.

In Phase 2, the words in your mind get heavier with the constant thinking. In this phase, we think about specific words or situations. We usually cannot identify if these words are negative or positive. We could be obsessing about negative or positive words and meaningful or meaningless words. What is important is that if you know you are obsessing about words, it is necessary to realize it so that you can move on to the next Phase.

The Third Phase is mostly concerned about mixed thinking. What I mean by this is that we feel lost with words. It is like a puzzle to find the right pieces or to identify the right versus wrong words. We may search for the purpose of living, it could be contained within a word. We could have a word in mind and determine whether the word can help or stop us from hurting ourselves. For me, my word was "Destiny". I tried to find why I have chosen the word destiny or why it came into my mind. For me, destiny could simply mean that it is my destiny to be born with Schizophrenia. The word destiny brought to think about accepting or neglecting the condition. By knowing the difference I had an assumption about what I really wanted. Knowing how to differentiate the real from unreal protected me from doing something wrong.

In Phase 4, we think about the purpose of life by determining the most important thing, obstacle or even goal in our lives by choosing one or many simple words meaningful to us. For example, the word "Destiny" had an important meaning to me. Therefore, I tried to find out if there is a word more valuable than the word "Destiny". By obsessing about words, we can add other words that could be as meaningful but less than or equal to the word "Destiny". To be more precise take a sheet of paper and draw a line down the middle of the page. On the left side write down important words that you value the most and on the right side write less important words come into your mind.

In Phase 5, once you have written the words and are able to classify the words you will be able to see your own thought processes. Knowing the meaningful words that you have chosen will help you realize your actions. In thinking about words, you pay more attention on the situation then the action. You are able to justify and clarify your thoughts and empty your mind. By writing them down on a piece of paper, you would be able to see with your own eyes the words that empower your mind. By writing down your thoughts, not only will if reduce your worries, tension, or doubts but it help you think more precisely, positively and rationally. By now the words that were meaningful to you became regular words. For me when I chose the word destiny it took me many months to accept it.

Immortality of the Soul

Philosophy

If the soul survives regardless of how the life ends, then we should not treat those who commit suicide differently from others. In the next section, I will explore the philosophical arguments that the soul survives after the body cause to survive. In the Oxford Dictionary and Thesaurus, the 'soul' is defined as the spiritual or immaterial part of the human being, often regarded as immortal. It can also be the moral, emotional, or intellectual nature of a person or animal. It is the personification of pattern of something. 'Immortal' means to live forever (Tulloch p.748 & 1482). The following will focus on Plato Phaedo's ideas on the immortality of the soul. It is based on a critique of Plato's proofs by examining both the strengths and weaknesses of Plato's arguments.

Phaedo reveals two themes by involving supernatural or imaginary and embodying popular phenomena. The first statement that he made is that 'we live in a hollow of the earth and are ignorant of the splendor of its real surface and of the purer life there; and the second describes what happens to immortal souls after death' (Grube p.3). He describes both myths artistically and elaborately.

The first argument is that the soul exists before birth Socrates explains that the soul learned all that it could learn from the Forms. The Forms are discussed at length to be intangible, divine, perfect, ideals of things such as Beauty, Good and Truth. All things in the world derive from their existence and identity. Plato explains his theory by using the word 'simple' and 'composite'. He believes that humans are a mixture of body and soul. To be more precise the body is a composite of many things and it dies at the end, whereas, the soul is simple and it stays alive after death.

In Plato's perception, "simple" is indestructible, it can't be broken down. If it is indestructible, then we can say that it is immortal. "Composite" can be broken down, therefore, it is destructible. For example, a vase can be smashed into tiny pieces and ceases to be a vase. What remains are vase parts, shards of glass and glass dust that made up the vase. This is the way destruction takes place in our world, and Plato claims it in the only way.

If the soul is immortal then there is life after death. If there is life after death then there is immortality, and if this is true then there is an existence of a supernatural form after death. Plato believed that there is life after death. In Hinduism, people believe in reincarnation. One must die but the soul never dies, and due to this that person soul is used to reincarnated someone else or something else. In Phaedo's arguments, he mentions that we must escape from the body and observe things in themselves with the soul by itself.

The second part of the first argument is that our souls exist after death. Socrates showed this to be true by constructing a logical proof. For example, he uses the doctrine of opposites: according to him, the opposite of hot is cold, opposite of large is small, then the opposite of life is death. If the body is controlled by the mind, and the mind does not function, then the body will stop functioning. However, the soul will remain alive and try to find another body, which is controlled by the mind. In another word, in order to be alive, one had to have been dead in the past. If this is true then life after death is also true. If all endings are beginnings and human death is an ending, then human death is a beginning.

The materialist will not dispute that human death is a beginning. With it you begin to be a corpse or you begin to be history. No particular reason has been given or thinking that you begin a new form of conscious, personal existence in some new metaphysical realm. Human death may just be too disanalogues to, or different form, any clear cases of transformation within the continuity of ongoing individual existence that we can see elsewhere in life, for this argument to carry any weight at all.

According to Plato, the soul is to forms what harmony is to lyre. However, harmony is destructible, when the lyre is destructible. For example, consider musical note being sounded by the trumpet. As long as the trumpet is blown, that particular musical sound exists. But smash the horn, and the sound will cease to exist. That particular sound's existence is dependent on the existence and proper functioning of the trumpet. Once the entity on which something is dependent is destroyed, that something is extinguished as well. In my opinion, consciousness with thoughts are like a note being blown on a trumpet. They are dependent on the existence of the body. Destroy the body, and the note will disappear. Death, in this analogy, robs the soul of its source and support, and thus it ceases to exist.

If human beings survived death, then many people who have already died would be communicating to us. There is no such communication from beyond the grave. Therefore, human beings do not survive death. Even if the soul can come apart, how do we know for sure that dismantling it is the only way for it to stop existing? Why can't something just fade away? Pluck a piano string, and the sound that results will eventually fade away. Existence could end in other ways besides dismantlement. In my perception, Plato's argument are not convincing enough to address the immortality of the soul.

Marriage

We get influenced to marry when we see a happy couple getting married. We tell others and ourselves that our turn will come as well. We feel eager and wonderful to see two people kissing. We value and honor someone who feels the same joy. It seems that we share their happiness when it happens. Based on my perception, there are a few types of marriage. Love Marriage, Arranged Marriage, Commitment Marriage, Reproduction Marriage, and the most the Commercial Marriage. There are also two types of gender marriage heterosexual and homosexual.

In a Love Marriage, you and your partner have known each other for a long time, both of you have been going out for months or years, you are serious in your relationship, both of you may have discovered each other's body or are just waiting for the proposal. More precisely, both of you have shared good times together, have known each other quite well, and each other's weaknesses and strengths. Therefore, you choose to follow your heart by marrying your partner.

Commitment Marriage is a type of marriage on commitment. Mostly, immigrants face Commitment Marriages more than non-immigrants. For example, you or your partner decide to move to another country. Therefore, there is a gap where both of you cannot see each other for a certain period of time. This creates a hole between two couple. For some the relationship turns out well for others it is ruined. For me, I am a Canadian citizen who went to foreign country to marry my native person. The process of immigration for my partner took many months, and depending on the country it might take many years. I had the choice to communicate only by telephone or internet. Those who are living my example would understand and even visualize the mental pressure that one lives through in this process.

Reproduction Marriage is a sensitive issue. Most people love children and dream to be a father or a mother. Most of the time an individual is aware of the responsibility of being a father or mother. It happens that a mother or father or both would shirk off the responsibility of being parents. Some people marry purposely to reproduce. We are all human and want to leave our names, traits, genes, behind. In many cultures, reproduction is not permitted before marriage. Therefore, the individual that does not care if the relationship will work out well or not, their only concern is to see their child on Earth.

Lately, in Montreal, people have been marrying for commercial purposes. It was reported that between 2009 to 2012, more than 700 couples married to stay in Canada. In other words, marriage is for the papers or documents. The matchmaker makes money for every couple they marry, and the bride or groom also makes money from the third party. These are the people who marry purposely to become a landed immigrant or to enter another country. According to the law, this marriage is considered fraudulent.

In Asia, the term Arranged Marriage is well known. In many cultures it is honorable for a father or mother to approve their son or daughter in choosing their mate. Sometimes, the father or the mother is introduced to the candidate by only spending a few moments chatting before a decision is made. In arranged marriages there is a matchmaker, who discusses with the parents about marriage. They talk about financial security, culture, and how it is perceived in other cultures. Even though the candidates are from the same country, many live in different casts systems. Religion and divorce are also discussed. More details are as follows:

- Matchmaker: They could be the parents, or someone close to the family or an agency. The parents decide to reveal publicly that they have a daughter or a son and looking for someone to get married, in that case the matchmaker is needed. Some agencies have a vast collection of people with their information and it is available for anyone who subscribes to the matchmaker.
- Financial security: it is really important for a man to be financially secure when choosing for a bride. The bride's family may investigate and may ask for a certain amount of goods and asset when discussing about marriage. When come to financial issues, both the male and female sides may try to minimize the cost of the marriage.
- Culture: In some places there is a caste system, in other places people are divided into low, middle and high classes. Among each class or caste, there are certain limitations. Marrying someone from a lower class or caste could be seen negatively.

The system is less strict than it is in the past. Most of the time, couple from the same culture get married at least to follow their beliefs.

- Religion: Religion is a powerful bond in a relationship. Before a matchmaker even starts their duty, he or she needs to know which religion the candidate believes in.
- Divorce: This is discussed by both of the couple's families. It is typically mention in advance that the bride will get something when there is divorce. In this circumstance, there are many laws that protect the female. For example, the male has to agree that he has to give a certain amount of money, goods and maybe asset to his former wife. On the other hand, males will usually get nothing. The only thing the male may get is a custody of the child.

What are the advantages and disadvantages of the Love Marriage, Arranged Marriage, Commitment Marriage, Reproduction Marriage, and Commercial Marriage? In a love marriage one knows the partner so well enough that he or she may seek for other adventures. He or she may not get enough affection after such a long period of time spent, or feel boredom. The advantage is that one knows the opposite partner well enough that, there is a trust built: just the presence of your partner may be special. One may be truly in love that one become invincible. Love is pure, holy and all dreams are created from the first touch, first kiss, first hug, first tears. It is a joyful moment to be around the chosen person.

With the arranged marriage, when being with someone, one may agree to marry them for beauty, for not feeling lonely to please his or her parents or to show society that one has a partner. It seems that your partner is a total stranger. Looking on the other side of the page, there are many advantages when choosing for arrangement marriage. It could be seen as holy for some, especially those with mental illness. Certain people with a disorder may not be able to find a decent partner, therefore, being introduced to someone to openly discuss about marriage can give hope and life to a couple. In most cases, when marrying a person the partner is aware of the illness. It takes courage, gentleness, and kindness.

Commitment marriage, both in a couple have to be apart from each other for months to years, trying to build a long distance relationship. The proverb "out of sight, out of mind" cannot work in a commitment marriage because both parties have decided their destiny will be together regardless of what might happen. They are on mission. Both are committed to each other, the only thing that is missing is love, to build a relationship.

The risk of the reproduction marriage is that one person may not be committed to his or her partner. When marrying for the sake of having children, it is possible that one person ends up forsaking the relationship, leaving the other to raise the children on their own.

In commercial marriage, the relationship depends on money and the agreement between the matchmaker, groom or bride and a third party. On the surface, the new couple will be technically married even though it is really a fake marriage. If caught both would be severely punished, one might get deported, or might be charged with fraud.

In modern society, couples who share different cultures, and religions get married and it seems to bode well. They have built a bond and are willing to spend their life discovering each other's culture or religion and showing their children the both side of the beliefs, eliminating the negative sides by implementing the positive ones. Their children will have the advantage of understanding the both sides of the wall between two cultures. Moreover, their children will have the last say in choosing the culture and or religion.

Marriage

Having arguments is normal, but what matters is that the message is conveyed to the opposite side and how one deals with arguments. When verbally fighting one should be creative. Some example are, instead of disputing at home, one should go outside and talk about it. Changing the atmosphere can make a difference. You can even briefly walk away from the argument: leave your apartment or house and go for a walk. If this does not work, and you are still upset then write a letter to your mate and make him or her read the next day. If they do not want to read it then do not put pressure on them, read it yourself and then throw it away. At least the argument has deescalated between you and your spouse by then. It is necessary not to tease your wife or husband about the argument that just happened, there is no point of escalating the point again.

Take a deep breath if still you cannot let it go. Ask yourself what do you want to achieve from this argument. How do you want to send the message to your partner? Keep your temper low and never threaten your partner that you will leave him or her. Do not guilt your partner, there is no need to pin point their mistakes. In a tense situation, the best way to resolve it is by sharing something funny. It is important to remember that we are human after all and we all make mistakes and learn from them.

When you cannot maintain the relationship even after putting in the work, the next step is to see a lawyer and file for a separation and later, divorce. It is always better to try as best as you can to resolve the problems and continue the relationship. Now it is time for both of you to ask what really happened? What do you want from each other?

Showing that one truly loved being with her or him, how much affection he or she has for one and following by affirmation is important in a relationship. Positive reinforcement is really important. A lack of affection in a relationship could lead to divorce. Money issues be disastrous to a relationship. When both people in a couple work, this could help juggle bills and compromise with each other's finances. Discussions about money help build a strong relationship. If you are already married you should not inquire about the past. One has not committed a crime where one has to be investigated about one's past life history. There is no point in doing this as you are wasting your time and this will create more tension into your relationship.

Now I will discuss about how one should behave with loved one's family. It is preferable not to give negative comments about your lover's family. If one does not like the partner's family members just keep it to yourself or share, if needed, only with your own family members. One must understand your partner may have been raised by their family, therefore your partner will have the utmost respect and affection for his or her family. Ask yourself how much respect and affection that you have for your own family members. Should you have the same respect for your lover's family? Regardless how much one loves you, insulting one's parents or sibling with not be acceptable and will be seen as injustice in front of your partner's family. This could lead to losing your mate.

After a conflict, you may feel alone and wonder how you will heal. Take a big breath and talk to a friend about your situation. Tell them both sides of your story. If you have any anger, sadness, or worries, mention them to your friend until you have emptied your heart and your eyes of all your sorrow. Do not blame yourself or even your ex-husband or ex-wife. Be true to yourself and things will work out you do not want to share your secrets then you can write them in a journal or even write a book such as I am doing at this moment and you may read it and reflect on it in the future.

Love

Now that you know all the different types of marriage, have you thought about Love? Does love at first sight exist? When do you know you are in love? Can you truly be in love when you are married? Those are the questions that I will briefly discuss in the following paragraph.

Theory of the Cycles of Love

In this paragraph I will discuss about the Theory of the Cycle of Love. The theory is composed of Fantasy Love, Commitment Love, False Love, True Love, Obsessive Love, and Real Love.

Fantasy Love occurs out of a fantasy. One sees a person for the first time and forms an image of that person. Within a short period of time one fantasizes about the person and believes that there is love. One develops irrational feelings for that person. One starts dreaming of the person. When imagining that person constantly, one would start believing that the person is right for him or her. One can be attracted to someone without knowing that it is based on fantasy. At first, you want to know more about the person, but you do not want to hear negative comments about him or her; the only thing that you would hear or believe are the positives.

In commitment love, a couple who have been together will realize with time that they are meant to be together. Their love has grown and they now want to start a real relationship. Slowly they will build a sort of bond that matches each other's personality, character, and beliefs. One who believes in his or her relationship may feel love regardless of the absence of the person. The partnership is based on commitment, friendship, respect and care. In this particular situation, commitment is stronger then love.

False Love is based on a relationship that is based on lying to your partner. One may do everything to show how he or she love the partner. Some would spoil expensive gifts or shower them with affection. False love occurs when there is boredom between a couple. One may even cheat in a relationship. In most cases, cheating it is a sign that one is not happy with the other individual. The relationship become like a game in which two people manipulate each other. This type of love does not last long. However, one confuse the false love with true love.

True Love is when one understand, cares for, trusts and believes in one's mate. Love plays an important role is this matter, one could say that one has fallen in love. One wants to be true to oneself. One will be affectionate with the partner. One is able to distinguish between what is necessary and what is not to hold a healthy relationship. When sharing true love one become good friends with the partner. One wants to share his or her secrets. True love makes you faithful to your lover.

Obsessive Love is when one thinks constantly of the other person. One fantasizes about that person. One constantly wants to know what the other person is doing or where the person is going. One may show up in front of the person's house. One may frequently call that person, or email or fax simply to tell that person that he or she cares. The obsessive behavior starts with jealousy, uncertainty, or dislike for something or someone. When the couple are no longer together, the obsessive lover may treat his or her lover by the use of emotional blackmail, for example, saying bad things about him or her by creating speculation. If this fail, one could bring the topic to the next level with the use of force, more precisely, by being violent. One with an obsession may not know how he or she is behaving. When the relationship does not work out well, one will ask for forgiveness and try to get the sufferer on his or her side. One may say that he or she will change, will respect the way the victim want. The victim may be manipulated by the obsessive lover. Those who go through obsessive love may have a mental illness. When one performs obsessive behavior one should seek for help by a psychologist or a psychiatrist.

We all hear, talk and read about love and we deal with love every day. How often do we ask ourselves if there is real love within ourselves or our partner? Do we really love ourselves more than our partner or our partner more than ourselves? In this paragraph real love will be discussed. Real Love is a strong feeling. Love is just a word in this paragraph, but one can portray differently as everybody love someone or something more than the others. For many loving human beings is more important than loving other animals and objects. One cannot touch love but touch his or her partner; one cannot break love but can break the heart, one cannot see love but can see through body language, one can cheat love when lying to your companion, one can smell love by being near one's partner, one can cherish love by holding them, one can taste love by kissing someone you love, one can abandon love by losing your lover.

Self-Analysis Therapy

Have you tried many types of therapies such as Psychotherapy, Cognitive Behaviors Therapy, Group Therapy, Supportive or Rehabilitative Therapies, Psychosocial Therapy, Occupational Therapy, Family Therapy? Have you wondered if this will help you? You may not know how to begin. When discussing with your doctor they will suggest that you be enrolled in certain types of therapy and trying them to see if they suit your diagnosis. The effectiveness of a therapy actually depends on the person. Having any therapy is beneficial. The main goal is to make you better assist you with some medical support and guidance.

The more guidance you have, the better you can heal. Trust your health specialist. You have to realized that the diagnostic process it can take some time, especially when in mental illness, which is a sensitive issues and may not be a priority in the health system.

A patient was asking me what should he do when having a panic attack? It is not easy to consciously realize that one is having a panic attack. He was concerned about his behavior and his attitude in front of others. Both of us were enroll in Cognitive Behavior Therapy (CBT) and he was sitting just beside me. He was sweating when he asked me how to cope when having such distress. He wanted to know if there is any way to better work on the self. I mentioned that one can keep a record of action conducted daily. For example, one can write on a piece of paper about one's behavior and concerns in a situation. Keep note of all the information written for future reference. Use the information written when comparing with various scenarios.

There are many types of therapies; why would Self-Analysis Therapy work? Self-Analysis Therapy is a new form of therapy that can be used by patients all over the world. You can perform

Self-Analysis Therapy for example, if you are having a panic attack. If you are not aware of your action or reaction when surrounded by others, ask the people around you about how you behaved or reacted. Writing down the information shared by your peers or loved one can be valuable in a moment of distress.

Behaving improperly can be disturbing to others. People tend to remember negative memories more than positive ones. Therefore, you want to give a good impression to others and control your temper. The more you have control over yourself, the more people will appreciate being with you. Your family and close friends may forgive and forget but others may not. Again, if you are concerned about your behaviour, ask a person near you about your behavior and reaction. It is the only way to know yourself and better analyze the situation. For example, when arguing with your mother, during a panic attack, ask her after the fact what you mentioned to her and how you focused on this matter. With self-analysis, you will have a better understanding of yourself.

For some, it can be very complex to analyze themselves, whereas for others, it is a routine like brushing their teeth, or writing in a journal. Writing is not the only way to express and review complex situations. Therapists can also monitor the behaviour by tape recording, video conferencing, and listening to your sorrow, and pain. Therapists are there to help you. If they cannot provide you with such help how can you heal? Self-Analysis Therapy can play a role when you have tried everything, when you have discussed with various health professionals and are still not convinced with the system or you feel that they were not able to help you. You feel discouraged and do not know what to do. You want to be cured and you are motivated to keep your health in top shape.

Some ways for analysing the self by using Self Analysis Therapy are as follows:

1. Write down your current thoughts, actions, and reactions.
2. Record some angry conversations involving yourself.

3. Video record your behaviors and conversations.
4. Ask a person who witnessed the situation of your behaviours.
5. Go for a walk and try to remember what happened. Be critical in thinking about your problems.
6. Take a break from thinking about your problems, and distract yourself by doing something else.
7. If nothing seems to work pace while thinking until you feel tired or bored. You will start looking a new solution.
8. You need to ask the following question: What, When, Where, Who, Why and How? This is to gain more information about yourself.

What are the events that require analysis? Self-Analysis Therapy can be done anywhere at any time. However, there is no need for Self-Analysis if there is no trigger. When someone or something has hurt your feelings you may perform self-analysis. At first you need to find out if the event is even related to you and if it requires your attention. If it is not your fault, then you will know that you do not need to waste time thinking about it. If it bothers you by triggering deranged thoughts, you should keep track of them by writing them down.

Understanding the external and the internal environment helps you become aware of how you are feeling and how others see you. Knowing your external environment it will help you perceive the outside world. For example, someone with Schizophrenia believes mostly that people want to hurt them and that others are against them. Having these thoughts can turn one deranged and may make one slowly push away from reality. One will develop negative perceptions and will rely on them. He or she will become confident in an idea that could be wrong. Having false beliefs can be disturbing and long-lasting.

These cemented beliefs will worsen one's conditions and perpetuate further thoughts. With irrational thoughts, one misinterprets and thoughts. One may have many symptoms such as headaches or improper sleep. The person may feel agitated and often tired. This internal environment augments one's feelings. Having beliefs from the external will pit against one's internal feelings. It can take a lot of time to start thinking logically. When people do not trust you for some reason it takes time in order to gain faith and build a relationship from scratch. It is the same with trusting yourself. Being able to trust your internal events will make you better person.

There are internal and external types of emotions you may have to deal with internal emotions arise from your own thoughts, not directly triggered by others or thee environment. On the other hand, external emotions are those brought on by a stimulus. Some internal emotions are anger, worries, frustration, sad, regret, shame, and jealousy. Having these types of emotions will make you feel negative. When being angry one might become aggressive. Having thoughts of worries can make one agitated. Feeling frustration can be a sign of not believing in oneself. One may feel sad and this could lead for future symptom such as being depress. Not having something or not being with someone may create regret on a certain situation. Therefore feeling shame of ourselves can be embracing. Not knowing how to cope with something then one feels unconsciously jealousy. Having such feeling are bad for our health and the mind. It is necessary to cope with internal emotion positively. But it also depend on external emotion.

Example of the external are emotions trust, hope, love, happiness and appreciation. These are positive external emotions. When we feel that we are trusted we feel like continuing to build a better relationship. However, when you are mistrusted, you may feel awful. When feeling hope you feel secured and confident with others. On the other hand, it feels like nobody is on our side when we lose hope. Being in love can change our lifestyles. Happiness occurs when there is a sign of better emotional care. When being happy you may feel appreciated by your peers, friends, family members and the surrounding. Regardless of the emotions you may feel, it is important to balance them and cope with them, be they negative or positive emotions. It is natural to have external and internal emotions. By understanding the emotions, one can have some immediate and distant support.

Immediate support is provided by people who know you well. There are many different type of support both immediate and distant. You may get support emotional, mentally, physically, spiritually, and morally. With emotional support there are specialists such as a psychiatrists, psychologists or other professionals who are willing to help you feel better, give you some peace of mind, and make you aware of your symptoms. They are willing to listen to you until you are ready to face the outside world. When you are hurt emotionally, your vision about life and people become very limited. Professionals are there to guide you better adjust with society. When feeling better you will be able to cope by getting other types of support. If you are not ready, then you may need support mentally.

There is a percentage of the population that need mental support. Those who need support mentally have mental illnesses such as depression, psychosis, schizophrenia etc. Being able to identify immediate and distant support can balance one's mind. Practitioners are there to help patients or people for a certain time period. When telling others of your illness, some may have different reactions. Do not lose hope as your mission on earth is to survive as long as possible. When you are not accepted externally, it may hurt your feelings internally. It is a matter of time until you can stand up on you own. What matters is that you can cope with the support you have. Understanding why you need support by doing Self Analysis can put you in a better position.

What happens when you are hurt physically and there is nothing to boost your mood? Those who perform self-analysis are the ones who can cope and have high self-esteem. Accepting that one is physically handicapped is the first step. It is a tragedy to become handicapped but life continues on and you are fighting with all your strength to better function and get respect from others.

For many people belief in the spiritual world can make them feel better. Having a strong faith in God gives people the strength and mentality to feel invincible. The prospect of believing in someone superior to us is a form of self-analysis. People feel satisfied when having faith and following a guideline. Many may live in poor conditions but emotionally, mentally, physically and morally, they are stable due to a strong belief in the spiritual world. Believing in the divine can bring peace and share goodness among people. This can be encouraging and motivating when maintaining a daily life. With self-analysis, as long you are happy with your beliefs, you will have a positive attitude towards life.

For many people believing in moral agency is important. Honesty is mandatory in life. Doing good things to please others is right. What matters is to be decent within a society, cast system, social class, group, community. Be fair with people and people will be fair with you. Believing in morality can distinguish between an honorable person with a dishonest one. You do not need to do many things to be respected in society. Following an ethical conduct can bring about untouchable rewards such as happiness and peace of mind. Using the proper words with others can be a symbol of kindness. If you do good to yourself, at the end of day you will feel joy.

When performing self-analysis therapy, it is important to find out your strengths and weaknesses. This will give you a better preview of yourself. You will be able to judge your different angles. Your weaknesses and your strengths. Both weaknesses and strengths are actually in your favor. Do not assume that your weaknesses are negative, as in this context they will give you a better perception about your skills and what you need to improve on. When working on a weakness, it could give you a positive side in making a decision. The more you learn from your negative side the better you can do more self-analysis. If you take a sheet and divide your paper into two sides, one for the weaknesses and the other for strengths, you will be able to balance both sides. Write down both weaknesses and strengths and try to feel both positive and negative emotions. Find out if both emotions come from internal or external factors. One tends to feel more negative emotion than positive.

When things do not work out, one tends to feel like of doing nothing. When one's mood is better, one will tend to participate in various activities. Getting involve in the community can change many aspects of your life. Taking the initiative to be involved is a positive sign health-wise. The more one wants to perform a task the more one feels autonomous. The key point here is taking the initiative to do a certain job either at home, outside the home, or even at work. When you know yourself better, you will have a more accurate perception of others.

Creating a check sheet or tool box can better help you find out where you stand. Visualising the list, box, and sheet will help you better prepare yourself and motivate your moods. If you are not sure about yourself, then experiment with a new activity. This can be fun and interesting. Start a project such as writing a journal, manuscript or even book to distract your thoughts and keep busy by doing something meaningful for yourself. When you finish your project and you see the results start a new project with self-analysis therapy. You can see if you are able to complete what you have started or if you have lost interest and you would like to start something else. Take life as an experiment; the more you experiment the better the results in life. At the end, you will learn more about your capacities, motivation, achievement, and dreams.

Doing Self-Analysis Therapy can be time-consuming. The following information can be useful for you to manage time. When one has time, one may choose to spend it socializing. Being with friends, talking on phone or even being on the internet by chatting and discovering new people can be interesting. Instead of doing nothing, if one uses the time correctly one will feel happier at the end of day. One way to feel better is to give yourself time doing something significant. It could be sleeping for one extra hour or even waking up one hour earlier. Use this hour to do physical exercise, or to focus on your creative side. Spending one hour daily on an activity which will add up to 365 hours and 1/4 in a year. Using one extra hour will not even be noticeable. Creating tools can be beneficial for yourself and bring you to the path towards freedom.

Even though you dream of freedom, there are various obstacles and responsibilities in life such as environmental factors, your interest in daily life, pursuing a career, personal beliefs, your responsibilities at home, work and environment, as well as how you will cope in your daily routine. Having a responsibility such as being a son, husband, or a father can be momentous. Facing the outside world is challenging when the environment is against you. Having critical personal beliefs can help you look at both negative and positive sides of yourself. Focusing at work can be a symbol of reward. Therefore, work gives you motivation when you like a certain type of job. When you feel comfortable doing activities, you perform even better in them. You feel strength to follow your heart until you can achieve your goals.

Know Your Rights

Knowing your rights is extremely important, especially if you are mentally ill and there are people not treating you justly. There are three different process to deal with your rights. After many years of working and you have to stop to medical reasons, you may wonder what your company can do for you. In most of places, companies have an arrangement with insurance companies. When you get sick, the insurance company should cover your rights and advantages. On the other hand, if you do not work and you receive government assistance due to health issues, mostly you may be covered by the health department. If you do not work and you do not qualify for the governmental assistance you may face difficulty.

You must know that if you pay for insurance, you have the right to receive its benefits when ill. Your practitioner will decide if you should stop working for treatments. From that point on, you will be compensated until you are well. This could be for a short period of time or for a long period of time. Your health is important and until you do not feel well you cannot work and will not be capable to perform accordingly at work. It is necessary to be fully healthy before you undertake any responsibility. When you feel well, you will perform well at work. The better you are at work, the more likely you will get bonuses, rewards, money and self-satisfaction.

If you cannot work for good reason, you have the right to ask for government assistance. When you are sick, or you may not able to work or be productive. Therefore, you have no choice but to be supported by the government. After all we all pay our taxes and we all have the right to ask for support while suffering from an illness.

When one does not qualify for government support and does not have private insurance life becomes complex and difficult. Not having financial support can cause a lot of stress and put one in misery. Some become homeless, others start taking loans, from family, relatives, friends and some seek homeless shelters.

Returning to work after being absent for a mental illness can be difficult due to the taboo surrounding mental illness. It can be emotional to explain to others. It can be emotional to explain the situation. In many cases, people do not understand mental illness and they may have a negative perception about your situation. Some are afraid, for example, when one displays unconventional behaviors. A supervisor may not keep you on payroll after you leave.

If the company does not keep you after returning to works then you need to find another job. However, the market targets people with good health and wants someone who can be productive. You may have multiple interviews and may face discrimination due to the mental illness. I have applied to various companies and I have had to say if I had any medical condition and if I was taking any medication. It was my choice to be honest or to lie. Eventually, the employer would find out anyways. From the interviews, I felt I was discriminated by many companies as I am schizophrenic and I do take medication. After, many months, I would be rejected even though I met the company's requirements.

In Quebec, people with a mental illness could receive help from various organizations when looking for jobs. Some companies have begun to their doors to many unfortunate people with various illness. If you cannot find any jobs due to your illness you should contact your local employment centre to set an appointment with a counsellor.

It is necessary to take accommodate people with mental challenges by applying equal rights across the board. Canada appreciates and acknowledges those with illness by ensuring people with disabilities can have these equal human rights and privileges. Some communities have a better perception about illness and others just do not understand.

The health system and the government are attempting to educate the population by showing different ads and discussing on the media. Some people are gaining knowledge about the multiple types of mental illness. The media has an enormous power to educate the public about mental disorders. You should not feel guilty for being ill even though the media portrays you otherwise. You have the right to stand up for yourself. You have right to express your feelings and thoughts.

If people treated you unfairly then you should express yourself by telling them that it is not fair and that their actions contradicts with your thoughts, feelings, ideas, and rights. You have all the rights to make mistakes and being accepted by others. One should know that not everybody will see you the same way and not everybody will share the same opinion. Also some people may respect you for who you are whereas others may not. You have the control about how to express yourself, how to deal with your society, and how to love someone. Just because you have schizophrenia does not mean that you have no integrity, morals, values, respect.

Time Management

Managing time can be very difficult. It is really important to function by prioritizing one's tasks with Schizophrenia like me it can be especially difficult to follow a routine. At the onset of symptoms we do not realize how quickly or slowly time passes. It is necessary to realize this by managing time to perform various tasks, socialize, be alert, find time to study, exercise, and generally be productive. Planning can be a way to take the initiative in doing something. In the following paragraph, I will discuss about for better managing time.

When ill, one may not realize how much time is spent sleeping. I remember sometime I would sleep for 12 hours straight. Other times I would sleep for three hours. It was extremely difficult to stay after while not sleeping enough. Often people have side effects from certain medications. One may feel more tired. As a result, one sleeps for many hours. On various occasions I would wake up and realize that half of the day was already gone. But when I tried to sleep I could not keep my eyes closed. To manage this, I decided to create lists. I would write down what I plan on doing on specific days.

Assigning value to time was something I am particularly proud of. I would be able to multitask at work. I felt extremely productive and my boss at work was very proud of me. It did not matter if it was day or night, what mattered to me that I was able to monitor my time. This allows me to be punctual. People would appreciate seeing me on time. I usually do not like to do certain tasks at the last minute. I would panic at times if I am not capable of being on time. I fear what others will think about me and how they will judge me. I would put value on various tasks by rating then as high, medium or low priority. It was a way for me to keep track of my important to do lists.

Often it bothers me when I am interrupted during a task. I like to put 100% of my motivation into a single task. It satisfies me to accomplish what I had in my mind. Being able to fulfill someone by simply being present at a certain place can be rewarding. Also when one is on time makes me feel happy. I can easily get distracted by someone who is not punctual or does not care or value my time. If I cannot complete a task then I will extend my time or ask others if it is alright to perform the task later. I often like to plan my time ahead and how long it will take when finishing a simple task. Setting a goal for me works out well and I advise others to follow suit or try experiment with setting goals. This can benefit you by helping you save time and by leaving you with more time to do other things. Such as spending it with family, friends, or by yourself.

How does one manage distractions when performing a task? First of all we should decide on what task we need to work on or complete. When doing a simple task we may be distracted by the background noise, people around us, having different thoughts in our minds, which all lead to not focusing on a situation. It is necessary to set aside time for unexpected distractions. Deciding on what task one should work on can reduce anxiety and worries.

Asking question such as how should I spend my time can validate our minds. Some spend time thinking, others playing games, some daydreaming. Many can become obsessed with working. One can also procrastinate. Nowadays, people often are on the internet. One may ask to have more times. One needs to be motivated in doing a task, and others want to find responsibility. It is often recommended to write down in a journal or be organized when working on a task. The more expectations we have for ourselves, the better the output. The more input we have from our surrounding the better we can socialize, focus on our creative side and be successful. We often think about taking care of ourselves. We need to look for better hygiene. Many have assignments or papers due. Other need to have confrontation with others, which can lead to fear, anxiety and conflict. Taking initiative by exercising or spending time for ourselves can benefit our health, mood, and give us peace of mind.

Speculation

Speculation has various synonyms such as conjecture, rumour, gossip, assumption, theory, guesswork, thought, and supposition. Each could be used in differently and mean different things to different people. That is the gift of any word. Let's play a game called "mouth to ear". The rule is simple you have to find first as many synonyms possible with a word: In this contest I will use all the synonyms of speculation. After that I will focus on contrasting certain words by keeping and eliminating some words. Then I will try to find out which words are repeated often by describing the words as examples of speculation. If you choose to conduct this exercise you may use other words as well.

The word conjecture is also defined as guess, surmise, inference, speculation, assumption, supposition, imagine and speculate. When using the word conjecture, it has a close meaning to other words such as speculation, assumption, and supposition. Next, I will use the word rumour. The words synonymous to rumour are as follows:

report, story, gossip, tale, buzz, chitchat, anecdote and word. In this context there is one word describing speculation matching with rumour which is gossip. From the word gossip; it has synonyms such as rumour, hearsay, tittle-tattle, scandal, chitchat, talk, chat, conversation. This word matches the word speculation with rumour. Then the word assumption is seen as supposition, statement, postulation, hypothesis, guess, best guess, theory and conjecture. Here supposition, theory and conjecture are seen and has resemblance with the word speculation. Whereas, the word theory is defined by words such as; hypothesis, premise, presumption, conjecture, supposition, speculation, assumption and guess. In this context there are four words defining speculation such as speculation, conjecture and assumption. Following the word "guesswork", it is presented by the following words; conjecture, deduction, presumption, speculation, estimation and deductive reasoning. Describing the word guesswork are followed by conjecture and speculation. Now the word thought, is described by synonyms consideration, contemplation, thinking, deliberation, attention, refection, idea, and notion. At least one word had a similarity with thought to thinking. And the last word supposition is synonymous with belief, guess, idea, theory, possibility, hypothesis, assumption and deduction. In this situation there are three words relating to speculation.

Words matches with speculation:

Speculation: conjecture, rumour, gossip, assumption, theory, guesswork, thought, and supposition.

-Conjecture: speculation, assumption, and supposition,

-Rumour: gossip

-Gossip: rumour

-Assumption: Supposition, theory and conjecture.

-Theory: conjecture, supposition, speculation, and assumption

-Guesswork: <u>conjecture,</u> and <u>speculation</u>

-Thought: <u>thinking</u>

-Supposition: <u>guess,</u> <u>theory</u> and <u>assumption</u>

Now that the word speculation is defined more clearly, one must write all the words and find out which word has the most synonyms. In this matter, the word theory is describe with conjecture, assumption, speculation and supposition has the most words with four synonyms. The word assumption and conjecture have three words to each. Guesswork has two synonyms. The words rumour, gossip and thought are described by with one word. When saying something to someone, one will hear up to a certain number of words and will add or reduce other words depending on the sentence. One will not try to dictate word-for-word.

Let's make it more special by representing an individual with a word each. With "speculation", there are 9 persons involved. The person who is the prime master in this place is speculation. His job is to create a speculation or one has created a speculation about him or her. Basically, in a scenario where 9 persons will be sitting together speculation will tell each of the person a word; in this context the synonyms are used for describing each person. The person who represents speculation will speak a sentence more precisely by whispering the sentence to the next person. This person continues to do this by making sure that each mention the same sentence to each other. It's a chain of people whispering a sentence to each other. The person who represent speculation will be the first to tell a sentence and last one when telling everybody sentence again. At the end of the circle the sentence will be changed when it returns to the person who represents speculation.

If the first sentence matches the last sentence then you have a winner. On the other hand, if the sentence has changed then a real speculation has occurred. You just created a speculation. The main goal here is to make you understand how a speculation about someone or something can be created.

Distinction between male and female brain

The brain is a complex element. There are many ways to explain the brain, to make it very simple, I will divide the brain into two parts, the cerebral cortex, and the rest of the brain (which I will refer to as lower brain centers). When explaining the brain I will then explain the biological differences between male and female brains.

The lower brain centers are lower in two ways. First, they are physically located below the cerebral cortex. Second, they help structure and develop the brain. The medulla and the Pons are two important structures that make up the brain stem. The brain stem is the lowest part of the brain. Placed right behind the Pons, it is the cerebellum, and looks like a small brain. The major role of the cerebellum is to smoothen and coordinate rapid body movements. Often times, voluntary movements originate from higher brain centers and are coordinated by the cerebellum. If the outer region of the cerebellum is damaged, one will suffer jerky tremors, or involuntary movements.

The limbic system is important in controlling the human emotions. Consists of the amygdala, septum, and hippocampus. The amygdala produces reactions of rage or aggression when stimulated. The septum seems to have the opposite effect, reducing the intensity of emotion and is more involved with forming memories. The hypothalamus is located near the limbic system (Wade C. & Carol T. 1996). These major structures are part of the brain stem and are connected to the complex and delicate development of the cerebral cortex, which makes it us unique as a species. It is the center for the processing and storage of information about the world. Cerebral cortex is the starting place from which one performs voluntary action.

The cerebrum is more highly developed in human beings than in any other organism (Wade C. & Carol T. 1996). The inside of the cerebrum, below the cortex, is composed mostly of myelinated axons and appears white. The cerebral cortex is divided into the left and right cerebral hemispheres. In each side of the hemisphere there are four major divisions of the cerebral cortex. These divisions are referred to as lobes of the brain: frontal lobes, temporal lobes, occipital lobes and parietal lobes.

In a normal brain, the two left and right hemispheres communicate with each other across a large bundle of nerve fibers called the corpus callosum. Whatever happens in one side of the brain is instantly flashed to the other, so behavior is smooth and well coordinated. Movements on the right side of the body are governed by the motor cortex of the left hemisphere; movements on the left side, by the motor cortex of the right hemisphere. At the back of each occipital lobe is an area of the cortex important for vision, known as the visual area. The auditory area is situated on the surface of the temporal lobe at the side of each hemisphere, it is particularly concerned with the patterning of sound in time, as in human speech. In the left hemisphere is the 'language' area. In the right hemisphere is the 'special ability', which permits us to visualize objects in 3D. Dreams are also thought to occur in the right hemisphere.

Some researchers have long suspected, that men's and women's brains are different from each other (Byer C. & Shainberg L. 1994). Some examples of the distinctions are as follows: girls have better greater verbal ability than boys, boys excel in visual-spatial tasks and mathematical abilities and they are more aggressive. In other areas in which they find suggestive, but ambiguous evidence of sex differences are the following: 'girls have greater tactile sensitivity, and they are more likely or willing to report fear, timidity, or anxious behaviour' (Unger R 1979). On the other hand males are more competitive as well as dominant, compared to females who tend to be more complaint.

In women, functions such as language ability seems to be more evenly divided between the right and left hemisphere of the brains, while in men, they are more concentrated on the left side (Byer C. & Shainberg L. 1994). For a long time, people believed that females had better verbal and language abilities than males. 'Research has shown that this ability has grown smaller since 1973. Hyde, a researcher speculates that this may be because male and female babies are socialized less differently now than in the past'. Males are known to be more aggressive than females. It is seen in all cultures. Most experts agree that this is one undoubtable differences between males and females. According to researchers, "evidence indicated that both animal and human have aggression and it is rooted in the male hormone testosterone' (Byer C. & Shainberg L. 1994). Nurturing is another differentiation between males and females. Females seem to be more nurturing than males. Young females who are beginning to walk learn faster than males by being better able in picking up nonverbal signals from others. When the time comes for interpreting beauty expressions, females dominate males. In school, on many different types of tests, such as SAT, males have scored higher than females on mathematic ability. This has led people to believe that males are better in mathematics than females. Many of research results that males do better in visualizing 3D objects and in reading and comparing maps. Females are able to perceive details quickly and precisely. They are able to change attention from one item to another. Females perform much better than males on tests of perceptual speed.

Humans have gained lots of sophistication with the use of epistemology. According to neurologists 'the main difference [between males and females] is the size between brains. Female brains are, on average 10% smaller than male brains, but because, on average the bodies of women are more than 10% lighter then men's '(Biology & Medicine). This does not mean that men are smarter than females. When the time comes to focus on general intelligence, IQ tests are used. During their early education, females score higher than males, but in high schools, males were dominant. However, it is extremely hard to be precise on IQ tests. Many students have different cultures and come from different ethics, 'people of one gender will tend to do better on some questions while the other gender will do better on others. Over several years, IQ tests have failed to demonstrate on overall the average of both sexes' (Byer C. & Shainberg L. 1994). Furthermore, 'a technology that provides rapid-fire brain images by measuring changes in brain blood oxygenation levels, has created enormous advances in scientists' ability to look at the living human brain (Brach, M. 1998) such as sex-based anatomical in visual cortex, differences in visual processing, and hemoglobin levels. This new technology is not precise enough and therefore requires further studies to determine the exact cause of the varying levels of activity.

It is very difficult to differentiate both male and female brains, but if there is something to differentiate, then it would be that males have a more massive brain than females. They are also more aggressive and better adapt to logical concepts. Females have better language skills and respond more quickly to different types of situations. Both sexes are intelligent but they use their intelligence differently.

Does the distinction between the male and female brains have anything to do with mental disorders? Actual intelligence of someone is difficult to measure. While IQ tests are predominantly used as an analog to intelligent, affected by cultural, geographical and educational background. One can be extremely intelligent but may not necessarily do well on IQ test. While someone with a high education may perform well on an IQ test. People than use these results to generalize across groups of people. For example, males were thought to spend more time with males than females in math, thus perpetuating the stereotype. One with mental illness maybe seen as having a low IQ or even thoughts to be mentally retarded. We all know schizophrenics were once functioning human beings with "normal" mental capacities before they become ill. I believe that normal people may use both right and left hemisphere for "intelligence" whereas, the less advantaged ones, those with mental illness, may use either just the left or just the right. This could perhaps explain the drop in intelligence.

This is not proven scientifically, but the hypotheses can start from here. It is very hard to understand what an ill person what may go through. A person with a mental illness undergoes difficulties with mental tasks. When I had depression, my thoughts were different then they are now. With psychosis, my intelligence dropped radically. I felt like I was a little boy and I could not cope with reality. I needed support from people and guidance to communicate, to understand, to behave and to function better. Having schizophrenia made me feel like I had to fight every day to keep up with general information and knowledge to better live my life. The hardest time in my life was the past 10 years: I had to struggle with various types of uncanny behaviours that made my life unsuccessful. I think back at the time when I was healthy and could wondered what I become and how my life would changes if I had not gone through depression, psychosis and schizophrenia. Back then, I thought I had all the wisdom, intelligence, and charisma to do whatever I wanted to do. Now I look back at myself and I wonder if I was using my normal side of intelligence or abnormal side intelligence. Do you believe that both human beings may have both normal and abnormal intelligence and capacities?

When a person is deranged and cannot function with their normal side of intelligence, he or she uses the abnormal side of intelligence? Whereas, a normal person will use intelligence as it is and they will function normally. Could it be possible that we human species are fortunate enough to function with both abnormal and normal sides? We use either intelligence differently. In my case, I would not be able to function if I could not use the normal side of intelligence while I was healthy. Hence, when I become ill I had no choice to use my abnormal side of intelligence. Even though I had difficulty living my life, I feel that I was lucky to learn from my daily challenges. This made me who I am today and made my life better and better every day. I am capable to work and functions almost before I was ill. However, I did become dependent on my medications to keep me balanced from disturbing worries, thoughts and behaviours. Using my abnormal side of intelligence made me able to write this book. My intelligence is connected with my abnormal part of life. Could it be possible that my abnormal side is stronger than the normal part of my brain? This would allow to function like others. But if people can be successful regardless of their intelligence and regardless of their sanity, then who is to say that it matters? There is nothing wrong with using the normal and the abnormal side of their brain to function. If the abnormal part of your life can save you from insanity then you are fortunate to use it and live life well until the normal side of intelligence can take over.

Gambling

One might be astonished to know that the 'Net Revenues of Gambling in Canada, in 1995 was a total of $4,557.8 million dollars. Furthermore, the estimated Provincial and Territorial revenue in the 1995-96 fiscal year totaled $165.200 million dollars. The gambling percentage total revenue was about 2.7% (A Report by National Council of Welfare). The government is making a lot of money and one might ask, where does that money go? Is it correct for the government to run gambling? Gambling is a disease, and it is full of risks. Day and night, hour after hours, people leap into the uncertain. Most of the time, people lose money in the Casino and it ends up with the government. Is gambling really good for our society? Does it have any effect on violence or crime? Does it disturb the human brain? There are some benefits and disadvantage to gambling, however, it does not seem to stop people.

According to the Gemini Research, which 'specialized in studies of gambling and problem gambling' (Dr. Volberg), the government is under contract with the state and provincial agencies. Most of the agencies sponsoring these surveys are human service agencies although several studies have been funded through state or provincial lotteries. It show cases many adults, adolescents and Native American are involved in gambling.

First of all, 'gambling is bad for our society, it gives a bad example to children' (David. S). They observe their parents gambling and sooner or later they will do the same. Scientists have proved that we usually do what we see. If an adult doesn't demonstrate a good example then who will? Parents should keep their money and explain to their children that they should spend it for a good reason or for sensible things. One main thing that people forget is that there is only one chance in a million to win. 'We win ten dollars but we lose hundreds', that's the way it is at the casino.

Without doubt, after Casino is built 'the rate in violence has increased a great deal'. (David. S). The police have more work to do than before. Crime took the front page in newspapers. A few years ago, some criminals followed people who won money from the Casino and held them up as they were getting out of their car. A man kills his brother-in-law because he wants to take some winnings. Parents lose their fortune and come home very depressed, angry and overall unpleasant, and become violent with their children. Through this, one can conclude that just for some cash people will have the courage to threaten others, to kill an innocent person, or hurt children.

After losing money, one usually convinces himself, as an excuse, that he or she is earning money to make it. Others 'might became very addicted and it could have an effect to damage their brain if they don't win' (David. S.). They might experience sorrow, nervousness, stress and aggression. Some would commit suicide, provoke a divorce and break up the family. It's not a good idea to gamble, but it's rare to find someone who is not tempted by the prospect of money'.

I think that people like to take a risk in life but they should know when to stop and to use their logic. This way nobody will get hurt and they could spend their money in peace. Gambling is another way for the government to make more money. It is better to open casinos than raise taxes. There are always positive and negative things in everything, but most importantly, people should know how to think maturely.

Homelessness

Walking on the street of downtown Montreal can be very frustrating. Seeing so many homeless people shows just how the government is taking care of the country. Cutting major social services such as welfare or raising money on goods and services are the prime reasons for having a large number of destitutes. High unemployment rates, diminishing mental health services are also some reasons why there are so many without homes. Society has changed, everywhere one might go, people can be seen asking for money and sleeping on the floor. Should one accuse the government for having a large number of homeless people? In my view, it is impossible to resolve homelessness, no matter how the government attempts to help, there will always be people who will consider their home the street. One cannot merely blame the government, there are other factors to consider, such as employment prospects, education, drug use and so on. Anything can happen to a person. Is it possible to help homeless? Yes it is possible and people can change a life by being generous. I believe that we all should help those who need it. If one has a place for someone, then they should share that place with the homeless. If people cooperate together, we might reduce the homeless rate.

I may offer food but may not agree that a stranger come to lives in my apartment. Many of those who live on the street, have mental health issues. Some have Schizophrenia. If one does not have a guidance in this disorder, it is easy to be on the street as one is deranged with so many issues. Cooking, doing groceries, taking showers, preparing breakfast, lunch, or supper are things that are doable when one is healthy. When one is in top shape, it is possible to have a job, an apartment, a car or be able to travel by bus or metro (subway) or even get married or have a girlfriend or boyfriend. Also, one keeps one's body clean, for example, by cutting the nails, or doing a hair style or putting on makeup. One can afford to live a luxurious life, by having a cell phone, a landline, internet, cable, by decorating an apartment with furniture and accessories, by buying expensive cloths, by being able to go to a luxurious restaurant with someone one trusts or loves. How often does that happen to someone homeless on the street?

Most of the time, when we walk on the street or we cross a specific street at the moment we see homeless purposely passing in front of us we do not pay attention and walk away. We do not know what message they would like to send us, is he or she asking for help, asking for support, asking for guidance, asking for love? One thing is for sure, they would ask for money, yet how often do we give. It is nice to be generous for one but again how often one can be generous? All the information above could be seen as a nightmare, but a lot of people are living that nightmare. We should feel thankful that it had not happen to us.

Have you wondered how homeless people feel or think or why they have chosen this route? By now one should know that it could be because of an illness, lack of funds, or even lack of responsibility. I am sure that many of us have spoken to a homeless at least once by giving charity to an individual. We ask ourselves why do they do this, what will happen if we are in their shoes. One might say that it won't happened to us, or that we are well prepared to live a decent life. We have family that takes care of us.

Studies show that in Canada that homeless people are propagating, 'an estimated 157,000 people are homeless each year in Canada' (2009). An estimated of 1,350 people die chronically, either in car accidents, by abuse or suicide. More than 20% of the homeless remain in street for at least 3 months. In regards to life expectancy, for a regular man in Canada it is 70 years old and for women 78 years, but for a homeless person in Canada, it is 39 years old.

The article Homeless in Canada, categorizes the homeless: 'basically, there are two distinct types of homeless people: those who are temporarily homeless, the transitional homeless, and those who are chronically homeless, living on the streets repeatedly and for more than one year.' (2009). The majority at risk for poverty, some are transitional and others chronic.

Those homeless who are under chronic risks represent around 20% of the population, which is around 32, 000 people in Canada. Among the 20% of homeless, 75% are men without jobs due to a mental illness or drug addiction. Many spend almost a year in various shelters. It is one last option before going to the streets. Transitional homelessness occurs after losing a job, going to a new city to find a job, not being able to pay rent for an apartment, leaving a difficult relationship etc. Basically, the transitional homeless is estimated to have less than 3 months period of seeking shelters. Research shows that 'there are an estimated 3.2 million Canadians living in poverty who may benefit from social assistance, housing improvements, and low-cost housing' (2009). It is evidence on how Canadians help each other to maintain low poverty rates compared to other countries. The

Canadian system seems to work better than other system. Regardless, of how much we pay taxes each year, one cannot complain when there are 3.2 million Canadians getting support and some sort of help from the Canadian society and the government.

The Soul of our Minds

Every individual uses different ways to understand their inner self. These include meditation, journal writing, music or drama therapy, analysis, and alcoholics anonymous. Using one of these methods can help people better understand their problems. Recently, I interviewed two friends who have experienced a process that lasted at least six months. They told me that having different types of experiences helped them get to know their inner selves better. I will use the names Bounty and Nice to represent my two friends.

Bounty and Nice have each gone through a personal exploration but their journey was different. Bounty never expected to change so much. Nice felt that something was missing in his life and though a trip to a foreign country he found his happiness. I was taken aback to hear Bounty's hardships, and all types of situation he had in the past. It was really surprising to hear these events from someone who never expressed his true feelings. Bounty was one of my closest friends and I have known him since my childhood. He is a nice guy who is also hilarious. The moment, the environment, and how people were or are with him would define his behavior. Presently, he is satisfied being himself; more precisely, before doing something he analyzes things that would clarify his mind. Unfortunately, he is unsatisfied seeing some of his friends being so egoistical and hypocritical with him.

Since grade seven, Bounty has been doing unforgettable things. He believed that doing vile actions were a symbol of coolness, even though wicked behaviour was unwelcomed in our society. Stealing, taking drugs, fighting, having sex with many girls were a part of his everyday life. One might get shocked hearing that, but these were the type of actions that he was performing in the past. First, he was in a gang with other teenagers, together they were doing illegal things. An example of this is when Bounty and his friends were stealing food and clothes from many stores because they did not have any money on them. This was something I did not understand, as his parents were somewhat wealthy. In this situation he was influenced by other members of his gang. Then, he become involved with drugs. Smoking marijuana, taking cocaine and other types of artificial pleasure makers, made him believe that these 'candies' would help him become hyper and powerful. Unfortunately, the drugs were too strong for him, and he could not control himself. Fighting was also introduced in his early reaction to the drugs. From that point on, he did not know what he was doing anymore. Furthermore, he was taking advantage of girls who were shy. One example of this is when he was sleeping with virgin girls, and each time that he had enough of one, he would move on the sleep with another to satisfy himself. However, the deep dark behaviour of Bounty's was only one part of his character. The other part was that he was a clever guy and his grades in school were impressive.

Every night, before sleeping, Bounty would take a few moments to write in his journal about his behaviour during the day time. One day, he was involved in a fight in school in which he had a knife. That was it! He was suspended from school for one month and he had to face the law. The police arrested him for a few days because he had a lethal weapon on him with one gram of cocaine inside his pocket. Then he was introduced to a lawyer. His parents could not believe it, it was the end of their dreams.

Fortunately, Bounty's mother had hope for him, and she decided to bring a psychologist to help him understand the situation. A social worker was also involved under the direction of the school. Her duty was to make Bounty realize that what he did was wrong. Day after day, the process continued and the lawyer interviewed him. She wanted to know what exactly happened. The psychologist was also a part of this process, as he tried to understand the situation; Bounty's everyday life with his friends, family, girlfriends and school and what kinds of things he did during the day and night. The social worker asked a few questions such as why did the fight start, how was the relationship between his parents and friends. Basically, she wanted to be helpful by understanding the cause of his action. Moreover, Bounty's parents were depressed to see their son behind bars. It was a hard moment for both of them, but the astonishing thing was to see them supporting Bounty by telling him that they cared for him as well as loved him in spite of what occurred to him.

After a few months, Bounty presented himself in the court room, accompanied by his parents and his lawyer. Bounty was found guilty. As he was young, the judge put him on probation for one year with one hundred hours of community services, without missing any class in school. In addition, he had to present himself again in court after a year. Thereupon, the judge would decide to punish him again or to give him another chance, depending on his behaviour.

Time after time, everything seemed to become normal; Bounty was doing his community work, and he was nice to everyone. Every Wednesday after school he had an appointment with the psychologist. Every Friday the social worker would come meet him and his parents. Every month, the lawyer had to write a report about Bounty's daily behaviour, a report to be given to the judge. One day, the psychologist told Bounty to read over his journal and analyze it by pinpointing which action was right and which was wrong. As soon as he started reading his journal, he noticed that what he did in the past was wrong. Basically, the psychologist wanted to make him realize his actions. When it was Friday, the social worker and Bounty, along with his parents were together, discussing their life. She wanted to know anything was wrong between Bounty and his family. Time passed and Bounty was changing; he started to realize that his previous actions were wrong. He felt guilty about what he did in the past. Since then, he stopped stealing, fighting, and taking drugs. It took him at least two years to understand his behaviour. Without receiving help there would not have been any positive changes in Bounty.

Bounty was very clever; he had an average overall of 85% and he was planning to become a doctor. His behaviour has totally changed, also it's been three years since he has been dating his girlfriend. He stopped smoking and drinking and is glad to see that everything that he did in previous years is over. One thing is for sure; he is satisfied to learn from his mistakes. Nice on the other hand, had a different experience compared to Bounty.

One day, I asked Nice about his life and he told me about how he felt, that there was an empty void his early life. He was unsatisfied being himself because there was something missing for not motivating himself. He was looking for an adventure.

At the age of fifteen, Nice went to an Asian country. Since then it was the beginning of his adventure to gain lots of sophistication using the five senses. Being with his relatives made him satisfied. Seeing his extended family fasting and being vegetarian was something unexpected in his early life. Becoming vegetarian was something astonishing that he found at the beginning, but as soon as he got used to it, it became pleasurable. Afterwards, his grandmother explained how religion was important for each individual. It was important to go to the temple and pray until the gods heard. Since then, he believes that religion would bring him fulfillment. However, five months later come the end of his happiness. He lost someone whom he loved and this left him broken-hearted. When his grandmother died, it was a crucial moment for him because he was really attached to her.

When he came back to Montreal, he felt that he needed to do something different, because he was having a hard time forgetting his sadness. His parents and all the relatives were with him to share their emotions. They tried to make him realize that everybody has to leave this one day world no matter what happens. Then one of his uncles told Nice that he will teach him something new and it will help him forget the pain. Nice and his uncle went somewhere very quiet and clean and started doing meditation. Meditating helped him spiritually and later he felt better to be himself in peaceful harmony. He was able to forget the sorrow that he had and recalled old memories he had with his grandmother. From that point on, he was changing constantly. He was more conscious of his behaviour. Each time he felt bad, meditation helped him bring joy.

He believed that he changed in several ways: meditating, fasting, and paying more attention to his religion. All of these were a part of his benefits. He learned from his family and relatives, and it was an awesome adventure that he had in his motherland. Nowadays, he feels much better about himself and he is more in touch with his religion and roots. He has learned that no matter what he does, it is important to do it with the heart.

Bounty and Nice are two completely different persons. Through their self-explorations they both gained knowledge able it in different ways. Bounty learned to distinguish bad and good from being a delinquent. He also learned the real value of a person, all this by wisdom. Nice found what he missed in his life. Fasting, meditating, believing in his religion and changing his way of eating by becoming vegetarian gave him the desire to go further in his life. Bounty was able to change his behavior from being a vile person to a good person, all this by receiving help from a psychologist, social worker, lawyer, and most importantly from his parents who supported him until the end of his changing period. His journal also helped him analyze his past. On the other hand, Nice changed through his family, relatives, and the people who surrounded him. He was able to fill up the gap he was missing in his life. They are satisfied in learning new things and wish to gain more knowledge about life. Even though they have had different experiences, they are both intelligent and friendly. I respect and admire them for being honest with me.

Nutrition

If I had to analyze what I eat every day; I think that I would come up with something like: I eat what I must to stay healthy by following the Canadian Food Guide, but most of the time I have the tendency to cheat. For example, I eat fast food, junk food, and chocolate, knowing that these foods are not good for my health. I guess I'm stubborn; that's why I keep doing it. Usually, I like to eat at any time to feed my stomach. I drink more orange juice than milk.

According to my lifestyle, there are lots of things that I should change to improve my nutrition. In my conception, it is required that all human beings eat from the 4 food groups, which are: grain products, fruits and vegetables, milk products, and meat and alternatives. It is better to eat an appropriate number of servings, and to eat 3 to 4 meals a day. It is also required for an adult to drink 6 to 8 glasses of water per day. It is good to eat at a specific time, something that I often forget to do. First of all, I think that I should stop eating fast food, junk food, and healthy foods at specific times. Moreover, eating does not improve health without exercise. It is good to exercise at least 30 to 60 minutes per day. It could be anything that we like to do, such as weight training, running or jogging, sports training, or cross training.

The following is a list of vegetables that exist around the world, which you might taste whenever you feel like it: artichoke, asparagus, aubergine, beans, beets, bell peppers, bitter gourd, broccoli, Brussels sprouts, butternut squash, cabbage, capsicum, carrot, cauliflower, celeriac, celery, chard, collard greens, corn, cress, cucumbers, drumstick, kale, kohlrabi, leeks, lettuce, mushrooms, okra, onions, parsnips, peas, peppers, potatoes, pumpkin, radishes, rhubarb, rutabaga, shallots, spinach, squash, sweet corn, sweet potatoes, tomatoes, turnips, watercress, and yams

Fruits include: almonds, apples, apricots, avocadoes, bananas (ripe and raw), blackberries, bread fruit, bayberry, black cherries, black raspberries, cantaloupe, cashew fruit, cherries, coconuts, chickoo, cranberries, cucumbers, custard apples, dates, dragonfruit, elephant apple, figs, grapes, grapefruit, guavas, hardy kiwi, Indian almond, Indian figs, Indian prunes, Indian strawberries, jackfruit, Japanese raisins, Jamaica cherries, kiwis, kumquats, lemons, lychee, Lady apples, loquats, mangoes, muskmelon/cantaloupes, nannyberry, native cherries, nance, oranges, olives, palm, orangelo, pears, papayas, pineapples, plums, pomegranates, pumpkins, pineapples, peaches, prunes, peanuts, quince, raspberries, raisins, redcurrants, rosehip, red mulberries, Rose apples, strawberries, sapodilla, watermelons, and wood apples.

List of grain products:

beaten rice—rice flakes, Bengal gram, black gram (whole), black-eyed peas, broken wheat, chickpeas (brown), chickpeas (green), chickpeas (white), corn, green gram, finger millet, millet—sorghum, pearl millet, puffed rice, quinoa, red kidney beans, red lentils, rice, rice (parboiled), semolina—cream of wheat, split chickpeas—split Bengal gram, split green gram, split red gram, split red lentils, wheat chickpea flour, gram flour, finger millet flour, maize flour, mung bean flour, pearl millet flour, refined flour, plain flour, rice flour, whole wheat flour

Meat and Alternatives:

beans, cooked and canned (175 mL, ¾ cup); eggs (2); hummus (175 mL, ¾ cup); lentils (175 mL, ¾ cup); nuts, shelled (60 mL, ¼ cup); peanut butter or nut butters (30 mL, 2 Tbsp); seeds, shelled (60 mL, ¼ cup); tofu (150 g, 175 mL, ¾ cup)

Meat, fish, poultry, and shellfish:

beef 75 g (2 ½ oz) / 125 mL, (½ cup); bison/buffalo 75 g (2 ½ oz) / 125 mL, (½ cup); chicken 75 g (2 ½ oz) / 125 mL (½ cup); deli meat, low-fat, low-salt 75 g (2 ½ oz) / 125 mL (½ cup); duck 75 g (2 ½ oz) / 125 mL (½ cup); fish and shellfish, canned (example: crab, salmon, tuna) 75 g (2 ½ oz) / 125 mL (½ cup); fish, fresh or frozen (example: herring, mackerel, trout, salmon, sardines, squid, tuna) 75 g (2 ½ oz) / 125 mL (½ cup); game birds (example: ptarmigan, partridge, grouse, goose) 75 g (2 ½ oz) / 125 mL (½ cup); game meats (example: deer, moose, caribou, elk) 75 g (2 ½ oz) / 125 mL (½ cup); goat 75 g (2 ½ oz) / 125 mL (½ cup); ham 75 g (2 ½ oz) / 125 mL (½ cup); lamb 75 g (2 ½ oz) / 125 mL (½ cup); organ meat (example: liver, kidney) 75 g (2 ½ oz) / 125 mL (½ cup); pork 75 g (2 ½ oz) / 125 mL (½ cup); rabbit/hare 75 g (2 ½ oz) / 125 mL (½ cup); shellfish, fresh or frozen (example: clams, crab, lobster, mussels, scallops, shrimp, prawns) 75 g (2 ½ oz) / 125 mL (½ cup); turkey 75 g (2 ½ oz) / 125 mL (½ cup); veal 75 g (2 ½ oz) / 125 mL (½ cup)

Milk Products:

Yogurt, milk, cheese, pudding, cottage cheese

Now that you know the 4 food groups, which are grain products, fruits and vegetables, milk products, and meat and alternatives, you may prepare a delicious meal for your mate, sibling, parents, or guardians. The variety of foods that I have listed may not be found everywhere around the globe. Basically, every country has their own food and sharing is done through import and export. Some places are richer than others. If you can experience the vast variety of food, then you may consider yourself lucky that you can try the 4 food groups.

Eating is essential for every human being and for animals. Without food, one will not be able to survive. One will slowly decompose after a few days without food. Not eating enough, one can start to feel weak and will not being able to accomplish daily tasks. It is important for every single human to eat at least 3 to 4 meals daily. We should feel fortunate that we live in a first-world country where food is not a problem. Everywhere we go, there is a restaurant, there is a grocery store, there is a mall. Even if you do not have enough money, there is a system where one can benefit from food bank. There is help if you seek it.

Memory

The memory is 'the capacity to retain and retrieve information; also the mental structure or structures that account for this capacity, and the material that is retrained.' (Wade, C. & Carol, T. 1996). The mind is a complex organ that essentially bestows upon each individual the same level of memory, but each person uses their memory differently. There are a few conditions that some people might have such as a mental handicaps, brain damage, or even Alzheimer's. These people's brains are affected, so most of the time they have difficulty remembering their past or may forget something even right after doing it.

Most people can remember up to seven items at any given time; any more, and they are likely to forget something. Memorizing can be very difficult for some people if they do not find a way to help themselves remember what they have learned. Usually, most individuals have their own way to memorize; some people can memorize by visualizing a picture or a map, others by writing down what they specifically have to remember, others still by reading aloud to themselves. Other people like to create mnemonics, which are 'strategies and tricks for improving memory, such as the use of verse or a formula.' (Wade, C. & Carol, T. 1996). Usually, without studying, it is possible to get through the exam with a passing grade. You may ask how that is possible. For example, visualizing can help you remember things, and can also help some individuals to memorize a sentence or just a couple of words, but it only works when we have many multiple choice questions or images. It all depends on how each different person learns.

If someone wants to lean the seven continents, then that person could use a map or classify these continents, which are: North America, South America, Europe, Asia, Africa, Australia, and Antarctica. It could be very easy for someone who is very visual to remember these continents. It would also be very helpful to put some colour on the map. We remember things better when we use our eyes to observe colourful objects or colours on a paper. Furthermore, mnemonic is another way to remember something that we want to lean. In addition, we could use a word that we create to remember the seven continents, like 'AANAAESAA', where the A represents Asia, the second A is for Africa, NA is North America, the next A is Australia, E is for Europe, SA is for South America, and the last A is for Antarctica. It can also be turned into a sentence; for example, 'Artists Attract Noisy Americans At Every Art Auction'. The previous sentences mostly help people to remember a certain pattern. When I was in French school in grade 7, my geography teacher thought me a sentence to remember the names of the nine planets in order, which is: 'Salut Mon Vieux Tu Ma Jeté Sur Une Nouvelle Planète. The S represents the Sun, M is for Mercury, V for Venus, T for Earth in English (in French, Terre), M for Mars, J for Jupiter, S for Saturn, U for Uranus, and P for Pluto. That sentence worked perfectly in French. With this sentence, I have no trouble remembering the nine planets in order. Moreover, the memory is an integral part of the human brain.

Usually, when we have many definitions to learn for an exam, we study enough to do well, then we realize that we have forgotten most of the definitions. These definitions that we study were in our short-term memory or, more precisely, "in the three models for memory, a limited capacity memory system is involved in the retention of information for brief periods; it is also used to hold information retrieved from long-term memory for temporary use" (Wade, C. & Carol, T. 1996). What is the function of the long-term memory? 'In the three-box model of memory, [it is] the memory system involved in the long-term storage of information; theoretically, it has an unlimited capacity' (Wade, C. & Carol, T. 1996). In the last couple of days, I have been asking myself who my two favourite teachers in elementary school were? So I decided to take a moment to analyze my past. It took me a while to remember them, when suddenly, one of my teacher's names popped up in my brain. His name was André. He was teaching in grade 4, and I really enjoyed being in his class, because he was a great teacher. Then another name came to me: Kathy, who was my grade 6 teacher. I used to like her a lot because she used to buy ice cream for all the students that were in her class. After that, in a short period of time, I began to remember all of my teachers' names. There was Richard, who taught me in grade 1; Michelin, who taught grade 3; Louise, who taught grade 5; and Paul, who taught grade 2. I also remembered the name of the principal of the St. Cecil School. The first principle's name was Lauren.

These names were inside of my long-term memory all along. After finding their names, I had a feeling that it was like a flashback, and it seemed to me that it was only yesterday that I was with them.

I began to remember all kinds of things, such as the fact that André would often wear gray trousers, and that he was tall and very old. I used to like him because he used to do lottery in class, and the winner received a lot of things. Sometimes, all the students would receive something. Moreover, he was very patient and gentle. Kathy's characteristics were very different compared to the other teachers. She expected all our school work to be perfect, especially when we used to do our homework, but she was very nice with everybody, and to reward us, she used to buy lots of things for us, such as candy, chocolate, and ice cream. Being with her was like a dream come true, especially when we are young and we got spoiled by a teacher, which gave young students more motivation to study.

Some students from other classes used to make fun of her because she was a little chubby, but we used to defend her by showing them our chocolates, candies, and ice cream. I noticed that other students were jealous because they did not receive anything from their teacher. I still remember in grade 3, most of the students were afraid of Michelin, even me. She was like the devil to us. She was very strict, and if someone did not do their homework on time, they were in big trouble, because she would call our parents and tell them to come to the school and speak with the principal. Being in her class was like a nightmare, and after passing her class I was so happy. My grade 1 teacher was simple. Richard was neither too strict nor too nice, and he did his job well by teaching us things that we should know. When the class was over, he used to leave at the same time as the students. On the other hand, Louise, my grade 5 teacher, would stay after class if some students needed a little more attention. Louise would explain and explain until we understood. Paul was a weird teacher; maybe that's why I do not remember that much about him. If I analyze my long-term memory, I noticed that my favourite teachers were the first to come to my mind, and it seems to me that we easily remember the teachers that we like or dislike.

According to my long-term memory, my brain is organized by several functions, which are: hierarchical, declarative memories, semantic memories, episodic memories, and procedural memories, among others. When I was trying to remember my two favorite teachers, my semantic memories were used by creating a flashback with details. What exactly are semantic memories? They are 'memories of general knowledge, including facts, rules, concepts, and propositions' (Wade, C. & Carol, T. 1996). After receiving many details from semantic memory, I was able to determine who was who, and to remember their names, characteristics, ways of teaching, and who I liked the most, as well as who I disliked the most. I was startled by my fascinating way of receiving information. It also seems to me that it was organized by my hierarchical memories, simply because my elementary teachers were separated from my high school educators, and they in turn were apart from my college professors. To be more precise, it was like a three-box model of memory, where each box represents something: the first box represents the elementary teachers, the second box represents the high school educators, and the third contains the college professors. In addition, above these three boxes, the word 'teacher' is the key that granted my long-term memory access to these boxes by choosing the right one. This process is completed in less than a fraction of a second.

I am someone who is very visual and I also remember with uncanny precision emotional landmarks. I will again use my teachers as an example of visualizing. By visualizing, I was able to see my teachers in my mind. I do not have a perfect image of them with the exact details, but my brain tends to fill in the gaps in order to perceive complete forms. That way, I can clearly remember images of them by considering all the information that I received from my long-term memory. This is fortunate because we often need to decipher less than perfect images. Furthermore, because of closure, I was able to determine the colour of André's trousers, and some of my teachers' faces, their movements, and, more precisely, how they walked, taught, and behaved, and that gave me a clearer perception of them. One thing is for sure: I have many emotional landmarks. For example, if someone hurts my feelings or insults me, then I will be extremely hurt and it will stay in my mind. First of all, I will never be able to forget the situation; in other words, I am someone who is very unforgiving to a certain extent. Secondly, I have a tendency to become paranoid by thinking all kinds of thoughts in my mind. Not only that, I will become very depressed. Thirdly, by keeping all this inside, I develop a lot of pent-up aggression which I have not dealt with. Usually, to dig up my past events, I use emotional landmarks, visualization, and sensory memory. What exactly is sensory memory? 'The sensory memory is a memory system that momentarily preserves extremely accurate images of sensory information' (Wade, C. & Carol, T. 1996). To be more accurate, if someone hurt me in the past, I will be able to determine the moment that occurred, the precise time of that action, how it materialized, and where it took place, plus what it felt like.

It is very complicated for me to forget past events that have befallen me in my life, and that is the foremost reason for my strong emotions during the last couple of years. There were no solutions to help me forget past hurts that I harboured, and I have to suffer until it stops, which may or may not ever happen. However, I recently started believing that we should forgive and forget. Nowadays, I try to control my feelings by using my mental states, and my surrounding environments. I manipulate my mental states by telling myself that I must defy my fears, which are vile memories that I keep inside my mind. By doing so, I feel less burdened. On the other hand, the surrounding environment helps me to keep track of what is going on around me, and by observing it, I can hold on to more information. In addition, our long-term memory helps us to remember our past events. An example is when there is a bank robbery and we want to give some descriptions to the police by remembering the vile people who robbed the bank. At that moment, we try to remember the way they dressed, talked, and what their face looked like if they did not wear a mask. Some people do not remember their past events, so the other possibility is to remember by utilizing the environment; more precisely, the witness who viewed the robbery can go back to the same place and try to remember what really happened, who was there, and how many people were there.

In the end, I have discovered that how people do at school depends upon the study program they have created for themselves. Furthermore, our brain gives us many options, including helping us to create a better and more organized way of remembering. One of the ways that our brains can help us to remember is by using the mnemonic technique. It's used more often by students who have lots of memorizing to do and little time in which to do it. Together, these techniques combine to help us keep our important memories accessible until the end of our days.

Mass Media and Mental illness

In the Canadian Mental Health Association of Ontario, Dara Roth Edney writes that "public perception of mental illness is shaped by the news and entertainment media. Research confirms that negative images and stereotypes in film, television, advertising, magazines, and newspapers are directly connected to the public's negative attitudes towards people with mental health issues. Negative media portrayals also have a direct impact on individuals living with mental illness, as well as on how the government respond to mental health issues (2004).

Research conducted by from the National Mental Health Association of United States showed the following results on the influential negative and positive perception of mental health. It is obvious and transparent on the statistics and percentages on popular information about mental illness. The research shows how mental illness is portrayed in various ways and mentioned by different people from all kinds of social groups, people with different views on mental illness talk about mental illness and portray mostly negatively in various forms.

Statistically 70% of programs in TV news, newspapers, and magazines show stereotypes about people who deal with mental illness. These consist of scenes that are made "interesting" by mostly showing the negative side of a gifted person. It is proof that media representations of mental illness promote false and negative images and stereotypes.

"The media play an influential role in shaping people's attitudes about the world they live in and about the individuals who inhabit the world with them. Stories about or references to people with mental health issues are rarely out of the headlines in news stories or plotlines in film and television, yet research indicates that media portrayals of mental illness are often both false and negative (Diefenbach, 1997 [citing Berlin & Malin, 1991; Gerbner, 1980; Nunnally, 1957; Wahl & Harman, 1989])."

Basically, media promote mainly the negative aspects and showcases a negative perception of mental illness. Therefore, many people often get scared due to violent and disturbing shows portrayed by many shows. People then respond negatively to those with mental illness they are as portrayed negatively. This leads to stigma among those with mental illness. Due to discrimination one with mental illness is directly affected by negative reactions and responses.

The mental illness is influenced by the Mass Media in various forms. The media grab the attention of millions of people by portraying the negative aspects of the illness through many different news, TV shows, movies or even talk shows. On the radio, the mental illness is especially mentioned when something violent occurs. A suspect is typically pointed out to have a mental illness. This negatively affects people with a mental disorder. What is outrageous is not only does one have to deal with being ill is blaming them for crimes. When someone does not behave, they are automatically labeled with a mental illness. The media then reinforce positively people who have no knowledge about the mental illness and show instead inappropriate information. Those people with less education have a tendency to believe what the media has to say even though that it is not necessarily true. Some sort of information will be retained after watching, listening or even reading information. Hence, people may have assumption about a story due to the media and how the media portray it. Therefore, people may get scared or even angry just because they heard someone with an illness conduct a violent act. This leads to generalizations, stigmas and assumption of people with mental illness.

The media should put more effort to influence people with positive information about mental disorders. Sometimes, when something is shown in media, it is twisted to fit one perception. Some may say that the media has destroyed people's values, morals, respects, and kindness due to the negative ways of showing people with mental disorder. Mental health has a primary role in our modern society, it should not have a prejudice and should be open to the society with actual facts and information. Yet millions of people have misconception and false beliefs due to the extreme negative publicity. Mental illness is common worldwide, many people admit that they do have mental illness, and others may not know that they are affected with a mental disorder. On the other hand, some may not wish to tell the truth by saying that they are part of millions of people "infected with an illness such as mental illness". Those who try to cover up by saying that they do not have mental illness are usually the ones not willing to admit that mental disorder could be treated like other illness.

Mental illness is seen as one of the main diagnosis in the first and second-world countries. The illness is taken seriously and many people believe that there is hope for treatments. The following are some positive developments of mental illness in North America.

1. There are many research conducted in mental illness: To better understand the symptoms and find the proper treatments.
2. Many professionals are getting funds to study the causes of mental illness
3. Governments and Private companies give funds to researchers in mental illness.
4. In certain Media, some TV programs try to explain and prevent a mental illness such as depression.

5. There is less discrimination on TV by those explaining the mental disorder.
6. People are becoming more open discuss mental illness.
7. People try to find out why there is stigma on those with mental illness.
8. There are more professionals in mental health then before.
9. Doctors, Nurses, and other professionals take the illness seriously.
10. More and more medication are available for one with the illness.
11. In Canada, the government helps those with an illness financially.
12. Some companies also support people with disability.
13. People with an illness or without an illness can participate in various studies.
14. Nowadays there are many resources on mental illness such as library, magazines, books, newspapers, and internet.
15. If needed one can easily get counseling with a practitioner.
16. There are many associations available for help.
17. There are many non-profit organizations to support an ill person.
18. There are many hot lines for those who in crises.
19. People, family, friends, peers, and supporters are more open about discussing any types of illness.

People can have false beliefs and get confused by the information provided by the Mass Media on mental illness. Some may even have conflict due to the negative information shown and mentioned. Therefore, people who have no knowledge about mental disorders end up stigmatizing people with the illness. Therefore, people are less tolerant with the unfortunate people with mental illness. One with mental illness has negative emotions and fears prejudice when seeking treatments. Some may even feel that they are rejected from society due to being excluded from the surrounding and environment. A certain percentage may react differently in due to the difficulty facing society. People do not supporting those with the illness, some may even call them names by saying they are "insane, paranoid, losers, retarded and stupid". Hearing these words makes one feel really terrible and tearful. One is already going through a difficult moment and others seem not to understand and value the illness. People do not understand that it is an illness such as other types of illness. For an example, one may show a lot of sympathy or be understanding to a person with cancer, whereas someone with schizophrenia is seen negatively and the society blames the patient just because he or she is schizophrenic.

According to Dr. Taylor Alexander, from Canadian Mental Health Association, National Office

"in reality, mental illness is a poor predictor of violence. The majority of people who are violent do not suffer from mental illnesses. As a group, mentally ill people are no more violent than any other group. In fact, people with mental illnesses are far more likely to be the victims of violence than to be violent themselves. But media depictions of persons with a mental illness attacking a stranger do much to shape public opinion" (2009).

I myself am a victim of violence and people has taken advantage of me when they know that I have a mental disorder. An example of this is when someone would show me a gun and would ask me to do something. Another time, someone pointed a laser to my eyes until I felt weak and asked me to do a favor. Another example is when one asked for my signature for no reason. I did not understand why they needed my authority. For some reason, I felt that people would take advantage of me since they know that I will not refuse due to my anxiety and fear. Another example is when people injected me with a sort of poison. Based on what I have mentioned one might say that it is my illness that makes me believe certain circumstances or actions have been conducted on me. A psychiatrist or a psychologist may say that they could be hallucinations or even delusions. They can also be distorted emotions. However, I felt these things really occurred and for some reason people has taken advantage of me. What benefit was my obeying to people's orders I still wonder. Therefore, I am more cautious now than I was before. I have learned to say "no" to people. I show reactions when I feel something terrible is happening. By being sometimes rude with people I feel safer. It is some sort of a coping mechanism or even defense mechanism.

Dr. Taylor Alexander also argues that the

> "current research shows that people with major mental illness are 2.5 times more likely to be the victims of violence than other members of society. It is estimated that one in every four persons with mental illness will experience violent victimization every year, a rate that is eleven times higher than the rate of violent victimization experienced by the general population" (2009).

I have tried to change my thoughts on my illness but the more I think positively, the more I still feel that people have been taking advantage of my illness. Having Schizophrenia made me feel weaker. Therefore, I have decided to conduct research to better understand my symptoms and my rights. I no longer want to be walked-over and made to feel like I am retarded. I am someone with good-will and am very knowledgeable. My illness has weakened me and affected my intelligence. I want to stand-up for myself and achieve what other could not. I want to change people's perception on mental illness, especially people who suffer from schizophrenia. Regardless of what people think about mental illness, not everybody will support people with schizophrenia but sending a message is a first step and a sign where people may understand my point of view on my illness. There are many angles of a certain situation; one may see things negatively, others positively. Some may not take any side and many may say it is part of life, I hope that people who suffer from mental illness will somehow be part of a society that one day accepts them.

Dr. Taylor Alexander also explained that people who suffer from mental illness are affected through the Mass Media.

"Half of the respondents said that the media coverage had a negative effect on their own mental health, and 34% said this led directly to an increase in their depression and anxiety. A total of 22% of the participants said they felt more withdrawn and isolated as a result of negative media coverage, and 8% said that such press coverage made them feel suicidal. Almost 25% of respondents said that they noticed hostile behaviors from their neighbors due to negative newspaper and television reports. A further 11% said they required additional support from mental health services due to negative press coverage, and almost 25% of all respondents said that they had changed their minds about applying for jobs or volunteer positions due to negative media coverage" (2009).

People seem not to understand the illness and many do not care about getting educated and to learn both negative and positive side of the illness. We seem to forget about the positive side of being diagnosed with an illness. One has a chance to recover from the illness when he or she can access treatments. One can be followed by a psychiatrist, a psychologist or even other professionals. A person diagnosed with illness can be prescribed regular medications and can understand the limitations of certain illnesses.

MEDIA ANALYSIS: WONDERLAND

In the last few decades, the media's influence on the public's opinion, the public's belief system and the public's perception has grown exponentially. A substantial amount of research has been conducted over the last 30 years to determine the effect of mass media on public 'perception' (Edney, 2004). To summarize, bad news travel fast. As soon as something new occurs right away there is a reaction from a journalist, written on the internet, newspapers, articles, manuscripts, or shown on TV. It is impressive to acknowledge how much money has been invested in Mass Media. It seems that people will do anything to be on the front page. People are good in telling stories and some may not wonder what impact this may cause to the society. Hence, telling the true story can be seen as novelty. Helping someone or being a witness can help one in misery. After all there is nothing wrong with telling a true story. What matter is when a medium is used in a way to convey the negative side. It can affect people in various ways. Studies have concluded that mass media is one of the most significant influences in 'developed societies' when consider both the media's power to influence public perception as well as the degree to which people are exposed to media representations (Edney, 2004). Every day we are informed through all types of information. This information can affect our mood: one may become scare of all kinds of people. It is great to keep updated by knowing as much as information that one can gather. This helps one be more sophisticated within a modern society. Research has also indicated that mental illness is a common theme in mass media, (Wahl & Lefkowits, 1989) and mentally disordered people are 'disproportionally' portrayed as violent criminals and as having a negative impact on society (Diefenbach & West, 2007). People can be violent for various reasons. Therefore, not all criminals are mentally ill. The media should not put any kinds of blame just because an incident has occurred. Most of the mentally ill people suffer from various types of disorders and showing or blaming in media can cause a lot of stress and lower the self esteem. We should be an open society where one should not accuse anyone without knowing any diagnosis or even finding the true motive.

For the purpose of media analysis, I will first provide a brief description of a television drama called *Wonderland*. I will go into more details with one of its opening scenes, which is a crucial contribution as to why the drama has been cancelled. Secondly, I will discuss existing scientific evidence regarding the power that media has over its viewers' belief system, and the relationship between mental disorder and violence. The third part will consist of a discussion regarding the implications for the practice of social work.

PART 1: THE ISSUE

Wonderland, is a short-lived and controversial ABC television drama directed by Peter Berg, It depicts daily life situations in the psychiatric and the emergency room units of Bellevue Hospital of New York City, from the perspectives of both the doctors and the patients (Hale, 2009). On April 6th, 2000, this psych-ward drama lost 20 million viewers from its lead-in, "Who wants to be a Millionaire" (Hale, 2009). The factors in the cancellation include a brutal time slot opposite ER (Hale, 2009), protests by mental health groups such as National Alliance on Mental Illness (NAMI) who heavily criticized this particular series, as it portrayed a 'bleak life' for individuals who are diagnosed with a mental illness (Tartakovsky, 2009) and the stigmatization of the mentally ill (Hale, 2009). We should be aware that shows such as Wonderland, with its viewers, can greatly impact society. Portraying the negative side of mental health is not a decent action. A lot of people who suffer with mental illness are from all ages, genders, social groups, races, ethnicities and various cultures. You will never know when the illness will hit you. People with mental illness work in various professional place and some are well established. There are certain groups who are very educated and understand the value of human being. Someone with an extreme level of illness can become homeless or be very ill.

The opening scene from Wonderland is of a man who is diagnosed with Schizophrenia. The man was off his medications when he went to the shopping mall in Times Square and shot down five men.

"[The patient] was under the belief that he was saving the world from monsters" stated by his psychiatrist during a meeting with the patient's parents and lawyer (Berg, 2000). He then stabbed a pregnant physician (played by Michelle Forbes) in the stomach with a needle (Berg, 2000). This particular scene was a negative media portrayal of schizophrenic individuals, articulating them as being violent and dangerous, which are considered one of the major myths associated with mental illness. The truth however is that individuals with mental illness are more likely to be victims of violence than to be violent themselves (Edney, 2012). Based on the series, one may conclude that a Schizophrenic can be violent but it is only a certain percentage of people who suffered from a severe illness. In reality not all patients are violent. Some are just trying to understand their own symptom. When one is hospitalized there is no chance for a person with Schizophrenia to be violent. In the TV series the illness was exaggerated and targeted a minority of the population. This can affect the majority of the mentally ill people.

In an interview, Peter Berg stated that his motivation to tackle such a difficult subject was due to his childhood stories of his mother's experience at a psychiatric hospital in White Plains, New York (Berg, 2000). Berg's mother was "mesmerized by the whole environment of a psychiatric hospital—in a good way" as stated by Berg in the interview (Berg, 2000). He also said that she loved the patients, the doctors, as well as the experience. Berg therefore spent about six months "pretty much living at that hospital" (Berg, 2000), to conduct his research at the Bellevue Psychiatric Hospital in New York. The following paragraphs will discuss some of the reasons as to why we should pay attention to this particular issue of negative media portrayals of mental illness.

Wonderland is not the only drama series where mentally ill individuals are portrayed in a negative light (Edney, 2004). Dozens of studies that have analyzed both the news and entertainment media from around the globe, show that media representations of the mentally ill promote negative images and stereotypes—particularly the false connection between mental illness and violence (Edney, 2004). This emphasizes the immediate need of curbing the negative information shown on TV. Many people get scared after watching TV or reading articles. Hence, it is affecting the majority of the mentally ill people. There were many studies conducted on violence in TV and it is believed that people tend to be more influenced to be more violent when watching actions series or movies. Children minds are shaped and manipulated easily. When they grow up, can end up violent. Many other studies have also found a consistency between the media's negative portrayals of mental illness and the public's negative attitude towards mentally disordered people (Edney, 2004). Although Peter Berg's intention was not bad, the scene of the schizophrenic character shooting five men and stabbing a pregnant physician was not a wise direction as it added to the common "stereotypes of mentally ill persons as different and dangerous" (Wahl and Lefkowits, 1989, p. 521) and "there is strong belief that such stereotypes help to maintain the stigma which accompanies mental illness" (Wahl and Lefkowits, 1989, p. 521). In Canada, there are many ads on TV and radios discussing mental illness such as Depression. Notifying the audience that many people can become mentally ill, and therefore, we should protect each other and not discriminate each other.

In terms of the impact that negative media portrayals of mental illness have on government policies, sufficient evidence exists to indicate that if the public considers people with mental illnesses to be violent, government policies will look more toward containment as well as control rather than recovery and community living (Edney, 2004). The few mentally ill people who commit crimes are not given the chance to return to their community. It seems that Harper government does not care about mentally ill. Bill C-54 was introduced for those who are violent and offenders but are not necessary responsible for their criminal actions. The mentally ill people who have committed a crime, (which is small percentage of the population) are targeted by Bill C-54. They are not allowed to return to their community after committing a crime, and are labelled to be "high risk" of committing future crimes even though research has sown otherwise. Anne Croker, a professor of psychiatry, has data from study she conducted for which to care. Many mental organizations showed their concern to push back the Bill C-54. Obviously, there are a certain population of mentally ill people who may "not be criminally responsible" and may not be at "high risk" in conducting another crime. This legislation is a negative sign for the mentally ill. Anne Croker says that in the province of B.C, Ontario, and Quebec, the likelihood of a mentally ill person to commit another crime is less than 10 per cent. This is enough evidence that people who are unfortunate are labelled and stigmatized against. Government create laws and looks for people's safety. In Canada there are many organizations that help people in misery as well as homeless. There are many organizations that protect the mentally ill. A percentage of money is going to assist people with the mental disorders and there are various shelters for those who end up living on the streets.

PART 2: EMPIRICAL LITERATURE

According to Monahan (1992), the belief that "mental disorder predisposes to violence is culturally universal and historically invariant" (as cited in Levey & Howells, 1994, p. 314). As a result, the public holds inaccurate negative views about mentally disordered people as being dangerous, unpredictable, unworthy, unattractive, and unlikely to be productive members of their communities (Levey & Howells, 1994; Wahl, Hanrahan, Karl, Lasher & Swaye, 2007). In this context, it is true for a minority of the population. Not all patients are dangerous, unpredictable, and unworthy. There are various places such as Hospitals and Clinics that offer counselling and have a Mental Health Department. A person like me or others patients who suffers from the illness are treated and seen at the Hospital and Clinics. Just because one has commited a crime does not mean that other patients including me should be seen negatively. Wonderland's opening scene of the schizophrenic man who stabbed the pregnant physician in the stomach depicts an accurate example of the public's attitudes of mentally ill persons, especially schizophrenics, as being dangerous, violent and "liable to commit horrific crimes" (Levey & Howells, 1994, p. 314). As stated by Marie and Miles (2008), labelling "schizophrenia may induce more negative reactions from laypersons because they consider individuals with this disorder as being more likely to cause harm to others" (p. 131). The label of 'depression' however, is not associated with greater belief that these people are dangerous (Jorm, Reavley & Ross, 2012, p. 3). Having a depression is perceived as one becoming blue, whereas being schizophrenic is a sign of being out of reality. Both are two different mental illness but someone with schizophrenia is portrayed as dangerous and insane.

Mass media, being the primary source of information both regarding crime and mental illness, plays a vital role in our attitude formation and/or maintenance (Levey & Howells, 1994). Therefore for some people, media plays a large and influential role (Levey & Howells, 1994). Obviously, we are informed by learning and getting information from Media. There are many channels in TV or Radio or even articles on the Internet that provide information about daily news. We are more equipped than 20 years ago. As soon as something happens, we are informed. For instance, individuals who do not have any direct personal contact with someone with a serious mental illness such as schizophrenia (Morgan & Jorm, 2009) are more likely to rely on other sources of information (Levey & Howells, 1994), such as media related sources. Levey & Howells (1994) draws on writings of Asch (1987) who argues that attitudes are partly influenced ``by formal and informal sources of information such as the school, the media, the family and peers`` (p. 318). Although the media can have a significant effect on the attitudes of the audience towards the mentally ill, it may also be that the media simply serves to maintain existing public perception (Levey & Howells, 1994). Even though the media shows negative information, people do believe that the media attract a certain audiences. It is up to the audiences to make the final judgments.

Mental Disorder And Violence

There are a number of extensive recent reviews of the literature pertaining to the association between mental disorder and violence and between schizophrenia and violence (Levey & Howells, 1994). According to Rueve and Welton (2008), "Most patients with stable mental illness do not present an increased risk of violence" (p. 36) and only a small part of the violence can be ascribed to mental health patients (Rueve & Welton, 2008). Rueve & Welton (2008) describe the etiology of violence best by stating:

"Patients who are violent are not a homogenous group, and their violence reflects various biologic, psychodynamic, and social factors. Most researchers and clinicians agree that a combination of factors plays a role in violence and aggression, although there are differing opinions regarding the importance of individual factors" (p. 37).

Substance-use disorders however have been proven to increase the risk of a violent incident (Rueve & Welton, 2008). Not all schizophrenics take illegal substances or consume alcohols, it is unfortunate to be part of the stigma and to be labelled by the media. Sometime, it is discouraging to know that we are seen in a different ways compared to other illnesses.

Research over the last three decades has shown that a substantial minority of both professional and 'lay people' have negative as well as rejecting attitudes towards the mentally ill (Levey and Howells, 1994). According to a survey conducted by Nordt, Rossler & Lauber (2006), it was shown that "Psychiatrists had more negative stereotypes than the general population" (p. 709). The general population however accepted restrictions towards people with mental illness "to a much higher degree, with the exception of compulsory admission" (Nordt et al., 2006). Nevertheless, it is even worse at work. One with a mental illness can be discriminated by their coworkers and managers. Sometimes when searching for jobs, employers would requires medical tests and as soon as the recruiters knows about such illness, they would reject the job application automatically.

PART 3: SOCIAL WORK IMPLICATIONS

Mentally ill persons and their families nominate stigma as a major concern (Jorm & Oh, 2009). The impact of mental illness therefore is not only severe for the patients, but also for their families and the societies, as it leads to suffering, high costs, and 'lethal consequences' such as suicide and destructive behaviour (Baumann, 2007). According to the World Health Report (2001), stigma is defined as a "a mark of shame, disgrace or disapproval which results in an individual being rejected, discriminated against, and excluded from participating in a number of different areas of society" (as cited in Jorm et al., 2012, p. 1). As a result of the stigma attached to mental illness, mental health problems are often 'underestimated,' 'under-diagnosed' and 'untreated' (Baumann, 2007).

As seen in the second part of this media analysis, mental illness is feared and misunderstood by many people. Thus, the only way to diminish this fear is by changing and erasing public stigma. Some studies have identified three approaches to erasing public stigma: (1) protest (2) education, and (3) contact (Larson & Corrigan, 2008). Protest, which is a moral appeal for people to discontinue stigma, involves suppressing stereotypes about mental illness (Larson & Corrigan, 2008). Education entails challenging myths about mental illness with facts (Larson & Corrigan, 2008). Some of the myths include: (1) people with mental illness are violent, (2) teens with mental illness are just going through a phase and (3) they don't get better (Tartakovsky, 2009). A standardized curriculum should be designed (Larson & Corrigan, 2008) by mental health professionals such as social workers, psychologists and psychiatric and this curriculum should be exported to all elementary schools, high schools, CEGEPs, and universities across the country. Finally, contact "involves fostering interactions between a person with mental illness and the public" (Larson & Corrigan, 2008, p. 89). The following paragraph will explain how the elimination of public stigma can benefit mentally disordered persons, their families, and untreated individuals with mental problems.

In my opinion, erasing public stigma may help in diminishing the negative experience of people with mental illness or by family members, which is experienced simply through "association with their relatives" (Larson & Corrigan, 2008, p. 90). Family stigma includes the prejudice and discrimination. Such type of sigma holds a negative impact on families and relatives with mental illness (Larson & Corrigan, 2008). Since the feelings of shame (Lai & Surood, 2007) and fear of gossip, particularly among South Asian communities (Bradby et al., 2007) is associated with mental illness, many untreated individuals with mental illness and their family members may not necessarily seek help. Therefore, a more positive portrayal of mental illness in the media, including social networks such as Facebook, may create a more positive public attitude. As a result, this may encourage more individuals and families to seek professional help. The following paragraph will discuss how the need for more social services may influence the policy context.

I believe that a higher level of social acceptance of the mentally ill by community members may increase the number of patients in hospitals and the number of clients in CLSCs. As a result, there will be more demands in social services for the mentally ill due to the increase in the number of patients and clients. The provincial government may be forced to increase funding for community and social services. As a result of a higher level of acceptance, there may also be more job opportunities for mental health professionals and the development of more specialized mental health services.

As a human being, I believe we all have a duty to help mentally ill people in their journey towards a better life. If the public perception of mental illness is negative and is based on false images, there is a danger that the government responses and services in the mental health field will be totally based on these false realities perpetuated by the media (Edney, 2004). We must all work together towards the elimination of direct and indirect oppression at three levels: personal, cultural and structural. The three levels will definitely help people feel accepted in the reality and better assist people who suffer with mental illness. After all we are all human and have equal rights regardless of our illness and disorders. Just because one is unfortunate to have an illness does not mean that people should be treated or be seen in degrading ways. Anyone at any age can develop mental illness, therefore before judging one should think twice.

In the past few decades, there is more and more research on mental illness, which brings hope to the society. People may feel more secure knowing that many studies are being conducted and more people feel safe walking on the street knowing that they would not get hurt. On the other hand, people with mental illness also feel more hopeful due to positive advertisement on TV. It is a sign that some do understand people who suffer from mental disorder. Being able to distinguish a normal person from a mentally ill person can make a lot of difference. Understanding the symptom can make a person acceptable. Other people do not need to discriminate just because someone lives with a mental illness. For someone with schizophrenia to know that family members, peers, friends, neighbors and acquaintances have accepted him or her as part of their life, it could mean a lot. Being accepted will help an ill person live with dignity. Knowing that people care for someone with mental disorder can make that person emotionally stable and feeling secure.

Being able to balance his or her behaviours can make a big difference in our society. When one is capable of controlling his or her temper, it could help the person to not isolate him or herself. Being surrounded by people can make an ill person feel much better and help overcome a symptom. One with the illness may feel that one has gained a lot of respect from others and be able to socialize with normal people. If someone does not feel comfortable and does not want to communicate with someone with a mental disorder, then it is a matter of choice. As long as one does not hurt people, there is nothing wrong in choosing to not be with certain people. The more positive publicity on Mass Media, the better the chance for someone with mental illness to recover. It is essential to talk positively to send positive messages to the outside world. Sometimes it depends on of the environment for someone recover from an illness. Environment and recovery go together in healing. By having hope, acceptance, dignity, balance, respect, choice, and recovery, one will feel freedom.

Day Hospital

Admission

Congratulations, you have been accepted to the Day Hospital! Have you ever had both bad and good feelings at the same time? Both negative and positive inside of your heart intermingled and inexpressible. Knowing that you have to enter somewhere very dark to see the light at the end. How does the admission work one might ask? Well without a medical doctor's referral one would not be able to participate in the program in the Day Hospital. There are many advantages and disadvantages of being part of a medical system for those who need help the most. In my case I was fortunate to have many Doctors helping me to build myself. Yes . . . I, myself was admitted to the Day Hospital in Montreal. At first I had to meet a nurse who asked me many questions about my health. To tell her from the beginning about my illness, what exactly happened with my health and the thoughts in my mind. Basically, it was a medical interview to have a better idea of my illness and my mind. It lasted around one hour and half. The nurse was extremely kind and gentle with me, then she asked that I come the next day to have another interview. This time, it will be with a doctor.

The next day I was anxious about meeting the doctor, I did not know what to say or to do. One thing was for sure: I had to show up if I wanted to get better. I was in a closed room where the nurse had interviewed me the day before. Because of that, the place was already familiar. To feel better I needed to feel like home. The more time I spend in a safe place the more comfortable I feel. When the doctor arrived, we shook hands and greeted each other. I felt warm in her presence. Soon after, the interview began, and so did the questions. I did not know where to begin. In my mind, I was totally lost, mentioning from a to z but without making sense of what I was saying. My thoughts were extremely disorganized and I had trouble with my speech as it was disorganized as well. I had to start with something without making a fool of myself. Slowly, I took control of my emotion and my mind and bit by bit I was able to express what had happened to me.

My story began with Schizophrenia and depression. In the past, I felt emotionally blue and could not cope with reality. During my period of early adulthood, I started showing some symptoms of depression. I would become very emotional, often had headaches, I could not sleep enough, and I often felt tired. I needed to take medications such as Zoloft. One thing is for sure, one never knows when depression will hit or who its next target is. It hit me while I was attending College. I do not know if it was due to high stress in my life. Having a low self-esteem about myself did not help either. I used to wake up around 5:00am to review my notes and to study before going to college. During winter, this means that I would not see the sunrise and when I would come back from college I would not see the sunset. I may have needed some Vitamin D. For some reason I have taken an overload of courses: even carrying my college books were a chore. It was an evidence for me that I have excessively taken too many courses. I succeeded in all of course, but at a price.

Many years after my depression, I was hospitalized: I could not cope with reality, and become severely ill. It was a tremendous suffering for me and it was a hard period in my life. Apparently, I spent one month in the hospital according to my family doctor: I had no memories about what happened and why I was ill. Still now I wonder what exactly was the cause and why I could not cope in that special timeframe. Many health professionals had told me that usually when we do not remember about our past, it is due to good causes. Basically, our mind erases all the negative feelings and keeps the positive ones. It is the mind's way of healing naturally without interruption. It happens for the best of an individual. In my case, however I could not remember either negative or positive feelings, memories, thoughts. It took me years later to know that I had psychoses.

Before the Hospital, I used to see my family doctor. The more I spent time with her, and the more I was able to trust her. To open up by telling what was inside of my mind. A few months before the Hospital, I was diagnosed with Schizophrenia. As my family doctor became trustworthy, I was able tell her everything from the bottom of my heart. One day I told her that I would see things when I closed my eyes. For me it was like being in another world. The images that I would see would be so fast that I could not keep track of them. It was like seeing something in a speed of light. For me it was like turning on a light switch when I close my eyes. The pupils were like a theater screen for me. Closing my eyes, I would see forms, images, pictures, all of which seem to be a gravitating towards each other. Having these visions were uncanny. The symptoms worried my doctor, and she mentioned the Day Hospital.

While my family doctor was on vacation, I had an incident. While eating 'bread', I started to hallucinate that it seemed to me what I was eating was a child's arm. This terrified me. I had to see another doctor in a Clinique, who increased my medication. It took me several months for me to eat bread again without having any symptoms. What was good about the incident was that I was able to overcome my fears and hallucination by using natural learning. When the family doctor returned, she was stunned to hear what I had to say. She then suggested adding a new medication on top of the one that I had (Zyprexa Zydis). Since then I had to adjust with the new medication, Abilify.

It seemed to me that I was in a makeshift mafia project. I would often be wanted for some signature, and I would not know why. I still believe that people want my signature for something. It is a perception that I live with in a daily basis and it is very hard to change my point of view. Due to many attempts by strangers, colleagues or friends and mostly those who, I trust the most I was forced in some occasions to sign documents. I wondered why this would happened to me as I am not a famous person nor that I am known internationally by being a millionaire. What was the benefit of having my signatures? Was it because I work for a bank and people would need a second signature for a loan, line of credit, mortgages or even any kind of purpose that requires a second signature? I did not understand why they would need my approval; I did not have access to give loans, lines of credit, or even mortgages as I work in a different department, (collection). Would I be seen as a co-signer when one applies for some sort of money or credit from the bank? Knowing that my credit history is above the population, getting a co-signer would be easy for one to commit frauds. Will I be charged in the years to come or will they remove my name when getting a sort of credit from the bank. I still ask many questions to myself and leave my mind with no answer.

The medical doctor asked me if I had faith in any religion I told her I used to believe in Islam but my conception about religion has changed since my illness. There was a time where spiritually I was very motivated and I strongly believed what others preached. Now I do not practice, nor do I have strong feelings about any religion. I believe that religion was created for educational purpose before ancient times. At that time religion was needed to guide one from doing wrong. Still now between good and bad is mention in religion but for me one religion is similar to the others. It's like taking at the university 100 level courses, once succeeded we take 200 levels then 300 levels and so one. Therefore, each religion has their own levels; weakness and strength, has bad and good, disadvantages and advantages. I do not like to see mercenary trying to publicize a religion when most of the population have a sort of believe in a supreme creature. However, even though that I do not believe in religion I still believe in God as the supreme creator or even a force which is stranger then human beings.

After my illness I started believing that we all live in a multi-dimensional world. What can one say about multiple dimensions one might ask? From a religious point of view, one may say that god loves us very much and wants to cherish us by bringing us closer to him. Therefore having hallucinations would be how he choose to do so to me. Showing many different forms, images, and pictures would make us believe that there is someone above us. Seeing something when there is nothing could be phenomenal. Some even may say it is a gift from heaven. Showing me something is making me understand that there is someone and one should have faith in that someone. For example, consider the binary number from 0 and 1. Adding zero to infinity or one to infinity. On one side, the number will increase, and on the other side the number will decrease. The more the number decreases the smaller we get; the more number increase the bigger we get. It's like watching TV or playing games in the computer. If the TV size is smaller then we will see a smaller version of the image. On the other hand, the bigger the screen, the bigger the images, forms, pictures. If this is true then you will agree that we might live in a different types of dimension. There might not be enough evidence to make you believe in multiple dimensions. Therefore, you may not agree with me and may say that it is not possible. In the medical and psychological field it is called hallucination. Many doctors, psychiatrists and psychologists will agree that due to some health issue there is a misbalance of chemical in the brain that lead me to have hallucination. With medication we can reduce it from our body and mind.

The long interview felt quick. Later, I was introduced to other patients in the Day Hospital. The first thing came to my ears was 'welcome' by another patient. I felt great. Slowly, I was being introduced to everyone one after the other. Each of us said our name. I was quickly integrating with the patients. The next day I met with the director of the program of the Day Hospital. He seemed like a very intelligent and professional psychiatrist.

Weekend review

Weekend review is a way of telling others what exactly we did during weekend. All the patients at the Day Hospital told their story. All the patients had some sort of mental health issue, and they were treated in the Hospital with special care and attention. We would sit in a circle and discussed our weekend journeys. This is done once a week. I remember my first weekend review, it was right after coming from a trip to Ontario; my wife, daughter and I went to Thousand Islands, Toronto and Niagara Falls. It was a guided 3-day trip. I enjoyed it but I did not feel good about it as much as I should have. Everywhere we went we had a schedule and a certain timeline: when visiting a place, we would have a two-hour guided tour and then we would proceed to the next tour. This created some sort of negative feelings and worries of missing the bus for me.

Luckily, my family did not miss the bus. Visiting the three cities in Ontario was great. Even though I have visited them many times it was the first time with my family. My daughter who was at that time 11 months old along with my wife enjoyed visiting. The moment that I remember most is that I felt extremely stressful about not having enough time to visit certain places such as the CN Tower, Museum or even downtown Toronto as we had to take care of our daughter. Especially, when we were not allowed to use the toilet inside of the bus due to some issues. Therefore, changing my daughter's diaper was a hassle. Apart from that, everything went well. We all enjoyed our tours. These were the stories we shared at the Hospital and now I am sharing them with you.

Assertiveness

Being assertive is really important. Knowing when to say the right word to someone can bring a solid conversation, be it with your boss, your spouse, a neighbor, friends, your coworkers, your parents and even siblings. There is nothing wrong with saying "no" or "yes" to one or all of the above persons mentioned. When discussing about assertiveness, one can use it aggressively or passively.

Aggressive assertiveness usually occur when one is loud. He or she seems to be bossy or like to dominate when dealing with something. One does not fear to intimidate others. The aggressive assertive will violate your rights by reacting instantly. In a situation where you are a patient, it could be very painful to deal with the aggressive assertive. He or she will stab your heart by speaking loudly. The ill person may feel deranged when hearing that person. Not being able to take control can hurt emotionally. In a case where your boss seems to be too hard on you, you may feel extremely stressed about it, especially when you know that he or she has high expectations from you. Putting pressure on someone can damage their health. Not respecting one's morals and values can violate one's beliefs. Your parents may pressure you without understanding your condition and saying no is difficult. Sometimes saying "no" to different people may elicit different reactions.

Now the passive assertive. Most of the time, one is unable to talk about their rights or even about themselves. In a particular situation one can have no idea about his or her actions. People may take advantage of that person by trying to manipulate some conversations or even an action. He or she may get hurt by not being able to respond to the other person. In many circumstances, one does not even know what his or her rights are. When that happens usually people tend to exploit a naive person by stepping over them. It seems that some people decide to be hard on others. Sometimes it seems that even if one is well mannered, people do not care. Being soft can allow others to take advantage, you. Regardless of how modest you are, people can use passive assertiveness to dominate.

Now one can be assertive by being direct and honest. One can value and respect others' rights and recognizing his or her rights. One can talk without a doubt and pin point what he or she meant in a nice and gentle way. One then would feel positive about themselves and recognize and consider having a say in someone else's life or even in their own lives. One who is assertive knows what he or she wants, feels comfortable using the "I" word: to comfortably explain and say that "I want", "I believe", and "I think or I see in that way". When being assertive, one is very respectful and gives credit where credit is due. One seeks to have a better comprehension by trying to recognize people's feelings and perception by implementing their own. If one is confused, one will ask or even clarify to better understand others. One will not try to judge or blame others for no reasons. One will do what is needed to be done in a peaceful manner. He or she will expand self-respect towards others.

Art Therapy

During bad weather, the Occupational Therapist would foster creativity by having art therapy. It was a way for us to focus on ourselves and know the inner self through various types of art. We would be in a small group where patients would explore their talents. The art therapy was a process of developing each patient's creativity by reflecting on ourselves. This helped each patient to improve their mental, physical and emotional stability. The main focus was to explore and create ourselves by coping with our illness, reducing stress, and releasing trauma. When doing art therapy each individual would come up with their own idea by creating or drawing what they felt like. It was one of the creative ways to resolve our problems by understanding them in a different pattern. This was designed to increase our self-esteem and as a way of seeing our problems from a different perspective.

Usually people from all ages can practice art therapy. However, at the Day Hospital it was mostly used with adults, focusing on cognitive, physical and emotional aspects. Anyone from any cultures or even social groups were involved in art therapy. When sharing our 'piece of art', one would reveal what the picture, image, form or graph symbolizes to us, how it is meaningful, and how it reflects ourselves. Being able to express what is inside of our heart, mind and thoughts allows one to release it the stressors or tension. To participate in any kind of art, one does not to be artistically inclined whatsoever. It is exceptional how one can draw something without having any artistic skills. Making and sharing art allows one to share their perception about a creation and even to learn from others who have similar difficulties with their health.

Art therapy was not only to create art but also for healing purpose. Anyone had a choice to either draw, sculpt, paint or even to replicate a picture. It was one way of expressing the imagination. Creating art used the cognitive side of our brains, allowing us to perceive and describe our issues better. It is amazing how from a small picture, or illustration one can come up with a story or even share a painful experience. Being able to share our opinion or even listening what one had to say was therapeutic for each individual at the hospital. When sharing a piece of art with another person, I learned that there were many different types of art: one can do it with only dots, with only lines, some with shapes, other with pictures, many with multiple colors or even some selective colors, and mostly one will portray either people or animals. A picture is not only a picture, each picture or some sort of art has a specific meaning and it can mean different things to difficult people.

In art therapy, each of us interpreted our psychological state through revealing our emotions. It was one way for each individual to understand and discover ourselves to better manage our life handle our problems and understand our health issues. It helped each of us share our ideas, stories, and to feel comfortable in group discussions. Being surrounded by people has helped in many ways for me to give and grasp information. The therapist was present to encourage each of us by exploring our work and focusing on our strengths and weaknesses. This helped us take both criticisms and compliments from our peers and the therapist. In a group, you are there to provide answers about your art: Each part of the art and each color used had a special meaning. The important thing was that we were able to complete our art by expressing ourselves using our cognition, emotion, thus helping us be more physically stable.

Community Life

Most of the patients want to be part of a community life. However, some may not want to be part of such a community or do not want the responsibility. Community life stands for taking the initiative in the Day Hospital by volunteering in daily activities. It could involve watering the plants, making coffee, cleaning tables, washing the coffee maker, washing the blackboard, cleaning the fridge, organizing the magazines, or decorating for special events such as Christmas, Easter or any other holidays. The main goal here is not to force people to work by assigning them tasks but to get people to initiate the tasks themselves. They can then become responsible and manage their time by participating and getting involved with the system. Moreover, not everybody has a weekly chore, some could be every two to three weeks. Those of them who want to volunteer are chosen to do simple tasks designed for the patients. Instead of putting pressure on the nurses, the patients are responsible. If the tasks are, not done then the nurses help out. I must admit that the nurses of the Day Hospital are wonderful, very kind and delicate.

Deciding who will do the tasks is not an easy choice. What job can one choose and follow through a regular duty at the Day Hospital? Usually, the nurse will go over the everyday jobs that need to be done. Everyone is asked what they would like to do during the upcoming week. Everybody is welcomed to participate and share their opinions who or what task. When responsibilities are done accordingly, no one complains. Actually the staff do not even complain about unfinished tasks but complete the tasks themselves. When I first arrived at the Day Hospital, I wanted to show a good impression about myself by getting involved in doing diverse tasks. My first three months involved non-stop contributing where I volunteered for jobs on top of completing the ones I was assigned to.

I must say that I felt good taking initiative. Beside following all the courses and having an education at the Hospital about Mental Health, I also participated everyday from morning to 2 pm at the hospital. Being at the hospital kept me focused and helped me work within my limits and daily routine. For me, the end of the treatments became like a regular job. Sometimes, instead of saying I was going to the Hospital, I would say that I was going to work. It was a sign that I missed my old work. One might ask how I survived: well the bank paid for a certain period and then the insurance took over. I could not anticipate returning to work. I was not sure if I wanted to return where I worked, mostly, at the bank. At that time, I had many issues that was going on in my mind. I was not sure if I was ready going back to work. I still felt irrational about myself and about returning to my regular life.

In healing, the nurses are one of the reason why a patient recover quickly. Their training and experience with the patient makes the difference. Without being a professional, it would not be possible for patients to recover. When a new patient arrives at the Day Hospital one may assume that he or she will recover within a certain timeframe. However, not all patients recover quickly; some have very intense issues and, may need a lot of extra attention. Therefore, the professionals are there to decide who needs more time than others. For most of the patients that are about to leave the hospital, some need to be further observed due to various health reasons while, others may be discouraged from not having enough attention therefore he or she decide to leave the Day Hospital. The System is designed for everyone, but not everybody sees it in a similar way, and some may feel that it is not for them. Some may also feel that being with other patients might make them become more ill.

Being surrounded by doctors, nurses, educators, occupational therapists, social worker and other staff made me feel really warm. It was clear that they wanted to see us. The patients were getting better and ready to go back to their daily routine be them working, or studying or staying at home because of them. They often encourage us to participate in various activities. They would organize events and outing within the mental health group. Their dedication and motivation made many of us more motivated to get involved within the society. Some of the patients including myself even volunteer in another Mental Health organization. Helping others made me feel really good and so did knowing that the time that I am putting towards an organization is helping them somehow. Just the mere fact that we helped made us feel special and generous. We could not help them financially but helping them physically and emotionally felt more rewarding.

Stress Management

We all take life as is; we implicitly know how to manage a stressful life-changing event. Stress manifest itself in many ways: for example, when doing an activity or tasks, when planning for a vacation, when driving a car or preparing for school work when there is an increase of work, not being able to cope with our partner or even our children. Dealing with stress can make one feel uncomfortable and can make impair our judgment. Some may perform and excel well when being in a stressful event. Some people need to feel stressed to be more motivated and feel challenged. One may not be able to say "no" to others' request and may feel stressful about it. Some cannot stay for too long in a silent place, and they need to hear something to feel relaxed. Other may perform well under pressure, them always running behind their schedules. Some do well in a competition or knowing that there is a reward waiting for them. Other may need to struggle to reach perfection to not feel stressed about something. In the following paragraph I will discuss some reasons why people may feel stressed, some advantages and disadvantages along with side effects of being stressed and some strategies to deal with stress. Furthermore, stressors can be personal, environment, work leisure, activities of daily living, or family and social network.

Going through pregnancy could bring a lot of stress for a woman and a couple. Being pregnant is not an easy process, one goes through various changes in her body. Therefore, it is normal that the female would react accordingly. While the female partner has difficulty by herself, her partner may not know how to behave or react with his mate. The couple can misunderstand each other. Becoming parents can be a gift but this can have emotional and financial changes. This could have an impact by changing the roles in personal life. Furthermore, the couple may have difficulty in modifying their habits with lack of sleep or not being able to perform regular tasks or routines. Having an illness this could bring more tension and stress within the couple. One may not know what he or she should do when someone is ill.

Managing family and social groups can be challenging. Going through health issues such as schizophrenia can hurt a marriage, leading to a separation or a divorce. It all depends on how the person deals with their loved one. Not accepting one's illness can be very stressful for both in a couple. Not knowing what to do or how it affects one's life can change a major relationship. Ending and later starting a new bond with someone else can also be a cause of distress. This could bring a negative or positive outcome, especially when introducing the new mate to their children. Having a negative memory of the past relationship can lead to sexual misjudgments within a couple. Furthermore, this can create more stress and one may get hurt when not pleased sexually. Therefore one may doubt his or her relationship. Moreover, having frequent conflict with family members, such as mother-in-laws, father—in—laws or even brother—or sister—in—laws can disappoint the couple.

Having many conflicts with our partners could have an impact at work. One may not perform well at work as a result. The tension created between both male and female could lose a job. Searching for a new job can be difficult for some. Others may need to change their work load. Having a new job can change in hours at work or have difficult boss. Hence, one will have to build a new relationship with coworkers and superiors. When there is a poor schedule, one may misbalance work and activities. One may not be able to participate in activities and may become less social when having a hard time at work or at home. Not being stable can cause difficulty in completing his or her daily activities, like doing grocery, shopping or even cooking.

Some people's moods depend on the environment. Depending on the weather, one may be unaffected whereas others may react differently. Moving to a new environment could be stressful. Having a new house or apartment can be seen positively or negatively. Not knowing the neighbors can make one suspicious about the area or even feeling uncomfortable from not knowing who lives near-by. It could take many days, months, and sometimes even years to accustomed to one's neighbors. Moving to another city is also a big change in one's life. Changing languages or facing language barriers can be difficult for some. Not being able to communicate by not understanding the language affects us emotionally and mentally. When going to a new country, one can be shocked by a new culture. Some may be motivated to learn a new culture, while others may not accept it. Hence, it is important to balance stressful events and adjust accordingly with the environment.

Managing stress can be advantageous when dealing with certain things. Regardless of our job, we will encounter some sort of stressful event in our life. What is important is to recognize what causes our stress and how we can cope with it. Being able to balance our stress can benefit our health and help us maintain a good relationship with our peers, friends, family and the surrounding. Being able to identify the origin of the stressful event can ease one's life. Asking ourselves where the stress comes from can be one way of finding a solution. Knowing the symptom, either emotional or physical, can affect our health and mood and also bring balance to our state of being. Then we must ask how we can make ourselves feel better in is a stressful situation. Living peacefully by having a good response to stress can improve our lifestyle. The common causes of stress are conflicts with employers, conflicts with loved ones not having enough money, or losing money by gambling. One can also be dissatisfied for some reason, or death of someone which can bring a lot of stress. Losing jobs or being in between jobs can cause a high level of stress. Some get very stressed in traffic. Furthermore, some common symptoms of stress are being anxious or trembling for some reason. Some find solution in pacing, others may show mood swings. Sometimes people may sweat when or have an increase in appetite when in high stress. The main target here is to find solution to manage the level of stress.

Managing stressful events can have its disadvantages. The following information are some example of some coping stress management strategies to deal with stressful events that maybe detrimental. For some, smoking cigarettes on a daily basis can reduce stress but this can cause cancer or event damage one's health. Others may eat too much when under pressure. This can cause one to gain weight. Not realizing that we have eaten too much can damage our body structure. After becoming fat, thinking about dieting for certain period of time can put one at an emotional imbalance. One other method of removing stress from our life is to drink alcohol frequently. This can lead to serious problems. Furthermore, many tend to isolate from the reality removing oneself from peers, family members or even friends. One should always be responsible when drinking alcohol. Drinking could lead to severe accidents when driving.

Some side effects can occur while living in a stressful environment. People may not realized that stress manifest itself in physical symptoms such as headaches, and not sleeping well. One may perform poorly at work, school or even at home. Not being able to concentrate properly when doing an activity or a regular task is another physical symptom. When living with a partner or even with family members, one may have a short temper. One may feel that he or she needs to argue to accomplish what one wants.

This can make one miserable and cause conflicts with one's partner. Not understanding a stressful moment can cause damage within ourselves. Recognising what causes and what triggers our stress can help us cope better and reduce the stress's side effects. We all have problems; what is important is to find solutions to deal and face our problems.

One may ask how we can manage our stress to benefit our health. The following information will reveal some healthy ways to manage our own stress. When we are stressed out one way of leaving our stress is to go for a walk. Either 15 to 30 minutes of walking can lower the stress that we feel. Some other people use different methods. For example, some write in a daily journal to reduce stress. Many people listen to music or even watch TV comedy when stressed. One can be stressed when one is alone; therefore calling a friend can help reduce the stress. Discussing with a friend or loved one in a proper conversation can help one stomach stress. It is important to find a way to feel relax and overcome stressful period. Doing Yoga or Chi Kung can be an alternative solution to relax the mind and the body by removing all the tension, and anxiety.

For every action there is a reaction, for every problem a solution. What matters is having the right answer by having a strategy for realising and coping with stress management. When your emotion takes over your body and you have no idea what to do is important to stay calm and taking deep breaths. If this does not work, count for every time you breathe by taking deep breaths for a few minutes and you will feel good and relieved. Find something that will distract your mind when you feel stressed out. Most of the time, your mind may be invaded with negative thoughts that need to be replaced with positive ones. Remember, our mind tends to keep mostly negatives thoughts in our memory, hence doing something positive will take over the bad and unpleasant thoughts.

Many of us are addicted to coffee or tea. It is necessary to avoid drinking coffee while being stressed out or being in a stressful environment. This will increase your mental state by being more tense. Therefore, instead of drinking coffee one should find other things that help one feel better. Drinking water can be a solution. For some, meditating is a coping strategy. The more you are with negative people, the more your mind will keep negative information. As a result, you may be brainwashed negatively and you may not be able leave a stressful situation. For that reason, it will increase your level of stress. When being surrounded with unhelpful people, you will not know what to do or how to behave coworkers, friends, acquaintance can make you feel tense, worried or not able to think rationally. Finding a proper space, environment or somewhere where you will feel comfortable can change your daily life. Some stress symptom can also be identified as physical, emotional, mental, relational and spiritual.

Being under pressure can lead to various symptoms physically. The following information will describe the physical symptoms that one can undergo. Some examples are feeling fatigue. One may feel tired and may not perform well when doing something. For a smoker, one may increase smoking without realising it. Occasionally, one may have muscle tension, or muscle pain. Moreover, one can go through insomnia, not being able to sleep enough could lead one to feel more weak. Other symptoms could be identified by shortness of breath, this occurs especially during a long walk or while running. When being out of breath, one will feel that one should decrease smoking. This can lead to more coughing. When coughing, one may feel chest pain and discomfort. This may also be a sign of beginning of illness. Slowly with time, this can augment to more symptoms. Not feeling well physically could lead to emotional illness.

Stress is a major factor emotionally; it could lead to anxiety. One can become easily frustrated and not be able to control his or her temper. Not being able to control his or her temper can lead to arguments with partners or loved ones. When arguing with someone one may feel that no one give attention or even cares for that person. Slowly, this will worsen with depression. When depressed one will have decreased self-esteem. Many more symptoms may appear when depressed. Having low self-esteem can cause one to have poor self-confidence and not be happy with oneself. One may not be able to justify an action when having poor self-confidence. Being emotionally imbalanced can bring mental imbalances.

When under stress one may not perform well mentally. This could lead to one not doing well at work, where one is capable of dealing with regular tasks can put one in danger of losing his or her job. Furthermore, one may feel bored with repeating and completing the same task over and over. This is a sign that someone needs new ideas to better function. Not being able to focus or do certain things or tasks is another effect of having poor concentration. This can make one doubt oneself.

When having arguments or misunderstanding one may not be forgetful. Not believing in forgetting and forgiving can break up a relationship. Not being able to create new friends or having poor relationship skills can affect one's in daily life. When having high stress one can isolate oneself not face reality. In this case, one will be lonely if one choose to isolate oneself. One may feel defensive with people's reaction to the isolation. Others, may feel envious of seeing someone doing well or seeing one in a better position. Jealousy can break relationships and create conflicts among friends or couples. This could lead people to mistrust you. When being in a relationship that lacks intimacy, one may have lowered sexual drive. This could break up a relationship.

When everything seems to go wrong in our life or within ourselves, one may believe less spiritually. Not having faith or not believing spiritually can have an impact yourself and your relationships. Having doubt of his or her religion can bring a trigger within a family or loved one. It is like not loving his or her mate and not sharing what the opposite believe in. When things go wrong we mostly become unforgiving. We may wonder why we should believe in a god that punishes people for no reason. We can be punished by our loved ones. Even when we have done everything according to the letter by believing until then, it is difficult to cope with the surrounding and the loved one. We are left then wait for a miracle, for something good to happen or the beginning of a change in one's life.

Swimming

Swimming was excellent during the summer. I used to go swimming for an hour at the swimming pool of the hospital. The nurse would always encourage all the patients to swim. It was one way of exercising and connecting the mind and body. It was a good workout to burn calories and put my heart rate higher. My endurance was terrible: I would swim for only a short period of time and would have to stop in the middle of the pool. Luckily, there were life guards, I would wonder what would happened if I drowned. Some patients were meant to be swimmers, and they would swim like a fish. They were fast and could swim like professionals. I think swimming can help those with mental health issues by first improving their physical health. It was one way of forgetting and forgiving ourselves for being ill.

Hiking

Hiking was exceptional for my health. It made me feel good. We did it once every week, with a nurse or educator. Often we would go to the mountain in Montreal. We would walk for an hour before returning to the hospital. The best part about hiking was that we could walk and stop whenever we wanted and we could discussed topics throughout the hike. One advantage of hiking was to release and relief stress. It made the body and mind work together. When doing hiking one needed to be motivated and passionate, otherwise it is a waste of time. One thing that brings dedication to hiking is the chance to explore the beautiful nature. Being in a group helps to build bonds between patients, educators and nurses. Some would even become good friends. It was also one way of staying far from pollution. Surrounded by nature, we were able to breathe pure air.

Self-Esteem

Self-esteem is how you see yourself. How you see yourself affects your performance: if you perceive yourself positively, you would do positive things. If you had to judge yourself as "honest or dishonest", "winner or a loser", "credible or unpredictable", how would you rate yourself? Basically this means that you have doubt about your self-esteem. It could be that you are about to lose control of yourself. Your mood or temper could lead you to have lower your self-esteem. In time, this can damage you, and lead you to perform poorly when working, or in a relationship, or lead to financial difficulties and slowly tears you apart. It is astonishing how one can start healthy but slowly with time, one's changing can lower one's self-esteem. The environment has lead you to lose faith and make you struggle with self-esteem.

It is difficult to evaluate one's success, let alone one's self-esteem. Therefore, you compare your achievements with materialistic things such as gold, diamond, silver, bronze or even anything on which you can put a value. However, one cannot estimate self-esteem on a scale. It is easy for people to judge someone by looking at their valuables. For example, buying a luxury car would increase his or her self-esteem for a certain period, but the situation may change when one cannot continue paying his or her car. Therefore, one's morale is no longer the same. It can hit the ego and ruin the self-esteem. The self-esteem can also be extremely high for people who can manage their life successfully. Even if they are struggling, they would be able to cope with delicate subjects or even complex situations.

Based on studies, it is recommended not to rate others when having a low self-esteem or even high self-esteem. Subconsciously, one can be hurt and the mood may bias oneself to see certain things negatively. It is believed that most of people keep mostly in mind most of the negative events in their lives. Because humans have a consciousness, they can keep track of positive events in their lives. Hence, regardless of the negative or positive thoughts, one should accept oneself by adjusting with the environment and the surrounding. One should monitor how one behave, and maintain a certain state of mind. Based on your state you may become more vulnerable with the circumstances and may be more sensitive towards people's comments, praises or insults. When monitoring your self-esteem, you can understand the concept of self-acceptance. Both self-acceptance and self-esteem can balance and juggle the negative and positive moods, behaviours, attitudes and beliefs. It is a matter of time and acceptance when dealing with self-esteem.

How can we build our self-esteem? It is important to be optimistic and show some sort of positivity when asking for something, or when making decisions and to always look for the best by challenging one's consciousness. Often when being positive by saying that you are a good person, you are gaining self-respect and other value you for who you are. When expressing your idea with someone, you will gain admiration regardless of your status and beliefs. It is a matter how you portray your thoughts and beliefs towards others. If you can make and build a positive situation one may perform positively and share his or her successes with you. Be sympathetic, calm, and affectionate with yourself. You will be able to love yourself and love others by rejoicing in your growing knowledge. You should accept comments, and compliments based on your past performance and expect more for the future. Be yourself and accept yourself and you will have a balanced self-esteem.

Kitchen

Cooking and being in the kitchen has been a total ordeal for me. I was forced to cook in my second and third year of University. I had no choice if I wanted to survive. I would eat at the cafeteria or restaurants as I was too lazy to cook for myself. When I did attempt to cook, I had to call my mother each time I went near the stove. Being a chef is not easy, preparing for breakfast, lunch or even supper can be hectic. I do not have the patience to cook. Hence, I admire those who are chefs and can cook really well. I think that they are the best chemists. The preparation, timing, mixing and tasting make food so good and delicious. Being at the Day Hospital, patients must go through a cooking process. It is considered part of mental health:

each of us contributed to prepare meals once a week. However, learning to prepare meals for ourselves can be difficult for some especially for myself.

It is amazing how some patients are talented in cooking. One would be astonished to see patients and nurse preparing, planning and cooking foods. The nurses took the time to plan what we will prepare and for everyone at the Day Hospital. The talents are exceptional; if an investor ever comes to the Day Hospital, he or she would offer to open up a restaurant after trying the food there. Now you may have an idea how patients are creative and passionate to be in the kitchen and cooking for themselves as well as others. Most of the patients know how to prepare foods. I would feel for not being able to cook. Therefore I used to do the cutting part. Mostly I would cut the vegetables and prepare salad. I had to contribute my time, hence cutting became by specialty.

Art Workshop

What I liked about the Day Hospital is that you may not realize how talented you are until you participate in activities. Art Workshop is another subject to deal with mental health. People would go to the art workshop to learn and discover their capacity for doing something. It was the patient's hidden talent that was used to build something or to create an object from ground zero. The person leading the workshop was a retired engineer with expertise in carpentry among other skills. He was extremely gentle and kind like the nurses, educators, staff and doctors at the Day Hospital. My project was to build a wooden treasure box: I had to plan how I would create my treasure box, I had to draw a blueprint and brainstorm about how I would put my secret documents and materials when creating the treasure box. I planned on creating a secret compartment. At the beginning I thought I did not had enough talents, they were polished with the help of the retired engineer.

Health Information

The director of the Day Hospital would have a health information session for one hour weekly with the patients. He was extremely knowledgeable and a brilliant psychiatrist. You could ask anything and he would have an answer to it. Most of the time, health information was based on various questions that the patients from the Day Hospital would have. Depending on the session, he would explain to help us understand the symptom and the terminology. The topic could start from diabetes and would end with psychosis. The majority of the time, the topic did not have to surround mental health issues but could focus on every aspect of life and symptoms. Sometimes he would explain certain medications and their side effects. It was fascinating how bright the patients were too.

Cognitive skills

The cognitive skills group, I learned how to grasp information using my own knowledge and personal experience. It was a way for me to understand how the learning process works and how to send or receive information on a daily basis. Sharing information daily by speaking or thinking made me better understand certain situations. I was able to develop connections by practicing with others. Being stressed impaired my cognition. Therefore, I was less able to function. With the cognitive group, I was able to better manage stress and became much healthier. A few tricks that one can use when having cognition problems, playing brain games, meditating, exercising daily, eating healthy foods; reading anything that interest you, (e.g. news papers, articles, novels and knowledge books). Reading could help one to express what he or she learned with others. There are many cognitive abilities that can be improved upon such as memory, attention, perception and being able to use the language properly. Each individual use cognition differently, one may have cognitive skills in one aspect, whereas others may be skilled in other aspects. It varies from one person to another. A healthy person is capable to function properly without having any problems.

When using memory, one may be able to retain information better. When using short term or long term memory, one can better recall certain things. Playing games that challenge and stimulate the brain to be more efficient. Attention is also one skill that can be improved upon. Being able to concentrate on a particular object or situation allows one to focus. Therefore, if one is asked a question, one would be able to answer without hesitation. Perception is keeping tracks of the five senses, such as taste, smell, touch, hearing and seeing. If one is asked if this a rectangular, one would be able to respond quickly without any doubt. Language can also be essential when discussing about a certain condition by helping us understand others and to translate what one had mentioned or simply explain in another language. Being able to phrase correctly can be a sign of being healthy.

Brain Health

When assisting the Brain Health group, I learned how to understand what we go through when we have difficulty with our daily routine. The main focus was based on cognition. We often forget about our health and specially in regards to proper sleep and maintaining a level of physical activity. Being able to think properly is necessary, and maintaining information is significant. If we cannot focus, it would impair our memory. Having trouble remembering can be devastating. One reason why one may not be able to focus from not enough or too much sleep. It is important to find the reason why one has problems sleeping. Once we find out the reason then we can start working on improving sleep by setting goals. I will recommend a few examples of how to better sleep. When one exercises, it makes the body work and stimulates the mind. Furthermore, having a routine can facilitate our mind and help it function accordingly. When our body and mind cooperate, everything becomes easy. We would better function. Also reducing caffeine such as drinking coffee at night can help one sleep better.

To better function, it is essential to find what is best for our mind and body. Being in an environment where there is a lot of distraction can be difficult for a person to think or focus. The person may need to be in a quiet place to be able to better grasp information. Other people may perform well in a noisy place. Our brain is transparent to all and works differently for different people. What may be good for you may not work for me. When one cannot concentrate when reading or doing something, he or she has to find an alternative solution. One solution can be practicing reading or writing. If certain place seems to bring inappropriate behaviour one should change place or environment. Being in a safe place or a place where we are comfortable can improve our mood and make our thoughts more rational.

Having a strong goal can be a step in the hospital. Therefore, diversifying the work load or routine can make someone more stable. When unorganized, one can get lost in one's own world. Doing various activities and working can motivate a person to better function mentally. However, if you have tried your best and you were not capable to better performing then you need to trace the causes. Hence, when feeling monotonous, one should work on a project or even keep busy by participating in various activities. Basically, one should ask oneself what I need to do or even what I want to do, what my goal is and what will I benefit from participating in something or with someone. Asking question to ourselves can motivate our intention or influence us to do more.

To keep our brain healthier one should solve as many mental puzzles or games as possible. Solving mental puzzles such as crossword or Sudoku can be stimulating for the brain. Playing strategic games like chess can boost the cognition. We can gain this all having fun and feeling peaceful within ourselves. For some people, listening to music like classical music or even nature sounds can be beneficial for the health. Walking or jogging are good for the body and brain. It is also good for our cardiovascular health. When the body is healthier, our brain is better. At the end of the day, we will feel better and our mood will improve. When our physical body improves, so does our creativity and thinking process.

WRAP

WRAP stands for Wellness Recovery Action Plan. Sometimes, it can feel that even when you do your best, the opposite always happens. Instead of feeling better, you end up feeling worse. Luckily, you have some control over your health and yourself, therefore you are able to take action based on your situation. If you want to avoid crises, you must act immediately. How can we know when we are feeling bad? In this context, one should make a list of all the negative signs that make one feel bad. Depending on the person, the answers may vary. It is important to be true to oneself and take action seriously. After all, it is up to you to budget your health and how you intend to recover. Knowing why you feel worse can prevent you from feeling bad and help you take control of your situation.

One way of knowing why you feel bad instead of feeling good is to find your weakness and strength. One can list all the signs why one feels bad. Knowing your own triggers and finding your own solution can help. For example, you are feeling not well and you want to know why. You might feel paranoid and you have no control about yourself. In this context you need to write down why you feel bad and what triggered your inappropriate behaviour. When paranoid, one can become deranged; therefore writing it down can help one realize that the paranoia is only an internal effect within yourself. Another example could be having suicidal thoughts. In that case, it is really important for you to seek help and if you feel uncomfortable discussing your concern with others, then you must write down why you feel that way.

Listing all of your sorrows and the situations in which you feel blue can help you find an answer to your own question. I call this the wellness list box. What you write in this list box depends your symptoms. You may write that you feel lonely, or that you do not feel well, or that you consider harming yourself, slowly staying far from the outside world, or that you sleep more than usual, or figuring out if you can avoid using unwanted substances or even alcohol. In the list box you write about yourself and what are the most important things about you. Being able to see your own list can get you to ask questions about yourself. This could prevent future crises. Furthermore, one can then create a plan. If you trust someone, you can share your list box with that person and get some feedback. Remember, the more you get support, the better you may be at the end of your journey.

When using the list box one can also make a list of your plan and action. For example, you can write the following: I am happy. I am sociable. I like to make people smile. People give good feedback about me. At work I am very productive. My family feels loved and secure. The list can be used when things just do not go the way you plan and you need help. One can feel anxiety, being angry, being paranoid, having low self-esteem, not being yourself anymore. At least what is important is that you are able to figure the negative and positive signs. The major plan here is to help you find an answer when you do not feel good about yourself by finding a solution. Another alternative objective can be to write about your specific needs, such call your doctor, call someone who can help you, take some counselling sessions, use breathing methods to better relax, and find someone who can stay by you when you do not feel at your best.

What can really help when dealing with strange conditions? People handle each situation differently and by seeking help when needed. Based on the type of help from supporters, one can respond accordingly. There are various solution; one of them is to create a list box. Other solutions can depend on your surroundings. When people encourage you, reassure you, let you rest, do not create triggers, keep you from stressful places or from being hurt it can help you feel better. Doing physical activities can improve the mood and morals. Doing physical exercise can make one feel better and release tension. It is always better to get some fresh air. Other ways of improve your mood are listening to music, watching movies, and playing games.

Other actions in the list box can include writing a journal, reading an article or a book. Some people get inspired to do research to further their knowledge. Others may simply socialize with friends or acquaintances. Taking the initiative to do something or go somewhere with a friend or loved one can change you and make you feel better. Being active will lead one to be more physically active. Doing regular exercise can help one to feel calm, and feel relaxed, and be in a better shape. When focused one can better concentrate on things including on other people. Being ill can be difficult for many. To overcome illness and feel healthier, one must take control of the body and mind. In having control one will not have mood swings and will sleep better. In the process of treatment, one will need to be very patient and have self-respect.

There are many ways to recover. To overcome from a distress may take a long time. If the loved one does not help the person with mental illness, it could take a long process for healing. Having as much support as possible can speed up the recovery process. It is important to ask for help and to recognize problems by seeking new ideas. When people do not have any idea about an illness, and unfairly stigmatize and label, one should always explain your illness to others. By explaining they can become more educated about the illness. Not telling others could prevent others from being concerned for you for other reasons. However, telling too much can also cause negative feedback. You must give enough information those who understand you. There is no need to talk about your illness to those who do not care. You will be wasting your time. It is good to be honest but do not be too honest about yourself.

Those with Schizophrenia may feel insecure when talking about their illness. Therefore it is essential to be patient with those who are ill and to know that slowly they will heal with time. You must think outside of the box when accepting loved one with illness by helping and supporting them. When your partner needs more attention, it is time to give as much support by being there for that person. They may isolate themselves, but you must change this behavior by telling positive words and showing that you care for that person. One may think that making mistakes is normal for an ill person but making mistakes for a normal person is not appropriate. When being with the ill person, both can create triggers when not understanding or even criticizing one person. Hence, it is necessary to be open with having new ideas. If you can accept those who are ill, you will earn tolerance and respect towards you.

It is fundamental to write a daily wellness list or even write down what you would like to add on your agenda. After all you want to feel better and you want to show others that you are cured. Mostly you want to be cured for yourself and as it is your health, others will support you when they see that you are accomplishing something. If you have plans to do something, you will see that you will feel well and day by day you will feel much better and healthier. Keeping a list short and realistic can be encouraging. It is mandatory to eat at least 3 healthy meals daily. Drink at least 6 to 8 glass of water. Drink less caffeine, anything that has sugar, or even junk food. To be healthy, it is good to exercise for at least 30 minutes and get exposed to sun light at least for a certain period of time. You may feel even better if you spend some time practicing meditation, yoga or even simple relaxation for your body and mind. Avoid unnecessary things and keep taking regularly your medication daily.

Yoga

Yoga is one of the Indian traditional exercises and a method of feeling relaxed. There are various types of Yoga. People actually feel better emotionally and physically after practicing Yoga. It also depends on the Yoga teacher and how they teach you. It is one way of getting stress relief. Yoga took popularity within a few years in Montreal. There are a lot of places where one can perform Yoga at any time. When I first heard about Yoga I thought that it was just another exercise. After trying it, I quickly learned that it was something completely different. I enjoyed it and felt really good after taking it. However, to better practice at home I need some sort of guidance, someone to tell me which movements to do in sequence.

Practicing Yoga helps improve the emotions, body, and mind. Body-wise, it helps one to stretch every single part of the body. Emotionally, it helps stimulate feelings and control one's emotion. On the other hand, the mind is satisfied by being distracted and is relaxed when the body is occupied in movements. People also like to do meditation; it is a way for to increase the concentration. Most of the time when meditating one may feel joy, be peaceful within the self. What makes it interesting is the students are taught by professionals and develop skills to better guide other people on top of themselves. One example is learning how to breathe and using it when having difficulty in life. Being able to breathe properly by using some Yoga technique can benefit a person who is suffering emotionally, physically and mentally. When we feel better, it seems that everything goes the way we want. Our vision of life and finding solutions to a problem become simple.

Yoga does not only help improve the emotional, physical and mental aspects. Its advantages can vary depending of what one is looking for:

1. One will feel much more relaxed in doing various types of movement.
2. One will sleep much better.
3. It releases tension by improving breathing.
4. One will be much more energetic after doing Yoga and will feel more awake.
5. One will be able to balance time and schedule by having discipline.
6. Your immune system will improve after completing Yoga session.
7. One will learn to better trust, judge, guide and take care of oneself.

It's a matter of time and putting enough energy and motivation to have a healthy body and mind.

Chi Kung

It was fun doing Chi Kung at the Day Hospital. I also do it at home now. The more I do, the more I was able to concentrate on and improve upon specific aspects. Those who want to teach require many years of study and hard work. My Chi Kung Guru was an exceptional person with a lot of talents. He made me feel better each time I attended the Chi Kung classes. Each Chi Kung teacher teaches differently in different rhythms. It is an unique exercise. Chi Kung has existed for over 5000 years and it was practiced mostly by the Chinese. A few centuries ago Chi Kung was introduced to the world and now it is well known across Canada. When doing Chi Kung, I perform a lot of movement that keep me energized. I feel that the energy flow within the body. Chi Kung controls the external and internal energy and the force that circulates within ourselves. The great thing about Chi Kung is that anyone can participate at any age in any type of clothing.

Chi Kung has many benefits. The benefits also depend on the person and his or her experience. When doing Chi Kung, one is controlling energy towards the body by making different types of movement. This helps better deal with emotional, mental, and spiritual problems. The more we practice, Chi Kung the easier it is to reduce stress and tension. Furthermore, it could be considered a therapeutic exercise if one practices it daily. The exercise awakens the life force within ourselves. Practicing meditation makes us feel better mentally. We feel peace of mind by practicing the Chinese exercise. If one can breathe correctly, one will feel much better. Being able to breathe correctly is necessary and makes us much healthier. This type of exercise could bring a person to heal mentally, emotionally and physically.

Cognitive Behavior Therapy (CBT)

Cognitive Behavior Therapy is usually used with patients that have addiction, anxiety, depression, and phobias. When people suffer from a wide range of disorders, the therapy is used to improve one's daily functions. In CBT, one needs to analyze his or her feelings, behaviors, and thoughts. It is difficult to analyze ourselves; therefore having a professional can make one feel comfortable. Even though it is difficult, self-analyzing can be beneficial. Moreover, being able to analyze ourselves can be a great way to see our problems and learn how our thoughts and feelings work from internal to external behaviors. It is recommended to go through CBT when there are signs of mental disorders. The person can learn how to cope and develop skills helpful during their treatment or even in the future. For many people, it works by distracting or relaxing the mind. Others may prefer to do role-playing. Depending on the strategies one may use in thinking or behaving in a certain way, one can perform well when dealing with our internal problems within the self and with the external problems with others.

Usually the therapist starts helping patients who have complicated thoughts and unusual behaviors by finding the right beliefs. Sometimes, one may not be able to think properly and merely react. The process may take a long time, there are no timeframes in this therapy. Emotionally they may feel too overwhelmed can have a different reaction to certain situations. One way for the patient to cope is to realize when they have any disturbances in their thoughts. The main focus of CBT is to overcome and take control of the patient's negative thoughts. Some can become too emotional just thinking about a situation. Being able to control a difficult moment can be beneficial for a person who going through a tumultuous event. Being able to identify thoughts, emotion and behavior can be a sign of healing.

The main goal of CBT is to find what is necessary for each individual to find the right answer. One way to fight against the symptom is to find the stressors or triggers of the symptoms. One may use medication for healing purpose or simply to cure oneself completely. Others may medicate to prevent a relapse in serious illness. Being able to learn and cope using various techniques can motivate one to better function. One will be able to manage emotions by trying to balance anger in a stressful situation. Knowing how to communicate can help one better resolve conflict between couples. Identifying what causes physical symptoms such as fatigue, pain or even insomnia can later improve those symptoms. Being able to cope may help one to better handle a difficult moment. One may not have the patience when facing a difficult situation. Therefore the individual may have to stay calm by facing the emotional challenges head-on.

Interpersonal relationship

Interpersonal relationships are all about bonding among people be it if one is heterosexual, homosexual, or bisexual. Regardless of sex, gender, race, age and ethnic group, if you have had a relationship with another you have built some sort of interpersonal relationship. Interpersonal relationships one could include the relationship between colleagues, lovers, friends, or family. How one builds a relationship with peers and partners determine how one can keep the bond together. At the Day Hospital, some patients stay at the hospital for a long time because of their illness. They create an understanding with other patients by exchanging emails or phone numbers. This builds a bond between acquaintances to become friends.

For most people, being mentally ill can make one lose contact from the reality and cause one to slowly withdraw from friends. Therefore one may choose to keep very limited friends. The majority of the gifted patients are very sensitive and cannot take criticism or blame. When any of these happened, one becomes extremely in pain and tearful. To feel comfortable with the relationship one must be soft and share common goals, values and objectives. Many may agree that it is preferable to meet someone who share the same interest and think approximately the same way. One must feel trusted to be respected by sharing their point of views, laughter and sorrow. Without having an honest and clear relationship one will not be able to have a successful interpersonal relationship.

A relationship with someone needs to have trust, care, understanding and loyalty to build an interpersonal bond. If there is no affection, trust and care in a pair, there is no bonding between them. There will be something missing in their relationship. If there is no trust, between "friends", there will be no friendship. One who insults, criticises or spreads rumors about others does not want to create a healthy relationship with other peers and friends. In this context, the person could be considered toxic in their relationship. On the other hand, between a couple or lovers if there no love, attachment, and trust, the relationship will not last long. If one is truly in love with his or her partner, if both have faith, care, and desire for each other, they will be able to build an interpersonal bond with each other.

Wellness Program

When I was part of the Wellness Program, I was able to lose some weight appropriate to my height. This program was designed for those in the mental health centre. In the beginning, we were a group of 12 people supervised by nurses, occupational therapist, educators and nutritionists. The purpose of this program was to make us understand what is good and bad for our health. How can one learn from psycho-educational services, such as practical sessions, how to prepare meals, to go to the grocery and exercises? We covered almost everything from exercising, walking, doing activities, cooking, getting information on our health, nutrition, taking our pulse and keeping track of our cardiovascular health regularly. This program really helped me by increasing my knowledge on health. It was twice weekly. In the beginning, we would go outside and walk near the mountain in Montreal. We would walk for almost two hours in the fall. It was amusing walking with patients and health professionals. When walking, everyone would pair up with another person. Even though, we were a large group, the walks felt intimate and private.

We were 12 at first, then 8, then 6. It was amazing to hear about how people think of their illness and the sacrifices one has make to have discipline and autonomy for themselves. One has to adapt to a new environment and open up to others. It is fascinating how we all forget that it is necessary to walk at least 30 minutes to 1 hour daily. Some may not walk or do any exercises; for me it was like being in high school or even college again. Participating with a group of people doing physical exercises motivated me to do more. Feeling tiredness and having sweat on my forehead made me feel like 10 years younger. After becoming schizophrenic, it seems to me that I have forgotten how to have fun and enjoy my daily life.

My life was boring, and I needed to have some sort of challenge in my life and some stimulation from someone or something. Even though that I was married for 3 years it seems that I was not fully happy. My partner often mentioned that she was not happy in our marital life. This affected me negatively. She needed to have brain stimulation where she would be satisfied with our marriage. For me it was difficult as I was on sick leave for a certain period of time taking care of my health. I do not want to blame her as I myself was not 100% strong, motivated and functional. One thing is for sure I did not receive enough support, respect, and love. Because of that, I have not given enough value, respect and love. It seemed that both of us were not meant for each other. The Wellness Program helped me overcome my sorrow and develop strength. Walking made me feel good, so I would invite my wife to go outside and walk with me. Both of us spent some time outside during my time of trials. Having a proper conversation was necessary to keep our marriage safe. This lasted for a while but it seems that my illness was contagious and she needed a break. She needed to stay away from me.

My goal was to change by being more productive at work and home. Being a loving husband and a caring father were not just goals but a responsibility. Keeping track of activities by having my wife participate with me was another goal. I also wanted to build and develop an exceptional and meaningful relationship with my peers, professionals, parents, sister and mostly my wife. It was important for me to better manage my situation when people criticize and blame me for something. I was motivated to overcome my fears and trouble. My goal was not only to better manage my disorder by reducing my symptoms, but to convince my wife of our marital strengths and of our talent. By sharing my dreams and creativity to my wife I would feel and live a healthy lifestyle. The more time passed, the more I realized that we do not share common goals. To get something requires patience and discipline, and there can be none if there is no common goal. One can dream and fantasize about something even though one knows it would not be possible to achieving it.

Keeping track of our health could mean being healthier. Knowing what food to eat is not a simple task. When walking on the street, I am amazed how many restaurants there are in Montreal. Eating well could have many meaning depending what one's taste. One may enjoy eating something others dislike. A food may smell awful to one while another will be stunned by the aroma. There are no such things as 'bad' or 'good' food as most of the foods, recipes, ingredients come from outside of Canada. It is a multicultural city with variety of foods, beverages and drinks. One cannot criticize food just because he or she did not like it. Everybody has their own tastes and believes. However, it is important to balance what one eats, tastes and drinks.

Regardless of what we eat there are some foods that are forbidden to eat, especially for those who are on diets. It is recommended to eat healthy foods not fast foods. Even though fast foods seem to be tastier, it is always better to eat what is good for one's health. When one has a choice one should eat accordingly. When one wants to be in good shape he or she should follow a routine and manage a system on daily basis. Not eating enough or not eating 3 to 4 meals daily is also unhealthy. One may not be in position of eating healthy or capable to feed his or her stomach with every meal. In that case, one will live with empty stomach or become less healthy due to lack of nutrition. This happened more and more in Canada, especially among the homeless. It seems that they do not have their regular meals daily due to mental illness and lack of money.

Since we were young, our parents and grandparents have taught us to finish each portion of food regardless how full we feel in our stomach. It is mandatory for one not to waste foods. They would often mention how poor people suffer when not having proper meals daily. Therefore, it could be seen as a sin throwing food away. This happened especially during eating at home or in a restaurant. Sometime we order more than what we can eat. Some may eat according to their hunger but mostly there is a chance that people will waste food in many different occasions. Some were born to waste foods and money regardless of their status, economical situation and wealth.

Most of us like companionships, we like to go to a restaurant to eat together or even invite a friend to have lunch or dinner at home. Sometime it is important for one to be kind toward yourself by treating your friends and yourselves. When one prepares a meal, it must look delicious. You have two choices either you follow the dieters guides or for once you forgive yourself by making something tasty for you and your companionships. For someone dealing with mental illness, it is very uncommon to invite someone over to spend time together. It is believed that those with Schizophrenia like to spend time with their thoughts alone. In the process of healing, one may take a risk by calling an old friend or inviting them over just to be together and have a decent conversation. One realize that one has friends who treat one with kindness and respect.

It is important to balance nutrition. What we eat and drink can improve our fitness. Our body requires energy to function correctly. Therefore, we need to eat until we are full to fulfill our body and to do daily tasks. It is important to balance nutrition by following the Canadian Food Guide. Based on the food guide, each food provides different nutrients that feed our bodies. Having a combination of healthy foods can change our moods and satisfy for life. Having a full stomach gives us energy to pursue various activities. Eating regularly is mandatory; it is also important to drink at least eight glasses of water daily and exercise as much as possible.

Creative Writing

Being able to express yourself about anything that comes from your mind can be fun and exciting. Creative Writing at the Day Hospital was something I enjoyed attending. There were no limits as to how much we could write: we would start with a theme in the beginning by first describing one or many characters. We would create a structure by integrating plots or continuing to write to the end. It was up to us to find ideas with a topic or image. As we did not had enough more than an hour to write, we would spend the time sharing what we have written. It was very entertaining to hear other people's short stories. The main point was to start writing; once we were able to gather information and brainstorm what was on our mind, it became easy to write. There was no competition among each of us, if anyone wanted to share their story by reading out loud it was their choice. My first day in Creative Writing, I wrote a poem on Freedom:

When thinking about freedom,
I like to see the skydom,
It reminds me about my childhood,
Surrounded by brotherhood,
Looking at their faces,
By continuing my paces,
They all looked bright,
I did not want to fight,
Because I saw a cage,
It gave me rage,
I realized I was on the hill,
They were staring at me still,
Later inside of a room,
Did not want to broom,
I found inside of me skydom,
As I search for freedom.

Participating in the creative writing made me feel good. I was able to express myself in writing. It was something that I needed to feel better. It was a moment for me to find myself back after being out of reality. The following week the occupational therapist came up with some images for us to write about ourselves. The first picture was of a little boy sitting on a chair with an ice cream cone in his hand. The boy was sitting outside on a sunny day. From that perspective we had to write something. When I looked at the image, it reminded me of my childhood.

The picture reminded me of myself, of my past. The chair in the backyard reminded me about my feelings. This boy was a reflection of my memory. It felt like it was yesterday and I was sitting outside of my house tasting an ice cream. The face makes me believe that the boy was lonely, as if something happened . . . Something really happened that day I injured my forehead by playing baseball right before sunset.

We were then shown another picture of the rush hour at the subway. It made me think of when I had to go to the hospital with my mother in a taxi because the subway was busy at rush hour. At the hospital, the doctor too busy to take care of me. They only told me to put an icepack on my forehead. I was heartbroken . . . I did not know what to do; I had severe pain in my forehead, and I wanted to see the doctor as soon as possible but I felt impatient. I could not wait until the doctor tells me that it was only a bruise and to not worry about it.

I do not know if I had a concussion or if it damaged my brain. The injury gave me a large bruise on my forehead more than one-inch wide. After being hit by the baseball bat I started crying out loud. I had tears falling from my eyes non-stop. It was terrible. Right after the incident, I was brought to the hospital. I remembered that I suffered for a certain time but do not know if it was the reason for my Schizophrenia. I loved to play sports, to be surrounded by people I would take the lead by creating two teams to play hockey, baseball, soccer, volleyball, badminton, and occasionally cricket. It seemed that sport was in my veins; I loved moving. I quickly learned leadership.

One-on-One Follow Up

One-on-one follow-up can go for a short or long period of time with a nurse, resident or a psychiatrist. One discusses symptoms and medications and their side effects, to see if a new medication is helping or making things worse. In most cases, the residents were the primary care taker of my health. Finding the right doses with the right medication for the right time would benefit me for a certain period of time. It was useful for us to experiment because they did not know what medication can stop hallucinations or delusions. The psychiatrists were also there to make sure that everyone getting better day by day. Time to time I would meet with the main psychiatrist as well. He would make sure that I would function well based on his recommendations. The follow-up would be based on my personal experiences and my surrounding: how I behave with my peers, other patients, and my family, and also how the medications are keeping me stable and focused. Sometimes during the follow-up, I would not be able to pay attention on the sessions with the medical staff. When discussing about an issue I would tell my part, but when they start talking I would not be able to focus. It seems that the time became very slow, each second was moving in a speed where I could fall asleep.

Have you noticed that when we have a problem, other problems would occur at the same time. It's like slowly picking up books one by one until suddenly you realize how tired have become just by holding books. Personal sorrow adds gradually like the weight of the books. When one is not healthy, it seems that the surrounding seems to be not healthy. It is what I perceive when I feel down. If the surrounding do not respond well with an ill person, then the ill person will not respond well to the surrounding. For every action there is a reaction. Later I could not concentrate on something for too long because of this perception.

Some may be able to hide their reaction while others may expose them. Usually, when looking at me, one would be able to tell if I am feeling blue or joyful. A nurse or resident would ask me what happened if I had a good weekend or if something occurred that I would like to discuss. My facial expression would tell everything, and there is no way for me to repress it. I could not be able to hide it. It was too evident with my illness. Sometimes, I would feel like to put make up just to cover my facial appearance. For once, I would look like another person outside but truly I would know how I felt inside. When people camouflage their face, they do it for good reasons: either to not get attention from the outside world or simply because they do not want to face the truth. I feel like I do not laugh enough and this bothered others. I feel that I should put an artificial smile on my face so people would notice that I often smile instead of being sad.

When dealing with mental illness one has to be able to face criticism, critics, stigma, and gossip. In my case, I was not able to handle any of it. For many years I went through depression, followed by bouts of psychoses, then later the schizophrenia diagnosis. It was very heavy for my mental states. Not being able to cope with reality was not easy. I needed a strong back up, such as my mother, sister and father to support me to the fullest. With their support I was able to control by illness for a short period of time, during which I was taking daily medications and supervised by my family doctor and a social worker. I was able to work 40 hours weekly and I would even often agree to do overtime to please my managers. With marriage, I thought that everything would go away and I will feel like a new born baby. I thought that finding the right woman in my life would bring less tension, less stress, and less triggers to my illness. But my understanding about marriage was wrong, my belief unacceptable. My disorder and marriage did not go together, like two attractive forces that at first seemed harmonious, until one force overtakes the others.

I would spend a lot of time with the nurse, social worker or even the resident psychiatrist telling them my story of the time since I got married. Many unusual triggers would happen, and I was often stressed about them. I did not have all the answers, and I did not know what to do. My thoughts about life and love have changed and my behaviours have change in return. Even though I was not aggressive, I would shout and scream occasionally. Looking back now, I realize that I was a very kind and generous person who is agreeable with everyone and everything. But for some reason I had negative feelings and felt as if I was receiving severe negative shocks from others. When ill for too long, others may take advantage of us knowing that we are not capable of making the right decision. There is no easy solution to schizophrenia. If the partner does not accept the one with schizophrenia, then there is no chance of continuing the married life. By not accepting it, it's like saying it was nice knowing you but now I have made my mind to leave you.

At Day Hospital, we are often taught to control our self-esteem. It feels that when I reached the peak of building my self-esteem, I would take an arrow to the heart from my loved one. It took me weeks after weeks to control my mood and beliefs to boost my self-esteem, therefore losing it disappointed me. The nurses spent many hours explaining how we can reach the top peak to better control ourselves without judgment, by letting the judgment go from one ear to the other. It was important for me to take control of my life and myself by not letting others walk over my body and my soul. It seems that for three years I would built myself but every three to four weeks, serious arguments with the my loved one would insult my character and bring me down again. This continued over and over across various topics and situations. It seems that the devil enjoyed hearing two fools scream, insult, and charge at each other. How disgusting can one feel when deranged?

We would have many group discussions about our lives as all the patients were going through a complicated moment. He or she who would share something and would get feedback from other patients. We would sit and face each other. It was an open discussion where the patients could comment on your situation to find a solution. In the end, the nurses would have the final say. It was motivating and helpful to deal with various scenarios and solution and to hear comments from other patients whose views are completely different from yours. Hearing advice would make me feel tremendously good. It made me feel that we were again at school debating topics. The best part was that the patients varied from all ages.

Sometimes patients were very straightforward to each other to the point where some patients would cry. Being critical could be very hard on someone and others may prefer to have a different types of answers. In my perspective, it was a good exercise as it helped to prepare us all for the outside world. When we become repressed, it seems that we fall in a trap being inside of a box. Therefore, it is essential to find solutions to answers and to think outside of the box. The more rational our thoughts, the better we feel about ourselves. We are able to resolve complex problems better when our mind works better. Being outside of the box makes us believe that we are capable in doing something for us and we are appreciated by our surrounding.

Once reinforced, our mind makes a connection with the body, and one can connect the two and feel more healthy. The more we let go of our anger, frustration, and disappointment, the better we feel at the end of the day. Many believe that the more we think positively, the better the chances of positive things occurring. It is like a self-fulfilling prophecy. An example of this is when one decides that 'today it is a bad day, therefore the whole day will be bad'. On the other hand, the more we smile the more we feel that people smile at on us. With other patients, it seems that we are not alone in this world, they are people like us who think either inside of the box or outside of the box. Making good connections with patients could make us feel better by helping us realize that it is possible to feel what others feel as well. After all discussions, the most important thing is that we all value and respect each other. Hence, being as caring as possible about others feelings could make patients feel relax and secure.

When I see how the medical professionals are doing everything to help me build my future and erase my past sorrows. I realize how important it is to not hurt others. We all make mistakes and each of us learn from our mistakes. It is not our fault that we had to deal with mental illness. This illness has changed my life completely, it has change my lifestyle, my mentality and point of view of other people. It is very hard for me to trust people when I have known for many years. As I am too emotional, therefore I cannot handle their criticism or unwanted words. Many people have their own opinions about me and sometime I wonder if I should follow their way or keep to my own.

What motivates me to have one-on-one follow-up was that I was able to express anything that would come from my heart, and mind. I knew that there was someone who was listening to what I had to say and, I was not afraid of telling them. I felt that even if I would say nonsense, the nurses, or resident psychiatrists would encourage me to say something else or to tell them about my overwhelming feelings. I have the utmost respect for them even though that it is their duty and it is part of healing. They were trained so that they would be able to change the topic without anyone noticing it. For one to do this one to with extreme precision, one would need to be a good observer and listener.

Discharge

Being discharged can be good news for one and bad for another. It happens when a patient recovers from being ill. Being discharged simply means one does not have to attend the Day Hospital. He or she may still be followed by the psychiatrist. One will return to his or her regular routine either back at work, school, or home. There is a waiting list for people who need care, attention and affection at the Day Hospital. Therefore, one cannot stay for too long or get too comfortable at the hospital. The majority of people there end up developing some sort of fear of being discharged. It is a sign that they are not ready to face the outside world. The nurses or practitioners will mention in advance to the patients that they will be discharged within a few weeks or months beforehand so that the patients can mentally prepare themselves.

Every week, the nurse will bring together a group to discuss about the advantages and disadvantages of being discharged. One advantage of being discharged is that you will feel much healthier by being able to find a way to deal and live outside of the hospital. You have spent many weeks or months in the hospital to get better; now you have a choice of doing what you really want to do and succeed in life. It's time for you to look for a new challenge. For a period of time you have felt unwanted, you have had irrational thoughts and you have not been capable of dealing with daily routines. The Day hospital will train you and show that there is hope in the outside world and that you can choose to follow the right path and aim high in life.

In many occasions, many patients start working immediately after being discharged, only to realize that they were not ready to take on their daily lives and to face their bosses or their coworkers. They end up having no choice but to come back to the hospital. Fortunately, the system accommodates this and opens its doors for the ill patients to return. Even though patients would leave with hope and dignity, they might not be ready and would have no choice but to start from ground zero again. Going back to work or even living day-by-day can be very intense for those mentally-challenged. Patients from Day Hospital face various types of stigma, being labelled, feeling inferior, or even feeling insecure when surrounded by other people. Some may feel that they did not implement what they were taught at the Hospital or did not even learn anything at all.

I remember being treated in the hospital when many years ago; I had trouble concentrating, speaking, reasoning, and understanding and my self-esteem was extremely low. I could not function well or even distinguish between right and wrong. When I went to the bank to withdraw money, I had trouble signing the receipts. It seems that the body leads the way whereas, the mind stays silent. When the mind is in disarray, the body will signals to function properly. If the mind gets "lazy", the body will get "lazy" as well. What I mean by lazy is that the inability to function and distinguish between what's real and what is not.

It is really hard to tell if someone suffers from a severe mental illness. Sometimes, our facial expressions tell others that we are fine. Other times, we can conclude that someone seem extremely sad due to some internal or external factors. Not knowing the internal factors could lead to more illness and could delay recovery. Therefore, the nurses, would have to look as deep as possible to find the real reason behind the sickness. In my experience, the majority of patients will mention only a few things about their symptoms. and would not able to express what they through and not reveal truthfully how they live. We must understand that it is not appropriate to talk about our fantasies or certain thoughts we may have. Sometimes, it is acceptable to say something, other times keeping silence is golden.

On the other hand, external factors could create excessive stress in our lives. People do not know when someone is going through a severe illness. Therefore, we react with an individual as if they are "normal". However, making a simple comment could devastate the mentally ill person, while, to normal people, the comment can be brushed aside. Those who know of our disorder need to consider with uncanny precision before saying or doing to us. External factors make a difference and shape our behavior and thoughts. The more we feel secure, the more we are able to bond with friends and the outside world. It is a sensitive situation. Not everybody can think our way, and not everybody will consider our illness. Most importantly, not everybody will wish to help us.

People react a certain way when they know we became mentally challenged regardless of our genetic background and health issues. Schizophrenia can be seen negatively within a community. Some culture may blame the victim for having a mental disorder. In my culture those with this illness will be stigmatised and labelled as insane. It is not acceptable to be mentally challenged. The culture and community do not support those with a mental illness unlike other types of illness. People just seem to not understand that we suffer from that illness and therefore they should not gossip about it or insult us. It seems that they do it purposely in front of the ill person to make it clear that it is our fault for becoming ill and for struggling with this disorder. Regardless you have done everything correctly to heal, there will be someone with a big mouth with unwanted words to purposely hurt our feelings.

Take a look outside, do you see the sky as blue and clouds white? Do both things stay continuously white and blue or does they change with time, especially during sunrise and sunset? One should be able to see various colors doing these period of time. People may see each "color" or symptom in a different light. The illness could be seen differently from different points of view. In the health care facility such as the hospital, people are used to diseases, disorders and symptoms. Consequently, they will not act surprised by them because they understand the diseases, disorders, and symptoms. When you do not understand a symptom or illness, you make the assumption that a mentally challenged person cannot cope with reality, and therefore is insane. What about someone with Metabolic Syndromes, or even other types of diseases? Do you label, stigmatize or reject their illness? Whether or not we are accepted depends on others' understanding of our condition.

In the Day Hospital, I had the privilege of participating in various types of educational learning based on a guideline for mentally ill patients. Many patients had severe illness and they were followed-up every 3 months to 1 year. It was intense; the program ran from 9:30 am to 2:00 pm from Monday to Friday in the Day Hospital. In most cases, many were there due for medication adjustments or for treatments. During the week various nurses, occupational therapists, and educators would teach us how to reintegrate ourselves in society. We would have 15 heavy and intense sessions weekly. There were no exams or assignments. For me it was like registering for a Masters degree in mental health. It helped me see the world differently.

Each of us patients, went through Admission, Weekend Review, Assertiveness, Art Therapy, Community Life, Swimming, Hiking, Brain Health, Self Esteem, Kitchen, Art Workshop, Health Info, Cognitive Skills, WRAP, Yoga, Chi Kung, Cognitive Behavior Therapy, Interpersonal Relationship, Wellness Program, Creative Writing, One on One follow up, Stress Management, Discharge preparation. Having followed these educational session gave me the courage and inspired me work on this book and find what I wanted 10 years ago. Attending the Day Hospital gave me strength, and motivation and I found myself returning from a natural disaster when it seemed that I was surrounded by hurricanes. Now, I have found calm in myself, in my heart, in my mind.

Recovery

There are four steps that need to be fulfilled to fully recover. According to a psychiatric nurse in the Day Hospital, we have to go through hope, healing, empowerment and connection to recover. When going through these steps, we will develop skills and learn new strategies to implement in our lives. Knowing that there is hope can ultimately motivate us to find ourselves to cope with the world. By having hope we will be healed and will continue to feel better. In the process of healing we will be able to feel empowered. When reaching the stage of empowerment, we can easily connect with others and we will have more rational thoughts.

When we feel hopeful, we tend to feel much better from within. When there is hope, we will wish for something or someone. We will become more social, more energetic compared to when one did not feel hope. Most of the time, we will be in good mood. We will realize that we will not feel sad. Hope is the idea that something good is around the corner. When we feel good; we may visit our friends, and family members. We will have a perception change in our minds. More precisely, the perceptions become more positive. Most of the time, we will be look forward to doing something by focusing on strength instead of weakness. Having hope will definitely motivate us in doing various things.

Hope will give you self-esteem, self-confidence, and self-acceptance. By attending the Day Hospital on a daily basis, we can slowly develop hope. Knowing that we can get out from an unwanted situation, bring us half way to recovery. Without hope, there is no reason to get better. With hope, we will see differently and overcome what we have left behind. One of the symptoms of losing hope is to isolate ourselves from the real world. As a result, we will not be able to cope with the reality or think rationally.

It is important to always think and act positively. If there is someone that you care about who is going through an illness, it is really important to support that person and not let him or her down. Having your support can boost their mood and help build their self-esteem, confidence and self-acceptance. With your support they will be able to overcome their illness even if it takes many weeks, months, or even years. Your patience is needed in this situation. When someone is ill they have to be prepared to win the battle to make them stable. To win the battle means to fight against the illness and to always think that we will be better even if it takes time for us to find ourselves. We are battling until we get our strength back and become invincible.

If you feel that you have an illness that needs special attention, take the initiative of doing something about it for yourself. Never blame yourself for having an illness; we are all human and in most of the cases, we will all get ill throughout our lifespan. Some get ill in their childhood, others in adolescence and most during adulthood. It is a matter of fighting against the illness. If you are strong emotionally and physically, even if you may be down or hurt physically, you know will overcome it in time. Keep knowing that as long as you can decide what is good for yourself, you will always have hope. When you reach the right state of mind, you will feel happy. You will be able to do various things. Surviving the moment takes hope, and when you feel hope, it will lead towards healing.

Healing is when you can remember who you were before the illness. When you are in the stage of healing, you will learn your strengths and weaknesses. You can go deeper by asking what really happened or why this happened to yourself. Knowing that we will feel better is a good sign of healing. It helps when people notice that you look good or that your health condition is improving. It seems that you have taken control of yourself. Healing does not happen all in one time; it takes a lot of time and work. You can feel lonely or insecure in the process of healing. In those cases, you should seek people, go outside, enjoy the company of friends, and family, spend time with trusted and loved ones.

It is important to love yourself. If you do not love yourself, how can you love others? In the process of healing you should look in the mirror and say positive things to yourself. Therefore, looking at the mirror appreciating each part of your body and your facial expression will help you build motivation and self-respect. You may even feel better when dressing up for special occasions. When you can take care of yourself and value your rights and beliefs then you will start to realize that other may feel the same way as you do. Slowly you will regain what you have lost from your illness. Now that you believe you have control, you will notice that you can control various situations. When you can fulfill your own needs, then you can realize other people's needs. It may seem impossible, but slowly everything may fall into place. If you give others a chance, others give you a chance too. It is a two-way street. The illness, may make you feel that you have lost many years of life. However, doing your best is a symbol of healing.

Sometimes we can be disappointed of not being able to be the best of ourselves. People may comment on certain things negatively, but it is important not to take it seriously. When sick, one mission we must fulfill is to overcome the illness. You are a soldier and you have to fight your illness until you win the battle. Having the illness can become an obsession, causing you thinking about it constantly. Not know what to do or how to solve it can make you very upset. You should ask many questions to find some answers. You will see that many people are still worse off then you. It is important to be optimistic in the process of healing. It is essential to keep a good judgment of something or someone. When healing, you can go to the next stage of empowerment.

Empowerment is to feel autonomy and courage. Being able to take responsibility or even trust yourself to do something is a sign of being health. Knowing your capacities can remove the boundaries of a challenge. You will feel that you can do anything. Empowerment is being able to act on your own behalf, and having the conviction and courage to face challenges

Connection occurs when you have perfected the three steps of hope, healing and empowerment. Connection is reconnecting with society by resuming social activities. When moving somewhere new, you may be afraid at first when you think that you will be rejected. You should not be shy, however; you have to interact with people and make friends. The more you socialize the better you may feel. You have to face criticism by having a better judgment. You may struggle in the beginning but you will be satisfied in the end with getting both good and bad feedback. You may get some power in a society or within a social group. When you are with positive people, you will get more motivated and feel more reliant to yourself. There is growth for everybody. To better get involved with people and yourself; you can start making a to-do list involving goal-setting, determination, reasons, self-analysis and looking for challenge by overcoming negative-thinking with positive-thinking.

Medication

There are many advantages and disadvantages of taking medication. Using the medication improperly is harmful. With a health problem, you must take medication regularly to better stabilize yourself. Some medication can prolong life whereas other types of drugs can be hazardous. It is important not to confused between medication and illegal drugs. Both have side effects. One may feel fatigue, dry mouth, less energetic and so on depending on the drug. It all depend of a medication taken or even one choosing to take illegal drugs. Some people may have negative reaction to a drug. The body can become dependent to a drug. Although it is best to heal without medication, medicine is sometimes necessary to balance the body and mind despite the many side effects. Some practitioners may start treatment without medication but the patient will be under observation. In my situation, I have tried many different types of medication by involving different doses. It took me many months of observation to better feel with the medication. The following information is based on my medication prescribed along with its advantages and the side effects.

Personally Zyprexa Olanzapine has helped me a lot. Zyprexa Olanzapine is a well know drug to treat Schizophrenia and Bipolar disorder. This drug is listed under antipsychotic/antimanic agents. According to E. Bruce Goldstein, this drug is used for balancing neurotransmitters: the chemicals that link the nerve pathways in the brain (2008, p.35). This drug has many brand names and are available in various forms. Based on the patients' choice, the medication may be taken orally or by injection. The side effects may include not being able to sit still, constipation, dizziness, and drowsiness. It is recommended not to share this medication without a consultant's approval.

Another drug I tried for a few months was Abilify. Abilify is an antipsychotic medication. It works by changing the actions of chemicals in the brain. (2012). It is used to treat psychotic conditions such as schizophrenia and bipolar disorder. Those who are going through major depressive disorder especially in adults are also given this medication.

Abilify has many side effects. They include fever, stiff muscles, confusion, sweating, fast or uneven heartbeats, uncontrollable jerky muscle movements, sudden numbness or weakness, headaches, vision or speech problems, increased thirst or urination, appetite loss, drowsiness, dry skin, occasional nausea and vomiting, thoughts of hurting the self, feeling like passing out, weight gain, anxiety, and insomnia.

I have also used Wellbutrin XL. Wellbutrin XL is usually used for Major Depression. Most individuals think, that depression will go away automatically. Therefore, they do not go to see a Doctor and instead wait until it gets worse. The early and common symptoms of depression are: feeling sad, anxious, or empty, feeling hopeless, worthless, or guilty, feeling restless or irritable, loss of interest or pleasure in usual activities or hobbies, loss of energy, fatigue, difficulties in making decisions or concentrating, difficulties in sleeping, a change in eating habits, weight gain or loss, thoughts of suicide or attempts and long-term aches or pain' (2011). This disease is a common illness that touches most of the population. What are the causes of depression? Depression usually has psychological, biological, environmental, and genetic factors. Biologically, it involves a misbalance of chemicals in the brain. Many could feel depressed after a life-event trigger such as lost of job, family problems, death of a loved one and divorce. This medication will improve functioning and performance. Some patients believe that Wellbutrin XL has a good impact with depression and could help them to heal more quickly.

One of the major problems that couples face, when taking antidepressants is the gradual decrease in sexual desire. According to researchers, 'up to 73% patients on commonly used antidepressants experience side effects' (2011). They have trouble getting aroused, or have difficulty in being sexually satisfied. One might ask what one should do in the case of sexual dysfunction. In that case there's no need to be shy; one should speak to a medical doctor.

Pro Risperidone in another medication I took. Pro Risperidone has different types of side effects such as agitation, anxiety, constipation, difficulties in sleeping, dizziness, headaches, indigestion, joint aches, nausea, runny nose, unusual tiredness, and vomiting'(2012). At least 1% of those taking Pro Risperidone feel some sort of unwanted side effects. The mild or severe feelings could be temporary or permanent.

When taking Pro Quetiapine, some possible side effects are 'headaches, weight gain, dryness of the mouth, constipation or even drowsiness or dizziness' (2012). We may react to a medication in different ways. If one does not feel healthy after taking this medication, then one should consult with a doctor or a pharmacist. Furthermore, 'if you experience agitation, confusion, diarrhea, fever, tremor and muscular rigidity or contractions you should contact your doctor, (2012). Pro Quetiapine is usually used for psychosis, a mental disorder. It might take many days before it takes any effect.

Unlike other medications, Pro Zopiclone is one of its kind. It helps manage insomnia. It is a depressant for the central nervous system to help one better sleep during the night. The dosage required depends on the age of the patient. 'Common side effect are mood changes, clumsiness, confusion, lack of coordination, anxiety and restlessness. It can cause dizziness, weight loss, a poor appetite, indigestion, heartburn, constipation, trouble sleeping and stomach pain'. Obviously, one will not get all the side effects, it all depends on the person.

Medications, such as Olanzapine, Abilify, Pro Risperidone, Pro Quetiapine, Pro Zopiclone, and Wellbutrin XL were helpful to stabilize me. They helped me be in a better shape. Obviously, I had many side effects but all bad things have a good side. I had specific medications for a certain period of time. If you think that taking these medications is not necessary for you then you were not in my shoes and I hope that you will never be in my shoes. With mental health and illness, people get frightened. It is a sensitive subject. Many people can be labelled as insane but regardless of one's sanity we are all equally human. We all have equal rights. Never blame, judge, comment on, laugh at or accuse someone who is going through insanity as you never know if you would ever escape unscathed.

I have tried many medications, some have stabilized me while others have not. I used to take Zyprexa Olanzapine. If I forgot to take it, I could sleep at night. I really got addicted to this medication. The disadvantage is that more I become dependent of Zyprexa Olanzapine, the more it would hurt me later. More precisely, I was at risk for diabetes because of the drug. To not get diabetes I had the option of taking another medication, such as Metformin. But I did not want to become dependent on other medications when I was already on drugs. While taking medications, I had some side effects: sometimes I would have dry mouth, I had constipation, I would have headaches, and I would feel tired. Even with the side effects however, Zyprexa Olanzapine really helped me in a period of high stress. I have found that the more I was in a stressful situation, the more I would have delusions and hallucinations. Abilify did not stop my hallucinations, but I am sure that it might help other people. I could be part of the lowest percentage of the population where Abilify did not have any reaction on my body. Taking Wellbutrin XL helped me better sleep at night. I do not recall which of the medications made me feel like a zombie. I told my main psychiatrist of this and he right away recommended to stop the medication.

While trying many medications I really felt terrible: I was extremely disorganized, disorientated, I often felt tired and I was not motivated in doing anything or going somewhere. It was difficult for my wife as she often wanted to spend time with me and our daughter. I did not explain about my situation as I did not want to bring tension and worries to her. But I did a mistake by not telling her as it later affected our marriage. This really hurt me as I did not ask to become schizophrenic as there is no real cure from insanity. I thought I could get better by taking medications but my disorder did not go away. It would help me balance my mind but would hurt my body in various ways. When I finally explained to my wife that I had Schizophrenia, her reaction was different compared to that of other people, like my family and work colleagues. I felt really fortunate to get enough support from my employer and my insurance company. They helped me for many months by giving me enough money to survive during a time of suffering. My company and insurance company were generous and reasonable enough to help support me even before I was admitted to the Day Hospital.

Medication is for everybody but not everyone can afford it. What happens to those who cannot afford it or do not even have health insurance? In most cases people are still alive and many may not even know that they have mental illness. They may also suffer more than other people. People who are unfortunate to not have any medication live a different life due to their illness. In third world countries, many people may not even know that they have a disorder called schizophrenia.

Conclusion

Coming to the Day Hospital every morning from Monday to Friday gave me the opportunity to follow a regular routine by maintaining a fixed schedule. Being punctual made me have discipline about myself. I learned a lot at the Day Hospital. I will discuss my thoughts, my expectations, and goals on the program in the following paragraph.

For me, the Day Hospital was like a job, where I come to learn about my health, the coping mechanism in life, mental health, daily problems and solutions to them. I learned how to be organized, how to manage and to cope with difficult situations. This helped me to balance my emotion too. I think that it is a great place where one can be educated about health. I observed that people with mental issues get better and feel happier from ground zero. It is a holy place for mentally ill people or those who suffer from an illness. While it is an endless learning process, knowing that my illness will lessen in approximately 3 months to 1 year gave me hope.

What was my expectation at the end of my treatment? First of all my expectation at the beginning was negative because I was surrounded by people who suffered from various types of illness. I thought that I would be more sick but later I realized that this has helped me. I have found people from various continent and countries sharing their stories and perceptions about life and its obstacles. This made me feel that I was not alone.

Sharing my thoughts with nurses, occupational therapies and practitioners helped me to stand by myself and to build trust. When I was severely ill, it was a difficult and dark moment that I thought I could not overcome. By talking to other patients, I developed skills and used tools to face the reality. I was astounded to see so many patients with such knowledge to share. I felt happy to be part of many patients who shared their education and wisdom. It motivated me to spend my time by discussing about everything and nothing.

The more time I spent at the Day Hospital, the better my mood and the better I felt. I still had terrible moments and my life was divided in many pieces like a puzzle. I still wonder if I am ready to face reality. I have challenged myself to start working and to live my life as it was before I was ill. I still wonder if I am really ready to be with regular people to spend time with my friends, to meet new friends, to share my happiness with others. I question if I am ready to try to be the perfect son, husband, and father, to forget bad situations and to forgive others whom I see differently. I am who I am and if you accept me by knowing that I have Schizophrenia then I will accept you in my life. I will let you be in my puzzle by sharing my thoughts, emotions, appreciation, beliefs, knowledge, happiness, and love.

Bibliography

Internet

American Psychiatric Association: <u>Diagnostic and Statistical Manual of Mental Disorders,</u> Fourth Edition, Text Revision. Washington, DC, American Psychiatric Association, 2000. (p. 27)

Schizophrenia Society of Canada, (2012), World Wise Web: <u>http://www.schizophrenia.ca/</u>, Date retrieved December 27[h] 2012

Michael Benston, M.D., **(1992-2012), <u>Types of Schizophrenia,</u>** World Wise Web:

<u>www.psychcentral.com/lib/2006/types-of-schizophrenia/all/1/</u> *(p.1-2,* Date retrieved December 27th 2012*)*

Disorganized-type Schizophrenia

<u>Schizophrenia—disorganized type</u>: MedlinePlus Medical <u>Encyclopedia</u>, (2012), World Wise Web:

<u>www.nlm.nih.gov/medlineplus/ency/article/000937.htm</u>, Date retrieved December 30[h] 2012

Catatonic Schizophrenia

MediLexicon International Ltd, <u>What Is **Catatonic Schizophrenia**?— Medical News Today</u>, (2004-2013). World Wise Web:

<u>www.medicalnewstoday.com/articles/192263.php</u>, Date retrieved January 22th 2013

Undifferentiated Schizophrenia

<u>Undifferentiated Schizophrenia?>—Health & Wellness—Tree. com</u>, (2011). World Wise Web:

www.tree.com/ . . . /schizophrenia-diagnosis-types-undifferentiated.asp . . . Date retrieved January 22ᵗʰ 2013

Residual Schizophrenia

Residual Schizophrenia | BehaveNet, (1995-2013), World Wise Web: *www.behavenet.com* › . . . › *Schizophrenia*, Date retrieved January 22ᵗʰ 2013

Negative Symptoms of Schizophrenia

The negative symptoms of schizophrenia (2000-2006), World Wise Web:

www.health.harvard.edu/fhg/updates/update0706c.shtml *(p.1)* Date retrieved December 23ᵗʰ 2012

American Psychiatric Association: Diagnostic and Statistical Manual of Mental Disorders, Fourth Edition, Text Revision. Washington, DC, American Psychiatric Association, 2000. (p.302).

Language

What are **the disadvantages of being bilingual**, (2012). World Wise Web: *www.wiki.answers.com* › . . . › *Categories* › *Literature & Language*, Date retrieved December 20ᵗʰ 2012

Schizophrenia Society of Ontario

Who gets **schizophrenia?**, (2011). World Wise Web:

www.schizophrenia.on.ca/ . . . schizophrenia/ . . . schizophrenia/3-who-get . . . Date retrieved February 12ᵗʰ 2013

Relationship

Healthy vs. unhealthy relationships | Go Ask Alice! (2005-2012), World Wise Web: *goaskalice.columbia.edu* › Browse Our Q&A Library › Relationships, Date retrieved December 20th 2012

Ethnicity

Diff En, **Ethnicity** vs Race—Difference and Comparison | Diffen World Wise Web: *www.diffen.com* › *English Language* › *Grammar* › *Words*, Date retrieved January 11th 2013

Sexual Orientation

University of Alberta Health Centre, **Sexual orientation**, (2001). World Wise Web:

www.ualberta.ca/dept/health/web_docs/healthinfo/ . . . /orientation. htm, Date retrieved December 24th 2012

Verbal Abuse

About.com, **Verbal Abuse**: Is Your Relationship Verbally Abusive? (2012), World Wise Web: d*ivorcesupport.about.com* › . . . › *Domestic Abuse*, Date retrieved December 23rd 2012

Coping Mechanism

Yahoo! Inc. What does **coping mechanism** mean?—Yahoo! Answers (2012) World Wise Web: *www.answers.yahoo.com* › . . . › *Words & Wordplay*, Date retrieved December 23rd 2012

Strategy

Torchbox, **Coping strategies | Rethink Mental Illness, The Leading Mental . . .** (2009), World Wise Web: *www.rethink.org* › **How we can help** › **Our services,** Date retrieved December 30th 2012

Emotion

Emotion—Wikipedia, the free encyclopedia (2012) World Wise Web:

www.en.wikipedia.org/wiki/Emotion, Date retrieved December 31[h] 2012

Cognitive

WebAIM: **Cognitive** Disabilities: *(1999-2013) World Wise Web:* www.*webaim.org* › *Articles*, Date retrieved January 29th 2013

Information Processing

McLeod, S.A. (2008) **Information Processing, Retrieved,** World Wise Web:

http://www.simplypsychology.org/information-processing.html, Date retrieved December 30th 2012

Problem Solving

About.com, **Problem Solving**, (2013), World Wise Web: www. *psychology.about.com* › . . . › *Psychology Dictionary* › *P Index* Date retrieved January 19th 2013

Attention

What are **attention skills?**—Challenging Our Minds, (2006), World Wise Web:

www.challenging-our-minds.com/blog/?p=15 Date retrieved December29[th] 2012

Math

**Comprehending Math by Arthur Hyde—Heinemann Publishing,
(2013). World Wise Web:**

www.heinemann.com/products/E00949.aspx Date retrieved
December 28th 2012

Visual comprehension

Trevor H. Cairney Literacy, families and learning: **Visual
Comprehension** (2007-2011) World Wise Web: *trevorcairney.
blogspot.com/2011/04/visual-comprehension.html* Date retrieved
December 27th 2012

Behavioral Symptoms

Better Medicine, **Behavioral Symptoms**—Symptoms, Causes,
Treatments—Better . . . (2012), World Wise Web:

www.localhealth.com/article/behavioral-symptoms Date retrieved
December 18th 2012

Anxiety

Johnston, J.E., **The Complete Idiot's Guide to Controlling Anxiety**,
(2006).

Depression

Depression Symptoms (2011), World Wise Web:

www.depressionhurts.ca/ Date retrieved December 18th 2012

Smith, L., L., & Elliott, H., C, **Depression for Dummies**, (2003),
p.23-213

Metabolic Syndrome

Metabolic Syndrome—Canadian Diabetes Association (2012), World Wise Web: www.*diabetes.ca* › **Diabetes and You Date retrieved** January 19th 2013

Anger Management

Gentry, W. D., Anger Management for Dummies. (2007), p.67

Stigma

Opening Minds—**Mental Health** Commission of Canada, (2008), World Wise Web:

www.mentalhealthcommission.ca/English/Pages/OpeningMinds. aspx Date retrieved December 28th 2012

Canadian Mental Health Association. (2006). Understanding mental illness. World Wise Web: http://www.cmha.ca/bins/content_page. asp?cid=3&lang=1 Date retrieved December 27th 2012

Reduce Stress

Haycock, D. A. (2009), The Everything Health Guide To Schizophrenia, Adams Media, a division of F+W Media, Inc p. 237

Phobias

Korgeski, G. P., (2009) The Complete Idiot's Guide to Phobias, city: Penguin Group (USA) Inc.

Early Symptom 'Short Story'

Joseph Dobrain, (2000), A Lover's Dream World Wise Web:

http://www.josephdobrian.com/column/column4.html Date retrieved December 26th 2012

Suicide

<u>Why are **men more** likely to **commit suicide than women**</u>?—Yahoo! Answers, (2013), World Wise Web: a*nswers.yahoo.com › . . . › Social Science › Psychology* Date retrieved December 24ᵗʰ 2012

Immortality of the Soul (Philosophy)

Sara, T., <u>The Oxford Dictionary and Thesaurus</u>. (1993), p. 748 & 1482

G.M.A. Grube., <u>Plato Phaedo,</u> (1977), p. 3

Time Management

Time Management—<u>MindTools.com</u>, (1996-2013), World Wise Web:

<u>www.mindtools.com/pages/main/newMN_HTE.htm</u> Date retrieved February 19ᵗʰ 2013

Distinction between male and female brain

Wade, C. & Travis, C, (1996) <u>Psychology,</u> 4ᵗʰ (ed.) city: Harper Collins College, p. 135-155

Unger, R. (1979) <u>Female and Male, Psychological Perspectives,</u> city: Montclair State College p.86

Byer, C. & Shainberg, L. (1994) <u>Dimensions of Human Sexuality,</u> 4ᵗʰ (ed) city: Mt. San Antonia College p. 351-353

Material Accessed from a WWW Site:

<u>Biology & Medicine</u>, World Wise Web:

<u>http://www.campus.bt.com/CampusWorld/pub . . . ceNet/database/Biology/9610/b00675d.html p.1</u>

Brach, M., (1998), <u>Press Releases</u>, Internet, World Wise Web:

http://www.mcleanhospital.org/PublicAffaires/
MaleemalesBrainFuction.htm p. 1-2

Gambling

Dr. Volberg, <u>Gemini Research</u>, Internet, World Wide Web:

http://www.geminiresearch.com/cnt_home.html

Erika S., <u>Bad Odds For Legalized Gambling</u>, Internet, World Wide
Web: http://www.policyreview.com /rc/insight/is94jIcu.html

South, David., <u>One Gambling Guru Think the Province is Going Too
Far</u>, Internet, World Wide Web: http://www.idmagazine.com/feature/
article/casino.htm

A Report by the National Council o Welfare, <u>Gambling in Canada</u>,
Internet, World Wide Web:

http://www.ccsa.ca/gmbivhtm

Homeless

Homeless in Canada—<u>Charity Intelligence Canada</u>, (2009) World
Wise Web:

<u>www.charityintelligence.ca/images/Ci-Homeless-in-Canada.pdf</u>
Date retrieved December 24th 2012

Nutrition

<u>Alphabetical list of **vegetables**—List of **all vegetables**</u> (2007-2012)
World Wise Web:

http://www.vegetarian-cooking-recipes-tips.com/alphabetical-list-
of-vegetables.html Date retrieved December 21th 2012

Meat and Alternatives—Canada's Food Guide

Health Canada (2008) World Wise Web: http://www.hc-sc.gc.ca/ fn-an/food-guide-aliment/choose-choix/meat-viande/serving- portion-eng.php Date retrieved December 23th 2012

Discharge

Dictionary.com | Find the Meanings and Definitions of Words at . . .(2013), World Wise Web:

www.dictionary.reference.com/ Date retrieved December 19th 2012

Medication

MediResource Inc., Zyprexa **Zydis**—Uses, Side Effects, Interactions— Drug Factsheets—C . . . (1996-2012) World Wise Web: *chealth. canoe.ca › Medications*. Date retrieved January 10[th]2013

Side Effects of Zyprexa (**Olanzapine**) Drug Center—RxList (2012) World Wise Web: *www.rxlist.com › home › drugs az list* Date retrieved January 11th 2013

Abilify Information from Drugs.com (1996-2012) World Wise Web: *www.drugs.com › Drugs by Condition › Schizophrenia*. Date retrieved January 12th 2013

GlaxoSmithKline, **Wellbutrin XL Home**, (2011) World Wise Web:

www.wellbutrinxl.com/ Date retrieved January 13th 2013

MediResource Inc., **Pro-Risperidone**—risperidone (1996-2013) World Wise Web: *libraries.mackenziehealth.ca/Medications. aspx?bran_name_id . . .*

PRO QUETIAPINE., 25MG COMPRIME—Familiprix (2012) World Wise Web: *www.familiprix.com ›* Date retrieved January 14th 2013

Zopiclone Side Effects | LIVESTRONG.COM, (2012) World Wise Web: *www.livestrong.com › . . . › Drugs & Side Effects Y-Z.* Date retrieved January 15th 2013

Dr. Jacobs, T., Balance Brain Chemistry, Get Back Your Life— Summit Integrative . . . (2013) www.summitintegrative.com › Blog › Integrative Medicine Date retrieved March 1st 2013

Edney. D.R, (2004), **Mass Media and Mental Illness: Table of Contents—Canadian . . .,** World Wise Web: *www.ontario.cmha.ca › . . . › Stigma and Discrimination*

Alexander. T,.(2009), The **Media's** Impact on Public Perceptions of **Mental Illness,** World Wise Web : *www.cmhanl.ca/ . . . / StigmaMatters%20-%20Kismet%20Baun%20articl . . .*

REFERENCES

Baumann, E. A. (2007). Stigmatization, social distance and exclusion because of mental illness: The individual with mental illness as a stranger. *International Review of Psychiatry, 19*(2), 131-135. doi: 10.1080/09540260701278739

Berg, P. (2000). Wonderland [Television series episode]. In P. Berg, New York, NY: ABC Network.

Bradby, H., Varyani, M., Oglethorpe, R., Raine, W., White, I., & Helen, M. (2007). British Asian families and the use of child and adolescent mental health services: A qualitative study of a hard to reach group. *Social Science & Medicine, 65*(12), 2413-2424. doi: 10.1016/j.socscimed.2007.07.25

Diefenbach, L. D., & West, D. M. (2007). Television and attitudes toward mental health issues: cultivation analysis and the third-person effect. *Journal of Community Psychology, 35*(2), 181-195. doi: 10.1002/jcop.20142

Edney, R. D. (2004). Mass Media and mental illness: A Literature Review. *Canadian Mental Health Association*, 1-27. Retrieved from http://www.ontario.cmha.ca

Hale, M. (2009, January). A series reappears, if only for a while. *The New York Times*. Retrieved from http://www.nytimes.com

Jorm, F. A., & Oh, E. (2009). Desire for social distance from people with mental disorders. *Australian and New Zealand Journal of Psychiatry, 43*, 183-200. doi: 10.1080/0004867080265349

Jorm, F. A., Reavley, J. N., & Ross, M. A. (2012). Belief in the dangerousness of people with mental disorders. *Australian & New Zealand Journal of Psychiatry, 00*(0), 1-17. doi: 10.1177/0004867412442406

Lai, D.W.L. & Surood, S. (2007). Predictors of depression in aging South Asian Canadians. *Journal of Cross-Cultural Gerontology, 23*(1), 57-75. doi: 10.1007/s10823-007-9051-5

Larson, E. J., & Corrigan, P. (2008). The Stigma of families with mental illness. *Academic Psychiatry, 32*(2), 87-91. doi/10.1002/yd.23319873407

Levey, S., & Howells, K. (1994). Accounting for the fear of schizophrenia. *Journal of Community & Applied Social Psychology, 4*, 313-328. Retrieved from http://onlinelibrary. wiley.com

Marie, D., & Miles, B. (2008). Social distance and perceived dangerousness across four diagnostic categories of mental disorder. *Australian and New Zealand Journal of Psychiatry, 42*(2), 126-33. Retrieved from http://www.ncbi.nlm.nih.gov/

Morgan, J. A. & Jorm, F. A. (2009). Recall of news stories about mental illness by Australian youth: associations with help-seeking attitudes and stigma. *Australian and New Zealand Journal of Psychiatry, 43,* 866-872. doi: 10.1080/00048670903107567

Mullaly, B. (2010). *Challenging oppression and confronting privilege.* Don Mills: Oxford University Press.

Nordt, C., Rossler, W., & Lauber, C. (2006). Attitudes of mental health professionals toward people with schizophrenia and major depression. *Schizophrenia Bulletin, 32*(4), 709-714. doi:10.1093/schbul/sbj065

Rueve, E. M., & Welton, S. R. (2008). Violence and mental illness. *Psychiatry, 5*(5), 34-48. Retrieved from http://www.ncbi.nlm.nih.gov

Tartakovsky, M. (2009). Media's damaging depictions of mental illness. *Psych Central.* Retrieved from http://psychcentral.com

Wahl, F. O., & Lefkowits, Y. (1989). Impact of a television film on attitudes toward mental illness. *American Journal of Community Psychology, 17*(4), 521-528.

Wahl, O., Hanrahan, E., Karl, K., Lasher, E., & Swaye, J. (2007). The depiction of mental illnesses in children's television programs. *Journal of Community Psychology, 35*(1), 121-133. doi: 10.1002/jcop.20138